Sir John George Bourinot

How Canada is Governed

A Short Account of its Executive, Legislative, Judicial and Municipal Institutions.

Second Edition

Sir John George Bourinot

How Canada is Governed
A Short Account of its Executive, Legislative, Judicial and Municipal Institutions. Second Edition

ISBN/EAN: 9783744721561

Printed in Europe, USA, Canada, Australia, Japan

Cover: Foto ©Suzi / pixelio.de

More available books at **www.hansebooks.com**

How Canada is Governed

A SHORT ACCOUNT

OF ITS

EXECUTIVE, LEGISLATIVE, JUDICIAL AND MUNICIPAL INSTITUTIONS

WITH

AN HISTORICAL OUTLINE OF THEIR ORIGIN AND DEVELOPMENT

WITH NUMEROUS ILLUSTRATIONS

BY

J: G: BOURINOT, C.M.G., LL.D., D.C.L., D.L.

CLERK OF THE CANADIAN HOUSE OF COMMONS, AUTHOR OF A MANUAL OF CONSTITUTIONAL HISTORY, PARLIAMENTARY PRACTICE AND PROCEDURE IN CANADA, AND OTHER WORKS ON THE GOVERNMENT AND CONSTITUTION OF THE DOMINION

SECOND EDITION.

Toronto

THE COPP, CLARK COMPANY, LIMITED
1895

Dedicated

PREFATORY NOTE.

THIS little volume is intended to present such a succinct
review of the public institutions of Canada as will be
easily understood by all classes of her people. The first duty
of citizens in every country is to make themselves thoroughly
acquainted with the nature and operation of the system of
government under which they live. Without such a knowledge,
a man is very imperfectly equipped for the performance of the
serious responsibilities which devolve upon him in a country
where the people rule. No amount of so-called "practical
experience" can compensate a man for ignorance of the elementary principles of political science, and of the origin,
development and methods of his own government.

I have kept steadily in view the requirements of that great
mass of people, old and young, men and women, who have
few opportunities of obtaining special knowledge of institutions
of government. I have avoided all technical language wherever it is possible, and in every case have explained such
words and phrases which, although in general use, are not
always understood even by those on whose lips they are most
frequent.

I have attempted to make this citizen's manual as complete
as possible within the limited space at my disposal. I have
borne in mind the fact that a Canadian is not merely a citizen

of Canada, and as such has duties and obligations to discharge
within the Dominion and Province, but that he is also a citizen
of the greatest and noblest.empire that the world has ever seen.
Consequently one of the most important parts of this book
is devoted to a brief account of the onerous functions of the
sovereign, who, through her national councils, executive and
legislative, administers the affairs of Great Britain and Ireland,
and of her many colonies and dependencies. The third part
describes the nature and methods of the general government
of the Dominion ; the fourth part deals with the powers of the
several provincial authorities that compose the federal union,
and with the organization and procedure of the courts of law ;
the fifth part outlines the working of the municipal system, in
which all classes of citizens should be so deeply interested ;
the sixth part indicates the manner in which our public schools
are administered by the government and people in every province ; the seventh part briefly explains the mode in which the
territorial districts of the Northwest are governed before they
have reached the dignity of provinces in the full possession of
responsible government. In the Appendix I give the text of
the constitution or British North America Act of 1867, and
amending acts in full. At the end of each Part of the volume
I add references to such authorities as will be most useful to
those persons who wish to go thoroughly into the study of
institutions.

In closing the book I say a few words with respect to the
duties and responsibilities that devolve upon all classes of
Canadians as citizens of a self-governing country. These
words are very inadequate when we consider the wide scope

and importance of the subject, and all I can pretend to hope
is that they may serve to stimulate thoughtful men and women
—especially those young men just assuming the obligations of
citizenship—to think deeply on the problems of government
which are every day presenting themselves for solution, and
perhaps encourage them in a desire to perform their full share
in the active affairs of a Dominion yet in the early stages of its
national life.

J. G. BOURINOT.

OTTAWA : Queen's Birthday, 1895.

CONTENTS.

MAP OF THE POLITICAL DIVISIONS OF THE DOMINION OF CANADA.

FIRST PART.

GROWTH OF THE CONSTITUTION.

SECOND PART.

IMPERIAL GOVERNMENT.

[ix]

THIRD PART

THE DOMINION GOVERNMENT.

FOURTH PART.

THE PROVINCIAL GOVERNMENTS.

FIFTH PART.

MUNICIPAL GOVERNMENT IN THE PROVINCES.

SIXTH PART.

SCHOOL GOVERNMENT IN THE PROVINCES.

SEVENTH PART.

GOVERNMENT IN THE NORTHWEST TERRITORIES.

CONCLUSION.

APPENDIX.

ANALYTICAL INDEX.

LIST OF ILLUSTRATIONS AND AUTOGRAPHS.

FIRST PART

GROWTH OF THE CONSTITUTION

MAP OF THE DOM

ENCRA'

"HOW CANAD.

D? J · G · BOU

THE COPP· CLA

TOR

D FOR

IS GOVERNED:"

NOT, C.M.G.

Co., LIMITED.
ro.

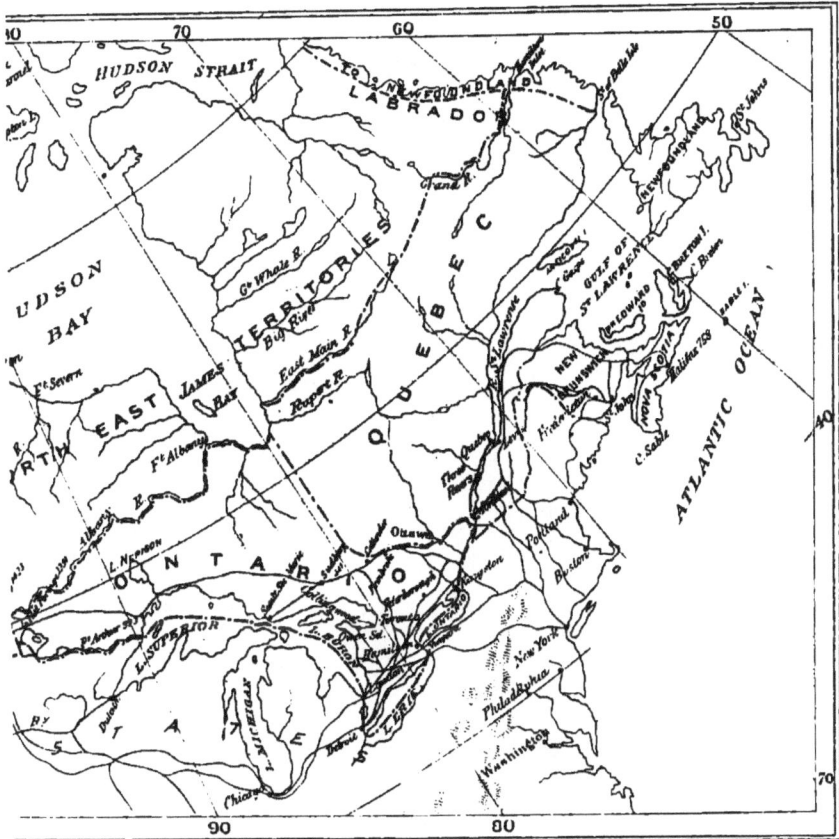

HOW CANADA IS GOVERNED

CHAPTER I.

DEFINITIONS OF WORDS AND PHRASES USED IN THIS BOOK.

1.—Introduction.

IN the course of this book it will be necessary to use certain words and phrases which are constantly in the mouths of those who speak of the institutions of government in a country. Among these words are "government," "law," "constitution," "administration," "parliament," "executive power," "legislative power," and "judicial power," the meaning of which it is important to explain at the very commencement, so that the reader may thoroughly understand the subjects which this book professes to treat. It is always difficult —indeed in some respects impossible—to give a short and exact definition of terms of government which cover so vast a ground of human experience as those in question. All that I shall attempt to do is to give such explanations as will suffice for the intelligent reading of a book which is not written for the scholar, or lawyer, or

DEFINITIONS.
DEFINITIONS.
professor, who has mastered these subjects, but for the student entering on the study of Canadian government and for that large body of people who are absorbed in the engrossing employments of life and have but few opportunities for reading of this class.

2.—Government.

In every organized society or community of persons like the Dominion of Canada, there must be some machinery, or system of rules, by which the individual actions of the members composing that society, and their relations with one another can be regulated for the good of one and all. The machinery or system of rules which performs this all important work is called *The Government*, which, followed to its old Greek origin, means to steer the ship. To steer "the ship of state"—that is to say, of a nation or people—means to govern or direct its movements. The instrument of direction has, by the usage of centuries, come to signify "the government." The true object of this directing power is the security of life and property, the well-being and happiness of the whole community. The forms that government takes are numerous. There is no more interesting study than that which traces the development of different stages of government ; from the earliest of all, the family, in which the parent rules, down to the composite forms which have grown up in the course of thousands of years to meet the varied conditions of modern society. It is sufficient for our purpose to show that Canada affords the most remarkable example that the history of the world has offered—in fact it has had no parallel—of the various forms of government that can and do exist in a community which is still in a state of dependency—that is to say, still dependent in certain matters on the parent or imperial state—and nevertheless exercises most extensive powers of self-government. In the first place, Canada is under a *monarchical* form of government, because at the head of her affairs and of the whole empire is a sovereign, not chosen from time to time by popular vote, but wearing the crown by legal right, and removed from all conditions of political conflict. In the second place, Canada is under a *parliamentary* or *responsible* form of government, because the sovereign or her representative in the Dominion does not exercise any power, legislative or executive, except through a legislature which makes the law, and an executive which is practically chosen by that legislature to carry out that law. In the third place, Canada is under a *representative* form of government, because the people—that is to say, all British subjects living in Canada and having rights under the law—choose from time to time a certain number of men to legislate for them in parliaments or legislatures or representative bodies. In the fourth place, Canada is under a *federal* form of government because she comprises within her territorial limits a number of provinces, or separate political communities, exercising distinct powers of government for provincial objects, and at the same time combining for general purposes for the promotion of the advantage of all those provinces. Each province has a local government, carried on according to prescribed forms. The whole of Canada has a federal or general government, conducted under prescribed forms. Nor are these the only forms of government of which we hear constantly. In every province there is a form of *municipal* government which provides for the comfort, convenience and security of the inhabitants of cities, towns, villages and other municipal divisions. All the schools of a province, which are supported by provincial moneys and municipal taxes, are also subject to a system of well-considered rules or machinery of government. Accordingly from the supreme government in England, which administers or superintends the affairs of the whole empire, down to the little village council in a province, which imposes taxes and provides for the general necessities of the citizens within its municipal control, we see how many forms enter into the machinery of the government of Canada.

3.—Law of the Land.

The principal duty of every government is to execute or carry out *The law of the land.* In its general sense the law is a collection of rules and orders, imposed by an established and recognized authority for the conduct of persons living in a political society or community. The fact that there is a government or power behind this law to enforce it, whenever necessary, is what really gives it strength. The law may be either written or unwritten, and it is both in Canada. The law which regulates the system of federal union, generally known as the written constitution, or British North America Act, is a written law or statute passed in 1867 by the supreme power of the empire, the parliament of Great Britain and Ireland. In addition to that written constitutional law, there are numerous constitutional rules, usages, and understandings, which have the force of law since they are accepted by common consent for

the direction of parliamentary or responsible government;
which regulate the formation or resignation of a ministry,
for instance, as the writer shall explain fully hereafter (see
Third Part, c. 1, sec.6). All the methods of government
which have been briefly described above, monarchical,
parliamentary, representative, federal, are secured and
regulated by this elaborate system of written and
unwritten law and rules, which forms the *constitution*
of the Dominion—in other words, a body of principles
constituted or established by the supreme authority of
the imperial state in accordance with the wishes of the
people of Canada. Then there is the statutory law of
the land, made up of the numerous statutes or legally
ordered acts* of the legislative bodies on the many
subjects under their control. Then there is that vast
body of rules and usages and judicial decisions which
have come to us from England and comprise the common
law of the country (see *Fourth Part*). The system of law
which we possess is consequently very complicated and
the result of the experiences of many centuries. Both
England and France have contributed their experiences
to our system, and we have built on that foundation a
large body of rules adapted to the conditions of a new
country.

4.—Executive, Legislative, and Judicial Powers.

The law regulates the division of the powers of government into what are known as the *executive, legislative,*
and *judicial* departments. The *executive* power carries

---

* Statute comes from the Latin word *statutus*, meaning ordered,
established, set up.

out and enforces the law of the land by the machinery which that law affords. From the governor-general in council of the Dominion and the lieutenant-governor in council of every province—or the supreme executive powers of Canada—down to the humble constable or peace officer executing a writ or order of a court, there is a large body of public officers engaged every day in enforcing the law of the land in accordance with the rules and usages laid down for their direction in every case. The *legislative* power makes law and alters it in Canada in accordance with the powers granted by the constitution or fundamental law (see *above* p. 5). In the Dominion there is a central legislative power or law-making body called a parliament—a name we derive from England (see *below* p. 7)—and in every province there is also a legislature with law-making rights, as well as municipal councils having certain legislative powers within their municipal divisions (see *Fifth Part*). The *judicial* power applies and gives a meaning to the law whenever disputes come before the judges in due form. This judicial power is represented by judges and courts duly authorized to administer justice and explain the law in such forms as the law has ordered.

5.—Administration.

Another word which is sometimes used for "executive" is *administrative*. The body of men who carry on the government is often called the " administration," and with some reason, since it is their duty to see that the duties of their respective departments or branches of government are carried out in accordance with law. For instance, it is the duty of the minister of customs, and the collectors at

every port of Canada, to administer the law passed by
parliament for the regulation and collection of duties of
customs on goods coming into Canada from other
countries. It is the duty of the minister of public works,
and of the engineers, architects and clerks under his
control, to look after the construction, repairs and maintenance of public buildings, like post offices and custom
houses, and administer 'the affairs of the department
generally. It is the duty of the commissioner of crown
lands in a province to carry out the regulations for the
sale of public lands and the licensing of " timber limits,"
and to administer all the functions devolving upon his
department by law. It is the duty of the warden, mayor
or other head of a municipal council to see that the
affairs of his municipal division are administered in
accordance with the general municipal law and the special
statutes or by-laws (see *Fifth Part*) governing municipal
divisions. A public official, in administering the law,
acts of course on his own motion, in accordance with its
rules ; a judge, in administering the law, does not act
until he is called upon to do so by a case or proceeding
which comes before him in his court in such form as the
law directs.

6.—Parliament.

The name of that great legislative body which has
performed so remarkable a part in the history of England,
and given a designation to the principal law-making body
of Canada, is said by one of the highest authorities,
Professor Freeman, to be simply the Norman French
translation of an old phrase which goes back to the time
of William the Conqueror. That king is said in an old

English record or chronicle to have had "very deep
speech"—*parlement*—with his national, or common
council (in Latin, *commune concilium*). This deep speech,
or *parlement* was "consequently a distinguishing feature of a meeting between king and people, and in
the end it gave its name to the assembly," which has, in
the course of time, assumed the somewhat changed form
of *parliament* (in low Latin *parliamentum*). The name
of the House of Commons—that body where political
power now mainly rests—does not at all mean that the
great mass of the people of England, "the commonalty,"
was ever represented in the early national assemblies.
On the contrary, the word "commons" was restricted in
meaning to a small and special representation of knights
of shires or counties, and of burgesses or citizens of a
few towns or boroughs, and cities, whose local bodies—
called *communitates* in legal Latin documents, because
their members had certain privileges in common —
elected the representatives in question. Gradually the
term "commons" came, as a matter of convenience, to
mean those classes of the people who were not lords of
parliament, and were not summoned to the upper
house, but could be elected to the lower or commons
branch. Even the sons of lords of parliament became
commoners—identified with the mass of people. In this
way, there grew up two houses of parliament: one
representing the classes or estates called "lords spiritual
and temporal,"—peers, archbishops and bishops,—and the
other, that estate which takes in so many people and is
now called the Commons of Great Britain and Ireland.
In Canada there has never been such distinctions of
"estates" or classes. The legislative councils of the

provinces, and the present senate of the Dominion, or upper houses of our parliaments, differ from the lower or commons' houses of Canada only in consequence of their appointment by the governors, representing the queen, and of their not being elected by the people who have a right to vote, for representatives. Under the laws that now prevail throughout Canada for the qualification of voters, all classes and interests can be represented in our legislative bodies. In fact, the representation of the commons or the people is far more liberal than that in the parent state, despite the great advances that have been made in this direction during the last sixty years—the period of the reform of the English parliament.

7.—Conclusion.

However imperfect the foregoing explanations may be, it will be well for my reader to bear them in mind and to refer to them whilst studying this short review of the governmental institutions of Canada. Other words and phrases that apply to the details of government will be more conveniently explained according as each branch of the general subject comes up in its proper place.

CHAPTER II.

1. The Dominion of Canada.— 2. Plan of the Book.—3. Periods of Political Development.

1.—The Dominion of Canada.

The Dominion of Canada forms one of the most important dependencies of the most remarkable empire known to the history of the world. It is properly called a dependency because its government, though complete within itself, is necessarily dependent on and subordinate to the supreme authority of Great Britain, whose queen and parliament preside over the whole empire. This Dominion comprises at the present time the provinces of Prince Edward Island, New Brunswick, Nova Scotia, Quebec, Ontario, Manitoba and British Columbia, as well as a vast area of territory in the Northwest divided into five districts of government. These provinces and territories are closely connected by a political system called a *federal union*, to which, as a whole, has been given the name of a *Dominion* from the fact that it forms a part of the dominions or dependencies subject to the government of the queen and parliament of England. It has a population of five millions of souls, of whom two millions and a quarter live in the English province of Ontario, formerly known as Upper Canada ; a million and a half

---

* The word *Canada* is a memorial of the time when the French discoverer, Jacques Cartier, found that the Indian inhabitants on the banks of the St. Lawrence called their villages *Kannata*, or a collection of huts.

in the French province of Quebec, formerly known as
Lower Canada ; nearly a million in the maritime provinces of Prince Edward Island, New Brunswick and
Nova Scotia ; one. hundred and seventy thousand in the
province of Manitoba, one hundred thousand in the province of British Columbia, and about the same number in
the Northwest Territories. In the province of Quebec
there is a French population of about a million and a
quarter of souls. In the maritime provinces there is also
a French Acadian population of over a hundred thousand souls. The remaining and larger population of
Canada is almost entirely of English, Scotch or Irish
origin. Of the whole population of Canada, nearly two
millions of souls are Roman Catholics, of whom two-
thirds live in the province of Quebec. Nearly three
millions are Protestants.

2.—Plan of this Book.

I propose to show the nature of the government of
this federal union of provinces ; in other words, the
nature of the political machinery which regulates that
political society or community of people, who live in
these several provinces and territories. My object is
simply to give such a concise and impartial account of
the nature and working of the executive, legislative and
judicial machinery of government as will be easily understood by the whole community, old and young, men and
women, and at the same time show them all that the
institutions of Canada are calculated to render the
people, irrespective of race or religion, happy and
prosperous as long as those institutions are worked out,
honestly and wisely by those who have been chosen by

the people for the administration or management of public affairs throughout this self-governing dependency of the empire.

3.—Periods of Political Development.

It is necessary that I should at the outset briefly trace the most important steps in the political development of the several provinces comprised in the present Dominion, so that every one may the more clearly understand the origin and nature of the system of government which Canadians now possess.

I shall first refer to the political history of the large country generally known as Canada until 1867, and now divided into the two provinces of Quebec and Ontario. So far there have been four complete Periods in the political history of those provinces :

1. The Period of French rule, from 1608 to 1759-60 or the Period of absolute government.

2. The Period from 1760 to 1791, when representative and legislative institutions were established.

3. The Period from 1791 to 1840, when representative institutions were slowly developing into responsible or complete local self-government.

4. The Period from 1840 to 1867, during which responsible government was established in the fullest sense of the phrase, and the federal union was finally accomplished as the natural result of the extended liberties of the people.

Since 1867 Canada has entered on the Fifth Period of her political history as a federation, the nature of whose institutions of government will be explained in the chapters following the historical review.

CHAPTER III.

1. French rule, 1608—1760.—2. English rule, 1760—1791.

French Rule, 1608-1759-60.

The country watered by the St. Lawrence and the Great Lakes of the West, and now divided into the provinces of Quebec and Ontario, and known as Upper and Lower Canada before Confederation, became the colonial possession of France by the right of first discovery and later settlement. Jacques (James) Cartier, a bold sailor of St. Malo, in France, landed at Gaspé in 1534 and sailed up the St. Lawrence in 1535, or more than forty years after the discovery of America by Columbus. It was not until 1608, however, that Samuel Champlain, of Brouage, on the Bay of Biscay, commenced the building of a town amid the rocks of ancient Stadaconé—

Champlain -

the name of a famous Indian hamlet of the days of Cartier—and actually laid the foundations of the colony which has developed into the province of Quebec.

Canada was for some years under the control of commercial companies to whom the king of France gave exclusive rights over the fur trade. By 1664, however,

[13]

the rule of commercial companies came to an end and
the king established a regular government in Canada
which became a mere province of France. In Canada as
in France the head of the province had only such powers
as were expressly given him by the king who, jealous
of all authority in others, kept him strictly subordinate to
himself. The governor had command of the militia and
troops; the *intendant* was an official, almost equal to him
in rank, and of larger authority in the colony, since he
managed its financial affairs, and acted also as judge and
legislator. A council, exercising legislative and judicial
powers, assisted the governor and intendant, and acted
as a colonial court of appeal in civil and criminal cases—
the king himself in council being the supreme court of
last resort or reference. Justice was administered
in cases of property and the rights of individuals in
accordance with the custom of Paris, or the French
system of law which is still one of the institutions of
French Canada. (See *Fourth Part.*) The bishop was a
member of the council, and the Roman Catholic Church
became established by the decrees and ordinances of the
government. The parish became a district for local as
well as church purposes. Tithes or regular charges for
the support of clergy and church were imposed and regulated by the ordinances or statutes of the government.
All education was under the control of the church and
its numerous religious bodies. An effort was made to
establish a class of nobles by the granting of large
tracts of land to lords *(seigneurs)* who granted them to
cultivators of the soil *(habitans)* on condition of receiving
certain payments. The king and council of state kept
a strict supervision over the government of the colony.

We look in vain for evidence of popular freedom in those days. Canada was never allowed representative government. Public meetings of all kinds were steadily repressed. No system of municipal government was established, and government was in every respect autocratic.

2.—English Rule in Canada, 1760-1791.

From the surrender of Quebec and Montreal in 1759-1760 to the English military forces dates the commencement of a new era of political liberty in the history of French Canada. Canada formally became a possession of England by the Treaty of Paris, of 1763, which allowed the French Canadians the free exercise of their religion. From 1760 to 1763 there was a military government as

a necessary result of the unsettled condition of things in a country that had suffered so much from war. Then King George III. issued a proclamation—a formal announcement of the·royal will—which established the first system of English government in the new possession of England. The people were to have the right to elect representatives to an assembly, but the time was not yet ripe for so large a measure of public liberty, if indeed it had been possible under the instructions to Governor-

General Murray which required Roman Catholics—then the great majority, and in fact the people generally of Canada—to take the same oath which prevented their co-religionists in England sitting in parliament. The government of the province was carried on for ten years by a governor-general, aided by an executive or advising council, composed of a few English officials and inhabitants, and only one French Canadian. The ordinances * or laws, passed by the governor and council, created much discontent among the French Canadians, since they practically laid aside the French legal system to which they had been always accustomed, and established the common law of England. In 1774 the parliament of England passed the Quebec Act, which gave the first constitution to the new province. The government was entrusted to a governor and legislative council appointed by the king, and the scheme of an elected assembly was postponed as "inexpedient," under existing conditions. The French Canadians were not yet prepared for representative institutions of whose working they had never any practical knowledge, and were quite content for the time being with a system which brought some of their leading men into the legislative council. But what made the act so popular in French Canada was the fact that it placed the French

---

* Ordinance is an old French word, which itself comes from the Latin *ordinare*, to order or regulate, and is generally applied in Canadian constitutional history to a legal order of the governor and council—a legislative body of only one house—common to all the colonies before the concession of a complete system of representative government. The acts of the Northwest lieutenant-governor and assembly are still called ordinances (see *Seventh Part*).

Canadians or Roman Catholic population on the same ⌐
footing as English Canadians or Protestants, confirmed
their right to full freedom of worship, allowed the
church as a body to retain their valuable property, and
restored the French civil law with respect to property
and individual rights. The criminal law of England was,
however, to prevail throughout the province. In the
legislative council both English and French were used,
and the ordinances were drawn up in the same languages.
The governor-general was assisted in the work of
government by an advisory body of five persons—chiefly
members of the legislative council—who were chosen by •
himself and called a privy council, in imitation of the
council that so long surrounded the English king. (See
Second Part, c. i, sec. 3.)

Old Bishop's Palace, Quebec, where First Parliament of Lower Canada Met in 1792.

CHAPTER IV.

3. Immigration of United Empire Loyalists.—4. Representative Institutions in Upper and Lower Canada, 1792-1840.— 5. Period of Responsible Government, 1840-1867.

3.—Immigration of the U. E. Loyalists.

While the Quebec Act continued in force, there was a very important immigration into British North America of some forty thousand persons known as United Empire • Loyalists—that is to say, men loyal to British connection— who decided to leave the old English Thirteen Colonies (now a portion of the United States), when they declared themselves independent of England. These men laid the foundations of the provinces now known as New Bruns- wick and Ontario, settled a considerable portion of , Nova Scotia, and exercised a large influence on the development of representative institutions in their new homes.

4.—Representative Institutions in Upper and Lower Canada, 1792-1840.

The Quebec Act lasted from 1774 to 1791, when the English government again interfered in the affairs of the provinces. By this time there was a rapidly increasing English population in the western parts of the country, and difficulties were constantly arising between English and French Canadians on account of the legal system not being made sufficiently clear. The British government considered it the wisest policy to form two separate provinces, in which the two races could work out their own future, as far as practicable, apart from each other.

By the "Constitutional Act," passed by the imperial parliament in 1791, the people were represented for the first time in an assembly elected by themselves. The act provided for a governor-general in Lower Canada and a lieutenant-governor in Upper Canada, both appointed by the sovereign. In each province there was an executive or advisory body, chosen by the governor of the province; a legislative council chosen in the same way, and an assembly elected by the people in certain districts on a restricted franchise. Members of both houses had to hold property to a fixed amount or lose their seats.

FIRST PARLIAMENT BUILDINGS, TORONTO, 1796-1813.

The great object of the act was to give to both Upper and Lower Canada a constitution resembling that of England as far as the circumstances of the country could permit. After an experience of some years, however, it was clear that the constitution of 1791, though giving

many privileges, had one source of weakness since
it professed to be an imitation of the English system, but
failed in that all-important principle which the experience of England has proved to be necessary for the
satisfactory working of the several branches of government ; that is to say, the principle which requires the
advisers or ministers of the head of the executive—in
other words, of the queen in England, and of a governor-
general or lieutenant-governor in Canada—to be chosen
from the political body that has a majority of the
people's representatives in the elected assembly, and to
be responsible at once to the queen, or governor-general,
or lieutenant-governor, and to the people's assembly, for
the work of administration and legislation. The English
Canadians in Upper Canada eventually understood and
pressed for the adoption of this principle, but the French
Canadian popular leaders appeared to consider the radical remedy was the election of the appointed legislative
council which was generally in French or Lower Canada
in conflict with the elected assembly.

   For some years, previous to 1840, when a new constitution was given to the two Canadas, there was a " war of
races " in Lower or French Canada, where the French
and elected element predominated in the assembly, and
the English and official or ruling element in the legislative council. The executive government and legislative
council, both nominated by the crown, were virtually
the same body in those days. The ruling spirits in the
one were the ruling spirits in the other. In this contest
of race, religion and politics, the passions of men became
bitterly inflamed and an impartial historian must depre-
cate the mistakes and faults that were committed on

both sides. But looking at the record from a purely constitutional point, it must be admitted that the majority in the assembly were right in contending for the control of the public expenditures in accordance with the principles of English parliamentary government. The voting of money is essentially the privilege of a people's house, though no measure can become law without the consent of the upper house, which may reject, but cannot change, a taxation or money bill. Another grievance was the sitting of judges in both houses. It was not until the assembly deluged the imperial parliament with addresses on the subject, that this grievous defect disappeared from the political system.

In Upper Canada the political difficulties never assumed so serious an aspect as in the French Canadian section. No difference of race could arise in the western province, and the question of money and expenditure gradually arranged itself more satisfactorily than in Lower Canada, but nevertheless the people at large had their grievances. An official class, called sarcastically "a family compact," held within its control practically the government of the province. The "clergy reserves question," which grew out of the grant to the Protestant Church of Canada of large tracts of land by the Constitutional Act of 1791, was long a burning question in the contest of parties. The Church of England and the Church of Scotland alone derived advantages from this valuable source of revenue.

In those times of popular agitation, the great danger arose from the hostility of the two races in the political field as well as in their social and public relations. At last, the political difficulties in French Canada ended

in the rebellion of 1837-38, led by Louis Joseph
Papineau, and Wolfred Nelson, the leaders of the popular
party. This insurrection never extended over any large
section of the French province, but was very soon
repressed by the vigorous measures taken by the civil
and military authorities. In Upper Canada, the popular
leader, William Lyon Mackenzie, attempted to excite a
rising of the people against the government, but it never
made any headway, and he was obliged to find refuge
in the states of the American federal republic. The
result was the suspension of the representative constitution given to Lower Canada by the act of 1791, and the
government of the province from 1838 to 1840 by a
governor-general and a special council appointed by
himself. The most important fact of this time, on
account of its influence on later constitutional changes,
was the mission of Lord Durham, a distinguished English

Durham

statesman, who was authorized by the imperial government to inquire into the state of the country as governor-
general and high commissioner with large powers.
Few state papers in English history have had greater
influence on the political development of the colonies
than the report which was the result of his judicial
survey of the political condition of all the provinces of
British North America. On no point did he dwell
more strongly than on the necessity that existed for
entrusting the government to the hands of those in
whom the representative body, or people's house, had

confidence. The final issue of the inquiries made by the imperial government into the affairs of the country was the passage of another act in the English parliament providing for a very important constitutional change in Canada.

5.—Period of Responsible Government in Canada, 1840-1867.

The act of 1840, which reunited the provinces of Upper and Lower Canada under one government, was the commencement of that Fourth Period of political development which lasted until 1867. The French Canadians looked upon the act at first with much suspicion. The fact that the French language was no longer placed on the same footing as English, in official documents and parliamentary proceedings, together with the fact that Upper Canada had the same representation as Lower Canada in the assembly, despite the larger population of the latter section at the time of union, was considered an injustice to the French Canadians, against which they did not fail to remonstrate for years. But so far from the act of 1840, which united the Canadas, acting unfavourably to the French Canadian people, it gave them eventually a predominance in the councils of the country and prepared the way for the larger constitution of 1867 which has handed over to them the control of their own province. French soon became the official language by an amendment of the union act, and the clause providing for equality of representation proved a security to French Canada when the upper province increased more largely in population than the French Canadian section. The act of 1840 was framed on the

principle of giving larger political privileges to the
Canadians and was accompanied by instructions to the
governor-general, Mr. Poulett Thomson, afterwards Lord
Sydenham, which laid the foundation of responsible
government. It took several years to give full effect to
the leading principles of parliamentary government, and
it was not until the arrival in 1847 of Lord Elgin, one of
the ablest governors-general Canada has ever had, that
the people enjoyed in its completeness that system of
the responsibility of the cabinet to parliament without
which our constitution would be unworkable. The
Canadian legislature was given full control of taxation,
supply and expenditure in accordance with English
constitutional principles. The clergy reserves difficulty
was settled and the lands sold for public or municipal
purposes, the interest of existing rectors and incumbents
being guarded. The great land question of Canada, the
seigniorial tenure of Lower Canada, was disposed of by
buying off the claims of the seigniors, and the people of
Lower Canada were freed from exactions which had
become not so much onerous as vexatious, and were
placed on the free footing of settlers in all the English
communities of America. Municipal institutions of a
liberal nature, especially in the province of Ontario, were
established and the people of the two provinces enabled
to have that control over their local affairs in the
counties, townships, cities and parishes, which is necessary
to carry out public works indispensable to the comfort,
health and convenience of the community, and to
supplement the efforts made by the legislature, from
time to time, to provide for the general education of the
country. The civil service, which necessarily plays so

important a part in the administration of government, was placed on a permanent basis.

The legislative union did its work until the political conditions of Canada again demanded another radical change in keeping with the material and political development of the country, and capable of removing the difficulties that had arisen in the operation of the act of 1840. The claims of Upper Canada to larger represent-ation — equal to its increased population since 1840, owing to the great immigration which naturally sought a rich and fertile province—were steadily resisted by the French Canadians as an undue interference with the security guaranteed to them under the act. This resistance gave rise to great irritation in Upper Canada where a powerful party made representation by population their platform, and government at last became practically impossible on account of the close political divisions for years in the assembly. The time had come for the accomplishment of a great change foreshadowed by Lord Durham, Chief Justice Sewell of Quebec, Mr. Howe of Nova Scotia, Sir Alexander Galt of Canada, and other public men : *the union of the provinces of British North America.*

But before I proceed to refer to the results of the convention of British American statesmen that met at Quebec in 1864, and framed a system of federal union, it is necessary that I should first refer to the progress of popular government in the maritime provinces, so that this historical sketch may be made complete until 1867.

CHAPTER V.

6.—Maritime Provinces: Nova Scotia, New Brunswick, P. E. Island, and Cape Breton, 1714-1867.—7. Newfoundland.

6.—Maritime Provinces, 1714-1867.

Nova Scotia, New Brunswick, and Prince Edward Island were formerly portions of the French domain in America. John Cabot, a Venetian in the employ of Henry VII. of England, appears to have discovered Cape Breton and Nova Scotia in 1497 and 1498, but the French were the first to make a settlement in 1605 on the banks of the Annapolis Basin. Nova Scotia, New Brunswick and a considerable part of Maine were in the days of French rule known as Acadie,* an Indian name. The present maritime provinces became the possession of England by the treaties of Utrecht (1713) and of Paris (1763). None of these provinces were ever given written constitutions by the parliament of Great Britain, as was the case with old Canada; but to all intents and purposes they enjoyed, previous to 1867, as complete a system of self-government as that large province. Their constitutions must be sought in the commissions of the lieutenant-governors, despatches of

---

* *Akáde* means a place, and was always used in connection with another Indian word showing some feature of the locality. Thus Anagwākáde is White Place or Point.

the colonial secretary of state, imperial statutes, and various official documents, which granted in the course of time a legislative system and responsible government.

In Nova Scotia, from 1713 to 1758, the provincial government consisted of a governor or lieutenant-governor and a council possessing both legislative and executive powers. A legislative assembly sat for the first time at Halifax on the 2nd October, 1758, or thirty-four years before representative assemblies met at Newark (now Niagara), the capital of Upper Canada for several years, and at Quebec, the capital of Lower Canada.

NOVA SCOTIA PROVINCE BUILDING.

New Brunswick, founded by Loyalists, was separated from Nova Scotia, and created a distinct province in 1784. Its first government consisted of a lieutenant-governor, and a council having both legislative and executive functions, and an assembly elected by the people.

At the time of the outbreaks in Upper and Lower Canada, 1837-8, there was still a considerable amount of dissatisfaction in the maritime provinces, arising from the existence of an irresponsible council exercising executive, legislative and even judicial powers, the constant interference of the imperial government in purely local matters, and the abuse of the powers of the representative and executive bodies ; but if there was in those sections less discontent and less obstruction to the regular course of government, it was because in them there was a nearer approach to sound constitutional practice. In New Brunswick especially, the political controversies that had been extremely bitter between the executive and legislative authorities were, to a great extent, ended by the grant of all the revenues to the assembly. Before 1840 the legislative council in the two provinces was no longer allowed to exercise both executive and judicial functions. By 1848 the principles of responsible government were formally carried out as in the province of Canada.

The island of Cape Breton, known also as *Isle Royale* in French Canadian history, was not ceded to England until 1763. It was under the government of Nova Scotia from 1763 to 1784 when it was given a separate government consisting of a lieutenant-governor and council having very limited legislative as well as executive functions. This constitution remained in force until the reannexation of the island in 1820 to Nova Scotia of which it still forms a part.

The island of Prince Edward, formerly known as St.
John, formed a part of Nova Scotia until 1769, when it
was created a separate province, with a government consisting of a lieutenant-governor and a combined executive and legislative council.   In 1773 an assembly was
elected.   Some of the lieutenant-governors were for
years, in the early history of the island, in constant conflict with the assembly, and during one administration
the island was practically without representative govern-

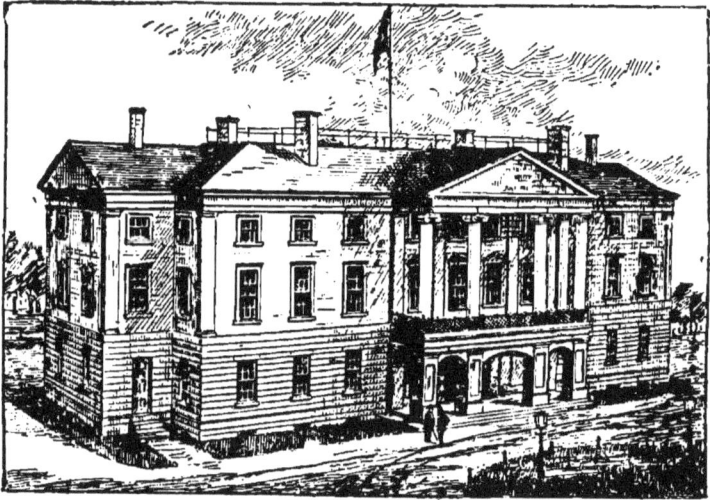

PRINCE EDWARD ISLAND PROVINCE BUILDING.

ment for ten years.   The political situation was made
much worse by the fatal mistake at the very commencement of its history, of handing over all the public lands
—in fact the whole island—to a few absentee proprietors,
and it was not until the admission of the province into
the confederation that this burning question was satisfactorily settled by the purchase of the claims of the

landlords. Responsible government was not actually
carried out until 1850-51, when the assembly obtained
full control, like the other provinces, of its public ✓
revenues, and was allowed to manage its purely local
affairs.

7.—Newfoundland.

The great island of Newfoundland, which stands at
the very gateway of the Dominion of Canada, became a
possession of England by virtue of the discoveries of
John Cabot in 1497, and of Sir Humphrey Gilbert in

LEGISLATIVE BUILDING OF NEWFOUNDLAND.

1583—the latter having formally received permission to
assert English jurisdiction over the island. For very
many years the island was only a resort for the fisher-

men of all nations and the scene of conflict between France and England. In 1713 the island was finally ceded to England, and English fishermen commenced to form settlements around its shores. Until 1832 the system of government was most arbitrary, and a few wealthy merchants in England and their agents in the colony practically controlled affairs. In that year representative institutions were allowed the people, and the government consisted of a lieutenant-governor assisted by an appointed council, with both legislative and executive functions, and an elected assembly. In 1854 responsible government was conceded. The government is placed in the hands of a lieutenant-governor appointed by the queen ; of an executive or advisory council of seven ministers ; of a legislative council of fifteen members, appointed by the governor-in-council ; of an assembly of thirty-six members, elected every four years by manhood suffrage by ballot. While the province is a colonial possession of England, France by virtue of the Treaty of Utrecht (1713), of Paris (1763), of Versailles (1783), and of Paris again (1815), enjoys certain fishery rights on a wide extent of the western and north-easterly coast, which have always prevented immigration and created difficulties which must be settled by the entire removal of those concessions if the province is ever to form a contented and prosperous portion of the Dominion of Canada.

CHAPTER VI.

FEDERAL UNION.

1. Summary of Political Rights.—2. Federal Union, 1867.— 3. Admission of British Columbia.—4. Acquisition of the Northwest Territories.—5. Three leading principles of Federal Union.—6. How Canada is Governed; Division of Authorities of Government.

1.—Summary of Political Rights, 1867.

As the previous pages show, when it was decided in 1864 to have a meeting of representatives of the British North American provinces to consider the feasibility of a union, all these countries were in possession of a complete system of local self-government, consisting of a governor-general in Canada, and a lieutenant-governor in each of the other provinces; of an executive or advisory council, appointed by the governor-general, or lieutenant-governor, and dependent on the support of the majority in the elected assembly; of a legislative council, appointed by the lieutenant-governor, with the advice of his council, in Nova Scotia and New Brunswick, but elective in Canada and Prince Edward Island; and of an assembly, elected by the people.

As we look back over the century that had passed between the Treaty of Paris, which ceded Canada to England in 1763, and the Quebec convention of 1864, we can see that the struggles of the statesmen and people of British North America had won from England

3 [33]

for all the provinces the concession of the following principles, which lie at the foundation of our whole political structure :

1. The establishment at an early period of Canadian history, of the principle of religious toleration and equality of sects.

2. The guarantees given to the French Canadians for the preservation of their law and language.

3. The adoption of the English criminal law in the French as well as the English provinces.

4. The establishment of representative institutions in every province.

5. The independence of the judiciary and its complete isolation from political influences and conflicts.

6. Complete provincial control over all local revenues and expenditures through the people's assembly.

7. The right of Canadian legislatures to manage their purely local affairs without imperial interference.

8. The establishment of municipal institutions, and the consequent increase of public spirit in all the local divisions of the old provinces of Upper and Lower Canada.

9. The adoption of the English principle of responsibility to the legislative assembly, under which a ministry or executive council can only hold office while its members have seats in that body and possess the confidence of a majority of the people's elected representatives.

2.—Federal Union, 1867.

Having had many years' experience of local self-government, having shown their ability to govern themselves, having recognized the necessity for a union which would give them greater strength within the Empire, and afford larger facilities for commercial relations between each other, and with the rest of the world, the governments of the several provinces, whose constitutional history we have briefly reviewed, united with the leaders of the opposition in the different legislative bodies, with the object of carrying out this great measure. A convention of thirty-three representative men was held in the autumn of 1864 in the historic city of Quebec, and after a deliberation of several weeks the result was the unanimous adoption of a set of seventy-two resolutions embodying the terms on which the provinces through their delegates agreed to a federal union. These resolutions had to be laid before the various legislatures and adopted in the shape of addresses to the queen whose sanction was necessary to embody the wishes of the provinces in an imperial statute.

In the early part of 1867 the imperial parliament, without a division, passed the statute known as the " British North America Act, 1867," which united in the first instance the province of Canada, now divided into Ontario and Quebec, with Nova Scotia and New Brunswick, and made provisions for the coming in of the other provinces of Prince Edward Island, Newfoundland, British Columbia, and the admission of Rupert's Land and the great Northwest.

Canada : *

Nova Scotia.

---

* The delegates to the Quebec conference, whose autographs I give above, held the following positions in their respective provinces :—

Canada : Hon. Sir Etienne P. Taché, M.L.C., premier ; Hon. John A. Macdonald, M.P.P., attorney-general of Upper Canada ; Hon. George Etienne Cartier, M.P.P., attorney-general of Lower Canada ; Hon. George Brown, M.P.P., president of the executive council ; Hon. Alexander T. Galt, M.P.P., finance minister ; Hon. Alexander Campbell, M.L.C., commissioner of crown lands ; Hon. Jean C. Chapais, M.L.C., commissioner of public works ; Hon. Thomas D'Arcy McGee, M.P.P., minister of agriculture ; Hon. Hector L. Langevin, M.P.P., solicitor-general for Lower Canada ; Hon. William McDougall, M.P.P., provincial secretary ; Hon. James Cockburn, M.P.P., solicitor-general for Upper Canada ; Hon. Oliver Mowat, M.P.P., postmaster-general.

Nova Scotia : Hon. Charles Tupper, M.P.P., provincial secretary and premier ; Hon. William A. Henry, M.P.P., attorney-general ; Hon. Robert B. Dickey, M.L.C.; Hon. Adams G. Archibald, M.P.P.; Hon. Jonathan McCully, M.L.C.

[36]

New Brunswick.

[signatures: S. L. Tilley; P. Mitchell; Charles Fisher; W. H. Steves; J. Hamilton Gray; E. B. Chandler; Jn. M. Johnson]

Prince Edward Island

[signatures: Wm. Gray; George Coles; T. Heath Haviland; Edw. Palmer; A. A. Macdonald; Edward Whelan; W. H. Pope]

Newfoundland.

[signatures: A. Shea; F. B. T. Carter]

New Brunswick: Hon. Samuel L. Tilley, M.P.P., provincial secretary and premier; Hon. Peter Mitchell, M.L.C.; Hon. Charles Fisher, M.P.P.; Hon. William H. Steves, M.L.C.; Hon. John Hamilton Gray, M.P.P., Hon. Edward B. Chandler, M.L.C.; Hon. John M. Johnson, M.P.P., attorney-general.

Prince Edward Island: Hon. John Hamilton Gray, M.P.P., premier; Hon. George Coles, M.P.P.; Hon. Thomas Heath Haviland, M.P.P.; Hon. Edward Palmer, M.P.P., attorney-general; Hon. Andrew Archibald Macdonald, M.L.C.; Hon. Edward Whelan, M.L.C.; Hon. William H. Pope, M.P.P., provincial secretary.

Newfoundland: Hon. Frederick B. T. Carter, M.P.P., speaker of the house of assembly; Hon. Ambrose Shea, M.P.P.

Newfoundland took no steps to promote union after the convention of 1864, which two of her representatives attended. Prince Edward Island joined in 1873.

3.—Admission of British Columbia.

British Columbia, which took no part in the convention, came into the federation in 1871. For many years the mainland was separate from Vancouver Island. That island was held in 1843 by the fur-trading corporation, known as the Hudson's Bay Company, and nominally made a crown colony in 1849, or a colony without representative institutions, in which the whole power rests in a governor and appointed officials. The official authority continued practically in the hands of the trading company for some years later. In 1856 an assembly was called, despite the very small population of the island. The island was united with British Columbia in 1866, and the latter name given to the united colonies. The mainland, known as New Caledonia and British Columbia previously to 1866, was also long a domain of the Hudson's Bay Company, and it was not until 1858 that it became a crown colony. In 1863 a legislative council was at first organized by the crown and was partly appointed by the governor, and partly elected by the people. By the act of 1866, uniting the island of Vancouver to the government of British Columbia, the authority of the executive government and legislature of the latter colony extended over both colonies. Until 1871, when the province of British Columbia entered the federal union of Canada, it was governed by a lieutenant-governor, appointed by the sovereign, and a legislative council, composed of heads of public departments and several elected members. Responsible government was not introduced into the province until after 1871.

4.—Acquisition of the Northwest and Formation of Manitoba.

Previous to the union of 1867 that vast country known as Rupert's Land and the Northwest Territory was under the control of the Hudson's Bay Company, who held exclusive trading rights given by Charles II. to his cousin Prince Rupert and " the company of adventurers " trading in that region. It was not until 1869 that the rights of that monopoly were purchased and the region formally transferred to the government of the Dominion of Canada. In 1870 a new province was formed under the name of Manitoba and invested with all the functions of self-government possessed by the older provinces. Subsequently the Northwest Territories were divided into the districts of Keewatin, Assiniboia, Saskatchewan, Alberta and Athabasca for purposes of administration and government.

5.—Three Leading Principles of Federal Union.

I have given a brief historical sketch of the constitutional development of the countries that compose the federal union of Canada, and I shall now proceed to direct attention to the framework of the government of that union.

The Canadian constitution, or British North America Act of 1867, is a statute of the parliament of Great Britain, before whom as the supreme legislative authority of the empire the provinces of Canada had to come and

express their desire to be federally united. In the
addresses to the queen containing the resolutions of the
Quebec conference of 1864, the legislatures of the
provinces set forth that in a federation of the British
North American provinces "the system of government
best adapted under existing circumstances to protect the
diversified interests of the several provinces, and secure
harmony and permanency in the working of the union,
would be a general government charged with matters of
common interest to the whole country, and local
governments for each of the Canadas, and for the
provinces of Nova Scotia, New Brunswick and Prince
Edward Island, charged with the control of local matters
in their respective sections."

In the third paragraph the resolutions declare that
"in framing a constitution for the general government,
the conference, with a view to the perpetuation of our
connection with the mother country, and the promotion of
the best interests of the people of these provinces, desire
to follow the model of the British constitution so far as
our circumstances permit." In the fourth paragraph it
sets forth : " The executive authority or government
shall be vested in the sovereign of the United Kingdom of
Great Britain and Ireland, and be administered according to the well-understood principles of the British
constitution, by a sovereign personally, or by the
representative of the sovereign duly authorized."

In these three paragraphs we see clearly expressed the
leading principles on which our system of government
rests :

*A federation with a central government exercising
general powers over all the members of the union, and a*

number of local governments having the control and management of certain matters naturally and conveniently belonging to them, while each government is administered in accordance with the British system of parliamentary institutions.

These are the leading principles which were made law by the British North America Act of 1867, and which I propose to explain in the course of the following pages.

6.—How Canada is Governed.

As the most intelligible mode of explaining the nature of the somewhat complicated constitution of the Dominion, I shall divide the whole subject—How Canada is Governed—into several Parts which will set forth in order the functions and responsibilities that belong to the following authorities, governing the Dominion as a dependency of England, and as a federation of provinces.

1. *The Imperial Government*, exercising executive, legislative and judicial supremacy over the dependency through a sovereign acting by and with the advice of a responsible council, a judicial committee of the privy council, and a parliament.

2. *The Dominion Government*, whose executive, legislative and judicial powers as the central authority of the federation are exercised through a governor-general appointed by the sovereign, or crown,* as legally stated, and acting by and with the advice of a responsible council, a parliament, and a supreme court.

---

* The word crown, where used in this work or any other, means the reigning sovereign, king or queen, who is represented by the governor-general of the Dominion and the lieutenant-governors of the provinces for purposes of executive government.

3. *The Provincial Governments*, exercising executive, legislative and judicial jurisdiction within their constitutional limits, through a lieutenant-governor, appointed by the governor-general in council, an advisory or executive council, a legislature, and a judiciary.

In the course of these chapters I shall necessarily explain the nature of the relations between the Imperial and Dominion governments, and between the Dominion and Provincial governments. I shall also give, as a matter of convenience, a special place to the government of the territories though it falls, strictly speaking, under the second division of powers, and to the government of municipalities and schools, though it also belongs to the third division of provincial authorities.

. BIBLIOGRAPHICAL NOTE.

I give at the conclusion of each Part of this book references to a few works which are most accessible to those students who wish to devote more attention to the subjects to which I have merely introduced my readers. For instance : Bourinot's *Manual of the Constitutional History of Canada* (Montreal, 1888), which is a text book in a number of colleges, and gives the constitution or British North America Act in full at the end. Houston's *Constitutional Documents of Canada* (Toronto, 1891), has the text of the Quebec Act of 1774, the Constitutional Act of 1791, of the Union Act of 1840, and of other statutes and official documents relating to the constitutional development of the provinces from 1760 to 1867. Dent's *Canada Since the Union of 1841* (Toronto, (1880-81), is correct. So is L. Turcotte's *Canada Sous l'Union* (Quebec, 1871), for readers of French. Professor Ashley's *Lectures on the Earlier Constitutional History of Canada* (Toronto, 1889), are useful. The official record of the *Parliamentary Debates on Confederation* in the legislature of Canada in 1865 (Quebec, 1865), should be carefully read. Every legislative and public library in Canada has copies of this book, containing the speeches of the fathers of Confederation in old Canada.

SECOND PART.

IMPERIAL GOVERNMENT.

CHAPTER I.

1. Introduction.—2. The Sovereign.—3. Origin of the Cabinet or Royal Advisory Council.—4. Working of the Cabinet System and Meaning of " Queen in Council."

1.—Introduction.

As the system of parliamentary government which Canada possesses is derived from that of England, it is important that we should clearly understand the principles on which that government rests. For the purposes of this book it is only necessary to refer briefly to the following supreme authorities of the empire:

The Sovereign,
Privy Council,
Judicial Committee of the Privy Council,
Parliament.

2.—The Sovereign.

In accordance with the constitutional usages and rules which have grown up in the course of centuries, the reigning sovereign of England, at present a queen, performs all executive acts through her privy or executive council, administers justice by her courts, and makes laws for the whole empire in her great legislature or parliament.

[45]

The crown is hereditary by English law. A statute passed during the reign of William and Mary, and called the Act of Settlement, settled the succession to the throne, vacated by James II., on the heirs of the Princess Sophia of Hanover—a German state—the granddaughter of James II. Her Majesty the Queen is a lineal de-

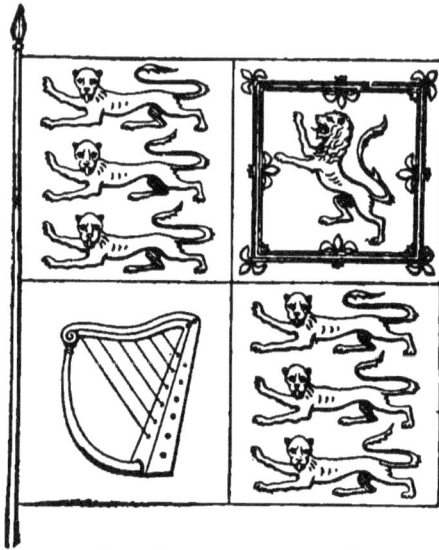

THE ROYAL STANDARD.*

scendant of this princess. The titles of her majesty at the beginning of her reign were " Victoria, by the Grace of God, of the United Kingdom of Great Britain and Ireland, Queen, Defender of the Faith." In 1877 she was proclaimed Empress of India.

---

* The Royal Standard, or personal banner of the sovereign, displays the arms of England (three lions "passant" or walking); of Scotland (a lion "rampant," or erect as if attacking); of Ireland (a harp,)—the English arms being repeated on the fourth quarter in accordance with the rules governing such heraldic devices.

On the death of the sovereign the crown descends to a male heir, and failing a son or son's son to a daughter or to a daughter's son or daughter. An uncle, nephew or male cousin of the sovereign only succeeds when there are no sons or daughters of the sovereign. The probable successor to the throne at the present time—the "heir apparent" as he is legally called—is the Prince of Wales, eldest son of the queen, who has a male heir, the Duke of York, to follow him.

Though the crown is hereditary in the family of the present sovereign, it is at the same time subject to the authority of parliament—that is to say, of the sovereign, the lords and the commons, acting together as a supreme legislature. From the earliest times in the history of England we see the evidences of the supreme authority of the English national councils in their assertion of the right to limit and regulate the succession to the throne in a national emergency. The great council of early English days, the Witenagemot or assembly of the wise men—Witan meaning wise men, and gemot, an assembly in Anglo-Saxon—elected the king, who was the chief among the nobles of the land,—the choice falling as a rule on a member of the family of the deceased sovereign. Even William of Normandy, the conqueror of England, felt it necessary to give some show of title to his claim to the throne by being chosen by a national council he called together. In later times kings were deposed and chosen by the will of similar councils of the kingdom. The revolution of 1688, which deposed James II. for his violation of the recognized or fundamental laws and rights of the people of England, and placed William and Mary of Orange on the throne, was the last example our history gives us of parliament asserting its right to regulate the succession to the crown. The laws of England declare that it is treason for any one to say that the parliament—that is to say, the king or queen, in conjunction with the two houses— is not able to make statutes of sufficient force to limit and bind the crown, and regulate and determine the descent, inheritance and government of the same. Every sovereign, at his or her coronation, solemnly promises and swears "to govern the people of this kingdom and the dominions thereto belonging according to the statutes in parliament agreed on, and the respective laws and customs of the same."

As the queen is by law the head of the executive power, all acts of gcvernment must be carried out in her name. It is by her will and pleasure that parliament is called together for the despatch of business, or is pro- rogued—that is, a session closed—or is dissolved,—that is, a new house of commons elected by the people. She is "the fountain of justice," since she is represented in her courts by her judges ; she alone can confer titles, distinctions and honours, she alone can pardon offenders against the law—this last being her highest attribute of sovereignty. All these and other prerogatives—that is to say, the ancient rights and privileges belonging to the sovereign as the head of the kingdom by law and usage —are not now immediately exercised by herself in person on her own responsibility. Every one has heard the maxim "The Queen can do no wrong." The meaning of this phrase must be sought in the constitutional history of the council who are directly responsible for the acts of the sovereign.

3.—Origin of the Cabinet or Royal Advisory Council.

From the earliest times of our history—for England's is Canada's history too—there were always councils around the sovereign whom he summoned to assist him by their advice. The several councils gradually developed with the growth of the kingdom into a parliament of two houses in which the commons had a representation, into law courts, and into a privy council. The latter was a permanent or continual council of officials and nobles, the confidential counsellors of the king. The sovereign for centuries, as late as the time of George I., sat in council. This was the executive body, as distinguished from the legislative body or parliament of which the king was the first branch, and which he alone could summon, prorogue or dissolve. This privy council became at last too large for purposes of consultation, and King Charles I. selected from its members a committee who were named a Cabinet Council because they met in the king's private chamber. In later times it was called also a "Cabal," or club of intriguers, in terms of derision. This smaller council had no special authority behind it—the privy council as a body was alone recognized by the law as the responsible executive council—but King Charles I. found it most convenient for his purposes in times when he was intriguing against parliament. In the quarrels of the Stuarts with the commons they were constantly asserting prerogatives in violation of the acknowledged rights of the people, and this council became very unpopular as the secret conclave, or cabal, for the king and his instruments. It owed no responsibility to any one but the

4

king himself. It was not necessary that its members should have seats in the popular house.

The practice of forming a committee out of the large body of privy councillors as a special or inner body of advisers of the crown has continued to the present time, and the term "Cabinet," once so unpopular, is now a title of honour and dignity. But the modern cabinet council is not the irresponsible instrument of the royal will and pleasure that it was in the days of the Stuarts. Since the revolution of 1688, when James II. was deposed, there has been gradually developed the principle that the cabinet must be composed of privy councillors not only chosen by and responsible to the sovereign, but selected from those men who have seats in parliament and have the confidence of the majority of the people's representatives in the house of commons, the elected body of the great legislative council of the nation. As long as they keep the confidence of this house they remain the counsellors or ministers of the king, and are responsible for the work of administration and legislation, but the moment they lose that confidence the sovereign must choose another set of advisers or ministers, who also must be privy councillors—for England has always clung to her old names and ancient institutions—and must have the support of the popular house. Sometimes a ministry, defeated in parliament, will be allowed by the sovereign to ask the opinion of the people at a general election. If they are supported at the polls and have a majority of the people's representatives, they remain in office. Otherwise they must give way to the men who have obtained the popular majority. Elsewhere, when I come to speak of the Canadian methods of government, which are copied from those of England, I shall explain how the prime minister or head of the cabinet or ministry, and the members of that body are chosen, (see p. 81).

4.—Working of the Cabinet System and Meaning of "Queen in Council."

From the foregoing necessarily imperfect summary three leading facts in the working of the constitutional system of England may be gathered :

1. That the privy council is, strictly speaking, the only body known to law and usage in England as the sovereign's council.

2. That in order to keep up old customs and maintain the law, the cabinet, or responsible council, is chosen from the large body of privy councillors.

3. That this responsible council must be members and have the confidence of parliament.

When members of the house of commons, who are not privy councillors, are called upon to form a ministry, they must be first sworn of the privy council.* Then they are called to the ministry or cabinet, and placed in charge of certain departments or offices of the government. One of these departments is entrusted with the supervision of the affairs of the colonial empire, and is called the secretary of state for the colonies (see *below*, p. 65).

The cabinet, or inner council, is the body that discusses

---

* English privy councillors are always styled " Right Honourable."

and decides all questions of public policy : *i.e.*, the nature of the measures to be introduced into parliament, the relations of England with foreign countries, treaties of peace, declarations of war, questions affecting the government of Great Britain and Ireland, India, and the dependencies, important appointments, and the countless matters that devolve on the government of a great nation. Its deliberations are held in secret, and when it reaches a conclusion, we see the results in executive, administrative and legislative action, according to the well understood methods of the British constitution. When the action of the head of the executive—that is of the sovereign—is necessary on any question of state, she is advised by the premier or responsible minister. When the sovereign has given her consent an order-in-council is passed, and has the effect of law. In other cases, the signature of the sovereign must also be given to the acts of the council—such as certain appointments by commission,* and other acts of royal authority. In all cases any document, which is an act of the executive, must be countersigned by a responsible minister or official and have the "great seal" or official evidence of the royal will affixed (see *below*, p. 86, for Canada's great seal). All orders-in-council, or other acts of executive power, are considered to be passed by the privy council—order-in-council means an order passed by the sovereign by and with the advice of the privy council—the only body known from old times as the permanent or advisory

---

* A commission is an authority or order to perform certain duties; all public officials, acting under the crown, have such an authority. It comes from the Latin word *committere*, to place or trust a thing somewhere.

body around the sovereign. The queen never acts alone. What she does in administration she does through the aid of a minister or ministry,—who are members of the privy council. In fact every act of the sovereign in her executive and royal capacity is done on the advice of a sworn counsellor. If the advice is wrong, or in violation of the law, the minister or ministry who gave it is open to the censure of parliament, or a particular minister may be brought before the ordinary courts of law. Consequently the maxim that "the Queen can do no wrong" has arisen from the adoption of the following constitutional principles :

1. That by no proceeding known to the law can the queen, herself the head of justice as she is of all branches of government, be made personally responsible for any act done by her in her executive capacity.

2. That every executive act is the result of the deliberation of a sworn council, who advise the queen thereon and are alone responsible for the advice.

3. That no minister of the crown can bring forward an order of the crown as a defence or justification of an act that is in violation of law.

4. That the minister who gives the advice becomes responsible and liable to punishment for misleading the crown.

The sovereign, it is well to mention here, has never sat in council with the cabinet since the days of George the First, who departed from the practice of his royal predecessors on account of his ignorance of the English language. What was in his case a matter of convenience has ever since become the settled practice. Now the sovereign—and the same is true of the governor-general of the Dominion and a lieutenant-governor of a province —is informed of the results of the deliberations of council, and acts on the advice of a responsible minister.

CHAPTER II.

1. Sovereign in Parliament.—2. Origin of Parliament.—3. Charters of English and Canadian Constitutional Liberties.—4. Strength of Parliamentary Government.—5. The Queen's Onerous Duties as a Sovereign.

1.—The Sovereign in Parliament.

Every statute or law passed by the supreme legislature or parliament of Great Britain and Ireland commences with these words :

" That it be enacted [*that is, made law*] by the queen's most excellent majesty by and with the advice and consent of the lords spiritual and temporal and commons, in this present parliament assembled, and by the authority of the same as follows." Here follow the provisions of the law or act of parliament.

I have copied these words because they show that the sovereign is still understood in law to legislate for her realm in a great legislative council known as a parliament, whilst she acts in her executive capacity in a privy council. The legislation she assents to as the first branch of parliament she executes or carries out in her executive capacity, through and by the advice of her sworn counsellors and officers appointed and sworn to execute and administer the law justly and faithfully, as I have shown above.

[55]

WESTMINSTER PALACE.

2.—Origin of Parliament.

The origin of parliament must be sought in the early assemblies of our English ancestors, who were Teutons or Germans who came from the sea-coast of northern Germany and of Denmark. The Witenagemot of old times, before the Norman conquest, was a national assembly of great nobles, and ecclesiastical dignitaries, summoned by the sovereign to consult and deliberate on the affairs of the kingdom. After the Norman conquest it became known as the "Great Council," and was practically the house of lords. It had executive, legislative, and judicial powers. The king's special or permanent council to which I have referred above, and the king's advisory law court *(curia regis)* became part of this great council at certain times, and together formed a common council of the whole realm. Eventually, the estates of the realm, the archbishops and bishops or the lords spiritual, the nobles of the kingdom or the lords temporal, and the commons, formed a parliament (for. meaning, see *above*, p. 7). It was a great noble, Simon de Montfort, of Leicester—a statesman much in advance of his age—who overthrew King Henry III. on the battlefield of Lewes, and first summoned representatives of the towns and counties to meet bishops and nobles in a parliament in 1265. This scheme of Simon de Montfort was adopted by King Edward I. in 1295, and has ever since formed the model of the parliament of England.

Edward accepted this great council, always thereafter known as parliament, as a most convenient instrument for raising taxes; it being the immemorial right of Englishmen to be taxed only with their own consent through their own representatives.   The representative principle, as applied to government, is essentially English.   Its origin can be traced to the "motes" or assemblies of the local divisions of England in early English times.   In the municipal system of Canada, as I shall show later (see *Fifth Part*), we have copied the names of those local divisions and of their public officers.

3.—Charters of English and Canadian Constitutional Liberties.

From the days of Edward I., a wise monarch, there was for centuries a constant struggle between sovereign and commons for the mastery.   The necessity for raising money by public taxation forced the most arbitrary sovereigns to summon parliament sooner or later.   At all times we find nobles and commons united to resist the unconstitutional efforts of kings to reign without the assistance of his national council.   Magna Charta, one of the great statutes of English liberty, wrung from King John, on the field of Runnymede in 1215, affirmed the fundamental principle of the constitution that Englishmen could not be taxed without the consent of the national council as then constituted.   Another great statute, known as the Petition of Right, grudgingly assented to by Charles I. four centuries later, when he could not resist the demands of parliament, again affirmed that no tax of any sort might be exacted without the consent of parliament.   The Bill of Rights, passed in 1689, when William and Mary became joint king and queen of England, was a strong declaration of the original rights of the people, violated by James II., who had fled the kingdom. This famous charter of constitutional liberty set forth among other things :

That it is illegal for the sovereign to suspend or execute laws without the consent of parliament.

That it is illegal for the sovereign to dispense with laws.

That it is illegal to levy money without the consent of parliament.

That petitions to parliament are legal and punishments for them illegal.

That parliamentary elections ought to be free.

That freedom of speech and debate in parliament is subject to parliamentary control only.

That parliaments ought to be frequently held.

These are the fundamental principles of parliamentary government in England as in all the dependencies of the crown.

4.—Strength of Parliamentary Government.

The great object of parliament is taxation in order to meet the needs of government. English sovereigns soon recognized the fact that Englishmen through their representatives in parliament must control all the taxes and expenditures of the realm. From the days of the revolution of 1688 the struggle between sovereign and the commons practically came to an end. With the development of the principle of ministerial responsibility—the presence in parliament of a body of ministers responsible at once to sovereign, commons and people—harmony was created between the executive and legislative departments. The cabinet is now the connecting link between the monarch and the people through their representatives in parliament. As advisers of the crown, as heads of the great departments of state constituting the government, as the recognized heads of the political party or combination of parties having a majority in parliament, this cabinet, which is legally a committee of the ancient privy council, are able to administer public affairs without that friction and conflict between executive and parliament which was the leading feature of old times of irresponsible councils and the personal rule of sovereigns.

When we come to consider the government of Canada we shall see carried out all the English methods and principles explained above. The queen in council, the cabinet, the parliament, are all to be found working precisely in the same way in Canada.

5.—The Queen's Laborious Duties as a Sovereign.

Although the queen performs all executive acts through responsible ministers dependent on the will of parliament and people, it must not be supposed that her functions as a sovereign are purely ornamental. On

the contrary, so high an authority as Mr. Gladstone, who has had a larger experience of government than any other living Englishman, tells us that "no head of a department performs more laborious duties than those which fall to the sovereign of this country." No despatch "is received from abroad, nor any sent from the country, which is not submitted to the queen." Her signature "has never been placed to any public document of which she did not approve." Cabinet councils "are reported and communicated on their termination by the minister to the sovereign and they often call from her remarks that are critical, and necessarily require considerable attention." In fact "such complete mastery of what has occurred in this country, and of the great important subjects of state policy, foreign and domestic," for the last fifty years is possessed by the queen "that he must be a wise man who could not profit by her judgment and experience." To these explanations of the active life of a great sovereign, it is well to add a fact not generally known to Canadians, that every governor-general is instructed to communicate directly to her majesty, from time to time, the fullest information on all questions of moment to Canada and the empire.

CHAPTER III.

*1.—Origin of Courts of Justice.—2. Judicial Committee of the
Privy Council.*

1.—Origin of the Courts of Justice.

We now come to the third division of government—
the judicial authority. The queen is the fountain of
justice, and it is administered in her name. In old
times, before government assumed its present forms and
methods of action, the sovereign dispensed justice
immediately and personally in a great council or court.
The nobles, lay and ecclesiastic, the great judicial officers
of the realm, the chief justice or justiciar—next to the
king in authority—and the chancellor formed a national
. supreme court of law (*curia regis*), over which the
sovereign presided.

In the course of many years after the conquest courts
of law were formed out of the great court or council of
the kingdom. The old names of these courts still exist
in English law, as I shall show when I come to refer to
Canadian courts (see *below*, p. 177). With the development
of parliamentary government, after the revolution of
1688, the judiciary were made practically independent
of the crown, and of all political influences. Their
tenure of office was made one of good behaviour,
and they can now be removed only on an address to the
crown by the two houses of parliament, after formal

[62]

impeachment * for grave offences and after full investigation of any charges made against them.

2.—The Judicial Committee of the Privy Council of England.

With the constitution and procedure of the courts of law of England Canadians have no direct connection. Justice is administered in their own courts, which have full jurisdiction over all matters of Canadian concern, and the queen is in theory as much present in Canadian as in English courts. But over the empire there is one great court of appeal, to which reference can be made in cases of important controversy and doubt. The origin of this court, called the judicial committee of the privy council, must be sought in the fact that even after the formation of the regular courts out of the great court or council of the sovereign in early times (see *above*, p. 49), some of the judicial powers still remained and were exercised in the permanent or continual council of the sovereign. The great council became the house of lords, which still has a remnant of its judicial powers, while the permanent council became the privy council. This latter was eventually divided into committees, which still discharge some of their old functions. One of these committees is the judicial committee, or supreme court of the empire (see *below*, p. 65). It is now regulated by statute and composed of the lord high chancellor and other legal functionaries, who must all be members of the queen's privy council. Here, again, we see the tendency of Englishmen to preserve the form of ancient institutions.

---

* To "impeach" means to prefer grave charges of official misconduct against a judge or other functionary, but its origin is obscure.

CHAPTER IV.

NATURE OF IMPERIAL CONTROL OVER CANADA.

1. Introduction.—2. Governor-General.—3. Secretary of State for the Colonies.—4. Judicial Committee.—5. Canadian Rights of Self-Government.—6. Making of Treaties.—7. When Canadian Legislative Acts may be Disallowed.

1.—Introduction.

With these explanations of the leading principles of the supreme government of the empire, I come now to explain to my readers in what manner and to what extent this imperial government can and does exercise authority or control over this dependency of Canada. The following principles and methods of procedure may be laid down as governing the relations between the imperial and dominion governments:

2.—The Governor-General.

The queen, as the head of the executive authority of the empire, acts through a governor-general appointed in council, and consequently an imperial officer. It is through him all communications between the imperial and Canadian government must pass. When the Canadian parliament requires any legislation that properly falls within the jurisdiction of the imperial legislature, addresses to the queen are passed by the former body, setting forth the nature of this legislation—such as an

[64]

amendment or necessary change in the fundamental law
of the Dominion or British North America Act of 1867,
which is an imperial statute, and can only be amended
in certain respects by the same authority that gave it.
This address is forwarded by the Canadian governor-
general with such remarks as are necessary, to one of
her majesty's ministers.

3.—The Secretary of State for the Colonies.

This minister, or privy councillor, is the head of the
department of colonial affairs and known as the secretary of state for the colonies,—all possessions of the
crown, except India, being designated colonies. It is
for this important minister, who has always a seat in the
inner council or cabinet, to bring the address or other
matter requiring the action of the queen and council
before that body in the manner required by usage. The
council on his advice will agree to introduce and pass
such legislation in parliament as will meet the difficulty
that has occurred in the Dominion. By the constant
interchange of communications between the imperial and
dominion governments, agreements are come to, as a
rule, on every question which requires adjustment, and
any friction in the relations of the two governments
prevented.

4.—The Judicial Committee.

The queen's courts in Canada administer justice in all
cases affecting Canadians, whether of a criminal or civil
nature, in accordance with the rights of self-government
accorded by law to the Dominion. Appeals are, however, made from the supreme and superior courts of the

5

Dominion to the judicial committee of the privy council under such conditions as have been laid down by that body under the law. The appellants, or parties who are not satisfied with the decision of the Canadian courts, petition the queen in council for leave to appeal, and if the appeal is allowed—for there are cases where the appeal may be refused—the whole case, as it appears on the record, is submitted to the judicial committee, composed of eminent judges—generally four, though three are a quorum—who hear arguments and finally report their decision to the queen in council. This decision is authoritative and settles the case. Criminal cases cannot be appealed from Canada to this court. Nor will the judicial committee admit an appeal from the supreme court of Canada, save where the case is of gravity (see *below*, p. 130).

5.—Canadian Rights of Self-Government.

It is a fundamental principle of the English constitution, as I have shown above, that a people under English government can be taxed only with their own consent, through their representatives, under the forms prescribed by law. The imperial state having granted to Canada a complete system of local self-government, with full control over taxation and expenditure, it is only in Canadian parliaments—and I here include provincial legislatures—that Canadian taxes can be imposed and Canadian moneys expended. If at any time Canada requires imperial legislation, on any subject not within her executive or legislative control, she applies to the queen in council in the way I have described above (see p. 64).¹ The imperial parliament cannot of its own motion constitutionally interfere with rights of local self-government granted to the dependency.

6.—Making of Treaties with Foreign Powers.

The queen's government alone, as the supreme executive of the empire, can commence and negotiate treaties with foreign sovereign nations. Canada' being only a dependency cannot of her own motion or action give validity to a treaty with a sovereign nation. It is through the imperial government and its representatives that all treaties immediately affecting her must be made. It is, however, now an understanding, or even maxim of the policy governing the relations between England and the Canadian Dominion, that Canadian representatives shall be chosen and clothed with all necessary authority by the queen in council to arrange treaties immediately affecting Canada, and all such treaties must be ratified by the Canadian parliament.

7.—When Canadian Legislative Acts may be . "Disallowed."

It is still a provision of the Canadian constitution that every act passed by the parliament of Canada should be submitted by the governor-general to the queen in council. This is a declaration of the sovereign authority of the imperial government, and only means in practice that it is within the power of the queen in council, responsible for the unity and security of the whole empire, to refuse to consent to, or in the constitutional words, "disallow," an act (see *below*, p. 163) which is in conflict with the interests of the empire at large, may threaten its integrity, and is at variance with treaties with England, a foreign nation, or with imperial legislation. It would be unconstitutional, however, for the imperial government to interfere in any matter clearly and exclusively within the authority of the dominion government. When the imperial parliament gave Canada a federal union and a complete system of local self-government, and the right to legislate on certain subjects set forth in the fundamental law of the constitution (the British North America Act of 1867), it gave her full control of all such matters, and constitutionally withdrew from all interference in the strictly local concerns of the Dominion. It is only when the interests of the empire are in direct conflict with the privileges extended to the dependency that the sovereign authority of England should be brought into action. This sovereign authority should never be arbitrarily or indiscreetly exercised, but should be the result of full discussion between the governments of England and the dependency, so that the interests of the two may be brought, as far as possible, into harmony with each other.

BIBLIOGRAPHICAL NOTE.

A useful elementary book on English constitutional history is David Watson Rannie's *Historical Outline of the English Constitution* (New York, 1881). Valuable books and articles for more advanced students are the following : Ewald's " *The Crown and Its Advisers* " ; or, *Queen, Ministers, Lords and Commons* (Edinburgh and London, 1870), Professor Freeman's *Growth of the English Constitution from the Earliest Times* (London and New York, 1884), Dicey's *History of the Privy Council* (London and New York, 1887), Mr. Reeve's article on *The Cabinet* in the 9th edition of the *Encyclopædia Britannica*, Professor Freeman's article on the *History of England* in the same work, vol. viii., pp. 263-368, with an index at end of subjects treated in the paper ; Professor Woodrow Wilson's sketch of the institutional history and administration of England, in pp. 651-821, *The State* (Boston, 1889). Carmichael's edition of Taswell-Langmead's *English Constitutional History* (London, 1890), is the best history for students in general, since it is both readable, intelligible and correct. Bagehot's *English Constitution* (London and New York, 1884), is a very clear treatise on the practical operation of parliamentary government. It was the first successful attempt to show the defects of the constitutional system of the federal republic of the United States, arising out of the absence of a political cabinet responsible for the work of administration and legislation, and having seats in congress.

THIRD PART.

THE DOMINION GOVERNMENT.

[71]

CHAPTER I.

THE DOMINION GOVERNMENT: EXECUTIVE POWER.

1.—Introduction.

IN the previous chapter, I have given a short summary of the different authorities that govern the empire as a whole, and now come to the government of the Dominion itself. This government is divided among the following authorities :

The sovereign, as the head of the executive, represented by a governor-general.

A cabinet selected from the members of the privy council for Canada, and forming the responsible advisory council of the sovereign's representative.

A parliament, exercising legislative functions over the whole of Canada.

A supreme court, exercising judicial functions as a court of appeal from the courts of the provinces, and for the settlement of constitutional difficulties.

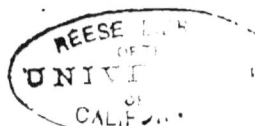

[73]

The duties of these separate authorities will now be explained.

2.—The Governor-General.

The queen is the head of the executive government of Canada. She is as much the sovereign of Canada as of England or of Scotland, or of Ireland, and her supremacy can be alone acknowledged in all executive or legislative acts of this dependency. As she is unable to be present in person in Canada she is represented by a governor-general appointed by her majesty in council.

This functionary, generally chosen from public men of high standing in England, has double responsibilities, for he is at once the governor-in-chief of a great dependency, who acts under the advice of a ministry responsible to parliament, and at the same time the guardian of imperial interests. He is bound by the terms of his commission, and can only exercise such authority as is expressly or impliedly entrusted to him by the queen. He must report regularly on all those imperial and other matters on which the secretary of state for the colonies should be informed, (see *above*, p. 64). In bills reserved for the consideration of the imperial government he forwards them to the secretary of state with his reasons for reserving them. The British North America Act provides that copies of all acts of the Canadian parliament shall be sent by him to the secretary of state for the colonies, that they may be duly considered and disallowed within two years in case they are found to conflict with imperial interests and are beyond the legitimate powers of Canada as a dependency. The governor-general, as the acting head of the executive of Canada, assembles,

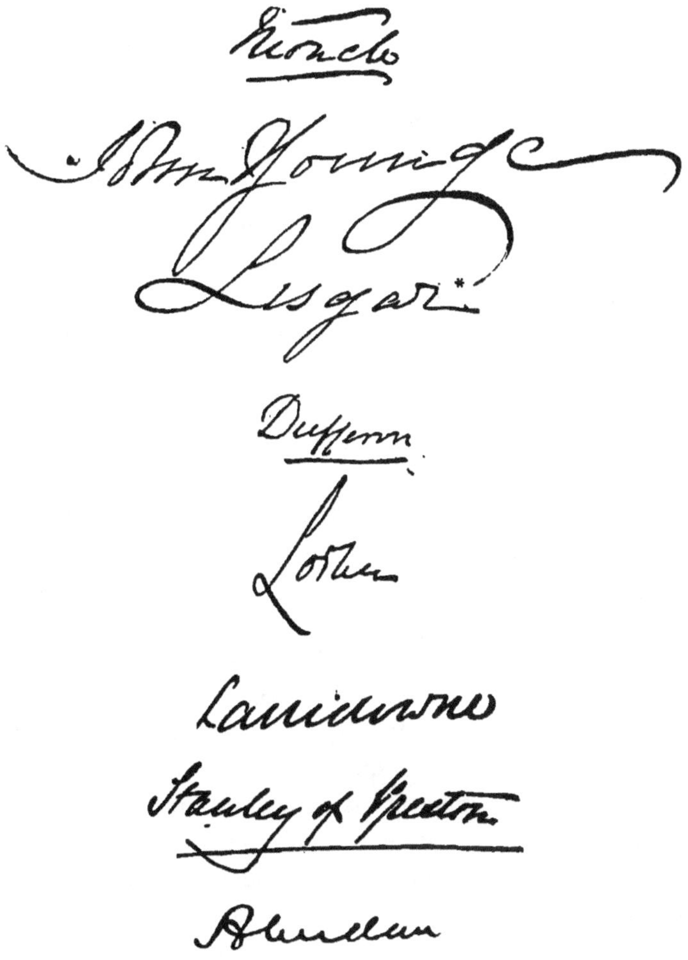

(handwritten autographs)

Monck

Wm Young
Lisgar*

Dufferin

Lorne

Lansdowne

Stanley of Preston

Aberdeen

AUTOGRAPHS OF GOVERNORS-GENERAL SINCE 1867.

---

* Sir John Young was created Baron Lisgar in 1870, while governor-general.

[75]

prorogues and dissolves parliament and assents to or
reserves bills in the name of her majesty; but, in the
discharge of these and all other executive duties, he acts
entirely by and with the advice of his council who must
always have the support of the house of commons.
Even in matters of imperial interest affecting Canada he
consults with the council and submits their views to the
colonial secretary of state in England. On Canadian
questions clearly within the constitutional jurisdiction of—
the Dominion he cannot act apart from his advisers, but
is bound by their advice. Should he differ from them on
some vital questions of principle or policy he must either
recede from his own position or be prepared to accept
the great responsibility of dismissing them; but a dis-
missal of a ministry is an extreme exercise of authority
and not in consonance with the general constitutional
practice of modern times, when his advisers have a
majority in the popular branch of the legislature. Should
he, however, feel compelled by very exceptional circumstances to resort to the extreme exercise of the royal
prerogative, he must be prepared to find another body of
advisers ready to assume the full responsibility of his
action and justify it before the house and country. For
every act of the crown, in Canada and in England, there
must be some one immediately responsible, apart from
the crown itself. But a governor, like any other subject,
cannot be "freed from the responsibility for his acts nor
be allowed to excuse a violation of the law on the plea of
having followed the counsels of evil advisers." Cases
may arise when the governor-general will hesitate to
come to a speedy conclusion on a matter involving
important consequences, and then it is quite proper for

him to seek advice from his official chief, the secretary of state for the colonies, even if it be a matter not immediately involving imperial interests.

The royal prerogative of mercy is no longer exercised on the sole judgment and responsibility of the governor-general, but is administered pursuant to the advice of the minister of justice. With respect to the allowance or disallowance of provincial acts, ever since the coming into force of the British North America Act, the governor-general has invariably decided on the advice of his ministers, and has never asserted a right to decide otherwise. Even in the exercise of the all-important prerogative of dissolution, which essentially rests in the crown, he acts on the advice of his advisers. Mutual consultation, as a rule, brings councillors of the crown into perfect harmony with their constitutional head.

Occupying a position of neutrality between opposing political parties, and having no possible object in view except to promote the usefulness and dignity of his high office, the governor-general must necessarily, in the discharge of his important functions, have many opportunities of aiding the interests of the country over whose government he presides. Although the initiation of public measures necessarily rests with the ministry, yet there are numerous occasions when his counsel is invaluable in the maturing of matters of the gravest political concern. If we could see into the inner councils of government we would be surprised at the influence a prudent and conscientious governor can and does exercise in the administration of public affairs. While he continues to be drawn from the ranks of distinguished Englishmen he evokes respect as a link of connection between the parent state and its dependency. In the performance of his social duties he is brought into contact with all shades of opinion, and wields an influence that may elevate social life and soften the bitterness of public controversy by allowing public men to meet on a common ground and under conditions which win their respect. In the tours he takes from time to time throughout the Dominion he is able to make himself acquainted with all classes and interests, and, by the information he gathers in this way, of the resources of the country he can make himself an important agent in the development of Canada. In the encouragement of science, art and literature he has always a fruitful field in which he may perform invaluable service.

3.—The Privy Council of Canada.

The British North America Act of 1867 provides that the council, which aids and advises the governor-general, shall be styled the " Queen's privy council for Canada," recalling that ancient council whose history is always associated with that of the king as far back as the earliest days of which we have authentic record (see *above*, p. 49). As in England, the terms " cabinet," " ministry," " administration," and " government," are indifferently applied in Canada to those members of the privy council who are for the time being at the head of public affairs. Privy councillors, when not in the government, retain their honorary rank, but it is simply one that entitles them to certain precedence on state occasions and has no official responsibility. When the governor-general appoints a body of advisers to assist him in the government he calls them first to be members of the privy council and then to hold certain offices or departments of state. It sometimes happens, however, that ministers are appointed to the cabinet without a portfolio or department, in accordance with English practice. The number of members of the cabinet vary from thirteen to fifteen, of whom twelve are heads of departments, whose duties are regulated by law and usage. At the present time there are the following heads of departments or divisions of the government for purposes of administration : .

1. *The President of the Privy Council*, who presides over the meetings of the cabinet, and has no departmental duties except those done under his supervision by the clerks, relating to the work of the council. ʻAll orders in council, and acts of the council, are sent from this office to those departments and persons who have to act under them.

2. *Minister of Justice and Attorney General of Canada*, who is the legal adviser of the governor-general and all departments of the government. He has the supervision of matters affecting the administration of justice in Canada, reviews all legislative acts of the provinces within one year after their receipt (see *below*, p. 168), and in short is the law officer of the Dominion government generally. He has also the superintendence of the prisons and penitentiaries of Canada.

3. *Minister of Finance and Receiver General*, who has charge of all matters relating to the finances and expenditures of the Dominion. He lays before parliament the "budget" (see *below*, p. 119) or official statement of the financial condition of the country, explains the policy of the government ʻwith respect to public taxation, the public credit, and the public currency. .

4. *Minister of Trade and Commerce*, who has control of all matters relating to trade, and a general supervision over the collection of customs and excise duties (see *below*, p. 134) and the officers entrusted with the administration of those departments (see *below*, p. 81).

5. *Minister of Agriculture*, who has charge of the following matters :—Agriculture, immigration, public health and quarantine, marine and immigrant hospitals, census, statistics, and registration of statistics, patents of invention, copyright, industrial designs and trade marks, experimental farms.

6. *Secretary of State*, who has charge of all the correspondence between the government and the provinces, and on all other official matters relating to government generally ; registers all documents issued under the great seal (see *below*, p. 86) ; has charge of public printing and of the purchase and distribution of stationery for all the departments of the public service.

7. *Minister of Marine and Fisheries*, who has supervision, under the laws of Canada, of the sea-coast and inland fisheries, lighthouses, beacons, harbours and piers, steamers ·and vessels belonging to the government, examination of masters and mates of vessels, inspection of steamers, establishment and regulation of marine hospitals, and generally such matters as are connected with the marine, fisheries and navigation of Canada.

8. *Minister of Militia and Defence*, who is responsible for the administration of militia affairs, including fortifications, armouries, munitions of war, stores, schools of instruction, military college at Kingston.   Under him is a major-general, chosen from the regular military service of England.

9. *Minister of the Interior*, who has control an management of the affairs of the Northwest Territories, of the Indians, and of all public lands belonging to the government, and of the geological survey of Canada.

10. *Postmaster General*, who has the management of the post offices and all arrangements relating to the postal service in Canada, and between her and all other parts of the world.

11. *Minister of Public Works*, who has charge of the construction, repairs and maintenance of all public buildings and works (except railways and canals).

12. *Minister of Railways and Canals*, who has charge of the Intercolonial Railway between the city of Quebec, Halifax, and St.

John, and all matters which the law entrusts to him in connection with railways throughout the Dominion. All the canals of Canada are also under his direction and superintendence.

Under all these political heads of departments, there are deputy ministers, permanent and non-political, appointed by the governor-general in council, and also a large body of clerks and officials, who are appointed and promoted in accordance with the rules of the civil service of Canada (see *below* p. 84).

4.—Ministers not in the Cabinet.

In 1892 a step was taken in the direction of the English practice of having ministers with seats in parliament, but not in the cabinet. By the present law there is a controller of customs in charge of the department of customs, and a controller of inland revenue, acting under the general instructions of the minister of trade and commerce. These ministers go out of office when the government of which they form a portion are defeated at a general election or in parliament. A solicitor-general, who is assistant attorney-general of Canada, has also a seat in parliament and is in the same political position as the two controllers. Such was the position of the two controllers until late in 1895, when they were made privy councillors and members of the Cabinet—an anomalous condition of things not yet (Feb. 1, 1896) satisfactorily explained in parliament.   X

5.—The Premier of the Cabinet.

As the members of a cabinet only occupy office while they retain the confidence of the lower house, the majority necessarily sit in that body, though there is always a certain representation (from four to two), in the

6

upper branch or senate. Since the commons hold the purse strings, and directly represent the people, all the most important departments, especially of finance and revenue, must necessarily be represented in that branch. The ministry, then, is practically a committee of the two houses. Its head is known as the "premier" or prime minister, who, as the leader of a political party, and from his commanding influence and ability, is in a position to lead the houses and control the government of the country. His title, however, is one unknown to the law, though borrowed from the English political system. It originates from the fact that he is first called upon by the sovereign (or, in Canada, by her representative) to form a ministry. The moment he is entrusted with this high responsibility it is for him to choose such members of his party as are likely to bring strength to the government as a political body, and capacity to the administration of public affairs. The governor-general, on his recommendation, appoints these men to the ministry. As a rule, on all matters of important public policy the communications between the cabinet and governor take place through the premier, its official head. Every minister, however, has a right to communicate with the governor-general on ordinary departmental matters. If the premier dies or resigns the cabinet is dissolved, and the ministers can only hold office until a new premier is called to the public councils by the representative of the crown. It is for the new premier then to ask them to remain in office, or to accept their resignation. In case a government is defeated in parliament, the premier must either resign or else convince the governor-general that he is entitled to a dissolution or general election on the ground that the vote of censure does not represent the sentiment of the country.

6.—Rules and Usages of Parliamentary Government.

In the rules governing the formation of the cabinet, its dissolution by death of the premier, its resignation when defeated in the commons, and the relations between the governor-general and his advisers, we see the operation of the conventions, understandings and maxims that have grown up in the course of time, and make parliamentary government workable. These conventions, rules and usages are not "rules of law" in the strict sense of the phrase. We do not find them laid down in the British North America Act, or in any statute or law of England or of Canada. The courts can hear and decide any case or action arising out of the provisions of the written law of the constitution, but they could not be asked to decide on such a matter as the propriety of a ministry resigning on a hostile vote in the people's house. These conventions and under-standings have now entered into the practice of parliamentary government as absolutely essential to its operation, and have now as much force in England and the self-governing dependencies as any legal enactment, since they have the sanction of public approval.

7.—The Governor-General in Council.

All orders in council, commissions, proclamations, and other acts of executive authority, follow the course of English precedent (see *above*, p. 52). The governor-general in council means the governor-general acting by and with the advice of his committee of the privy council of Canada—that is to say, the cabinet. Proclamations summoning, proroguing and dissolving parliament, writs of election, and commissions to office must be signed by the governor-general, countersigned by a minister or other proper officer, and bear the great seal of Canada (see *below*, p. 86). On every executive act there must be the evidence of ministerial responsibility and authority.

8.—Civil Service.

The effectiveness of administration largely depends on the conduct and ability of the civil service of Canada, which is the term generally applied to all classes of public officials and employees in the several departments of the executive government. " Civil service " is an old English phrase, used to distinguish the subordinates in the civil government from the naval and military services of the country.

All public officials are appointed by the governor on the recommendation of the ministry of the day. All appointments are "during pleasure"—practically, during "good behaviour"—and the great body of clerks and employees below the rank of deputy head (see *above*, p. 81) must pass an examination on their admission and serve a term of probation or trial of not less than six months before finally placed on the staff of a department. A board of examiners is appointed by the governor-general in council to examine all candidates for admission and give certificates of competency to those persons who pass·an examination successfully. Promotions are made under special examination in the departments of the

public service. But city postmasters, inspectors of post offices, inspectors, collectors and preventive * officers in the customs, inspectors of weights and measures, deputy collectors, and preventive officers in the inland revenue department, may be and are generally appointed without examination. These offices are given as rewards for political services. The moment, however, these men are appointed and show themselves capable in the discharge of their duties, they become the servants of the people at large, and not of a particular party or administration. Recognizing their obligations in this respect, the public officials of the Dominion must keep aloof from party conflict and intrigue, and confine themselves to the legitimate functions devolving upon them. When they have attained a certain age, or become incapable of performing their duties, they are allowed a fair superannuation or retiring allowance under the conditions laid down in the law. Civil servants and officers of the senate and house of commons must have served for not less than ten years, and have attained the age of sixty at least, though in practice over sixty-five is the minimum, except in case of incapacity. The allowance is calculated on the average yearly salary for the last three years of service. In case of special professional qualifications, the governor-in-council may add ten years to the actual term of service. A reduction of two per cent annually is made from the salaries of officials toward meeting the expenditures for superannuation. The revenue does not meet the cost of this allowance so

---

* Preventive officers are those whose duties are to prevent smuggling of goods into Canada, that is to say, without paying the duty required by law.

far. Whatever defects may still exist in the rules and practices that regulate the public service, it is not too much to say that the permanent officials of Canada are, as a body, an industrious and efficient class, whose services are indispensable to the administration of public affairs.

9.—Great Seal of Canada.

By her majesty's command the government of the Dominion of Canada has authority to use a special great seal, composed of the royal effigy, with appropriate armorial surroundings and a combination of the arms of the four provinces that first entered into a federal union. The provincial arms are not arranged on a shield in four divisions, or "quarterly" as set forth in the royal order, but the seal is actually composed as follows:

The queen seated upon the throne, crowned, and with orb and sceptre in her hands. Placed, apparently, upon the straight stems of two young oak trees on either side of her, the leaves and acorns showing between the shields, are four *separate* shields; upon her right hand hangs the coat of arms of Ontario, that of Nova Scotia beneath it; on her left the shield of Quebec, with that of New Brunswick below. Beneath her feet is a shield displaying her own coat of arms, without supporters, crown, or motto; in the tracery above the throne or chair of state is the motto "Dieu et mon droit" (God and my Right). In the circular margin of the whole seal, in large letters: "Victoria Dei Gratia Britanniar. Regina F. D. In Canada Sigillum. (Victoria by the grace of God queen of Britain, defender of the Faith. Seal in Canada.")

The illustration on the opposite page will give a better idea of the seal than a mere verbal description.

This seal, in accordance with the usages of English law, is the emblem of the royal authority in Canada, the

The Great Seal.

evidence of the royal will and prerogative exercised under the constitutional forms peculiar to our system of government. We can trace the use of such a seal to very early times in English history. Its keeper always was and is still the lord high chancellor of England —the highest judicial officer of the crown—who originally was one of the clerks or secretaries of the king, by whose order he affixed the seal to all official documents of royal command. Absolute faith is given to every paper that bears this seal. In Canada it is affixed to proclamations summoning, proroguing and dissolving parliament ; to writs of election, commissions of lieutenant-governors, judges, members of the privy council, departmental ministers, speaker and members of the senate, chief clerks of the two houses, deputy ministers, and numerous other public officers ; and in short to all official and executive acts of the queen, done under the authority of the governor-general in council. All documents bearing the great seal must be countersigned by a crown officer or secretary of state.

10.—Dominion Coat of Arms.

The arms of the Dominion are composed of the arms of the four original provinces—Ontario, Quebec, Nova Scotia and New Brunswick—quartered or combined in one shield, as is shown next page and on flag of governor-general on another page (see *below*, p. 90). It is not unusual to add the armorial bearings of the other provinces that have been brought into the union since 1867*—Prince Edward Island, Manitoba and British

---

* All the arms of the provinces are given in the Fourth Part of this work.

Columbia — but this cannot be done without express

DOMINION COAT OF ARMS.

royal authority, and until this is so ordered the correct
and legal Dominion shield of arms is as stated above.

11.—Dominion Flags.

The famous English flag commonly called the "union
jack" is flown from all the fortresses and garrisons of
Canada, whether under the charge of imperial military
authorities or colonial militia forces. The union jack is
a combination of three flags. The red cross on the
white ground is for England, the white cross with the
arms placed diagonally on a blue ground for Scotland,
and the red cross with the arms placed diagonally on a
white ground for Ireland. It is seen on the flags of
Canada illustrated on the following page.

The Dominion of Canada has also authority to display on all public occasions a national flag, viz., the red or blue ensign, a flag of plain red or blue having the

THE RED ENSIGN OF CANADA.

union jack in the upper "canton," or corner next the mast, and the Dominion coat of arms in the "fly" or field of the flag.

FLAG OF THE GOVERNOR-GENERAL.

The red ensign is displayed at the opening and closing of parliament, and on national occasions. The blue ensign is a distinguishing flag of the government vessels of Canada; the mercantile marine of the Dominion has a right to use the red ensign.

The governor-general has authority to use a plain union jack in the centre of which are the Dominion arms, surrounded by a garland of maple leaves and surmounted by a crown, as we show on the preceding page. Imperial regulations at present for some reason limit the use of this flag to occasions when the governor-general is "embarked in boats and other vessels." The union jack is ordered to be flown at the government house at Ottawa on ordinary occasions; the royal standard at the government houses at Ottawa and Quebec, and at the citadels in Quebec and Halifax (an imperial garrison) on the queen's birthday, and on the days of her majesty's accession and coronation. On the Toronto government house the private flag of the lieutenant-governor (see *below*, p. 153) is used, and other lieutenant-governors have presumably the same right, though the union jack is flown on ordinary occasions at Quebec. This provincial capital appears also, as I have shown, to occupy an exceptional position with respect to the uses of the royal standard.

PARLIAMENT BUILDING, OTTAWA.

CHAPTER II.

1. Senate.—2. House of Commons.—3. Speaker of the House of Commons.—4. Officers of the Houses.

We have now to review the nature of the functions of the senate and house of commons, who, with the queen (represented by a governor-general), constitute the parliament of Canada.

1.—The Senate.

Two houses always formed part of the provincial legislatures of British North America from 1791 until 1867, when Ontario, whose example has been followed by the majority of the other provinces of the confederation, decided to confine her legislature to an elected assembly and the lieutenant-governor. The upper house or senate of the Canadian parliament bears a name which goes back to the days of ancient Rome, and also invites comparison with the distinguished body which forms so important a part of the congress or national legislature of the United States; but neither in its constitution nor in other respects does it resemble those great assemblies.

Three great divisions of Canada, (1) Maritime Provinces, (2) Ontario, and (3) Quebec, were in 1867 each given an equal representation of twenty-four members with the hope of affording a special protection to their

[93]

representative interests in the upper house. Since 1867 the entrance of other provinces and the division of the Northwest Territories into districts has disturbed this equality and brought the number of senators up to seventy-eight in all, but at no time can the greatest number exceed eighty-four, even should it be necessary to resort to the constitutional provision of the law allowing the addition of three or six new members to meet a grave emergency, such as a deadlock in a political crisis. The senators are appointed under the great seal of Canada by the governor-general on the recommendation of his privy council, and must be of the full age of thirty years, and have real and personal property worth four thousand dollars over and above their liabilities. The president or speaker of the house is appointed by the governor-general in council. In legislation the senate has the same powers as the house of commons, except with respect to bills or measures imposing taxes, or expending the public moneys which are the proceeds of taxes on the people. Such measures should commence in the lower or commons' house (see *below*, p. 117) and the senate cannot even amend or make changes therein. Divorce bills are always presented first in the senate, but this is simply as a matter of convenience ; it has no greater legal power in this respect than the commons. The senators of the province of Quebec must reside in the divisions for which they are chosen, or have their property qualification therein—a provision intended to maintain French Canadian representation in the upper house—but in the case of the other provinces the law simply requires that members reside within their province. If a member becomes bankrupt,

or if he is absent for two sessions, or if he becomes a
citizen of another country, or if he is convicted of crime,
his seat will be declared vacant.

2.—House of Commons.

It is in the commons or elected house of parliament
that political power rests. Its majority makes and
unmakes cabinets. No ministry can remain in office
without its support and confidence. For some years
the number of members representing all the provinces
amounted to two hundred and fifteen, but by a law,
passed in 1892 after the taking of the last census of the
population of Canada, the representation has been re-
arranged as follows :—

PROVINCE.	MEMBERS.
Ontario	92
Quebec	65
New Brunswick	14
Nova Scotia	20
Prince Edward Island	5
Manitoba	7
British Columbia	6
Northwest Territories	4
In all	213

The representation must be readjusted after every
census, which is taken every ten years—the last in 1891.
The British North America Act provides that the
French Canadian province of Quebec must have always
a fixed number of sixty-five members, and each of the
other provinces is assigned such a number of members

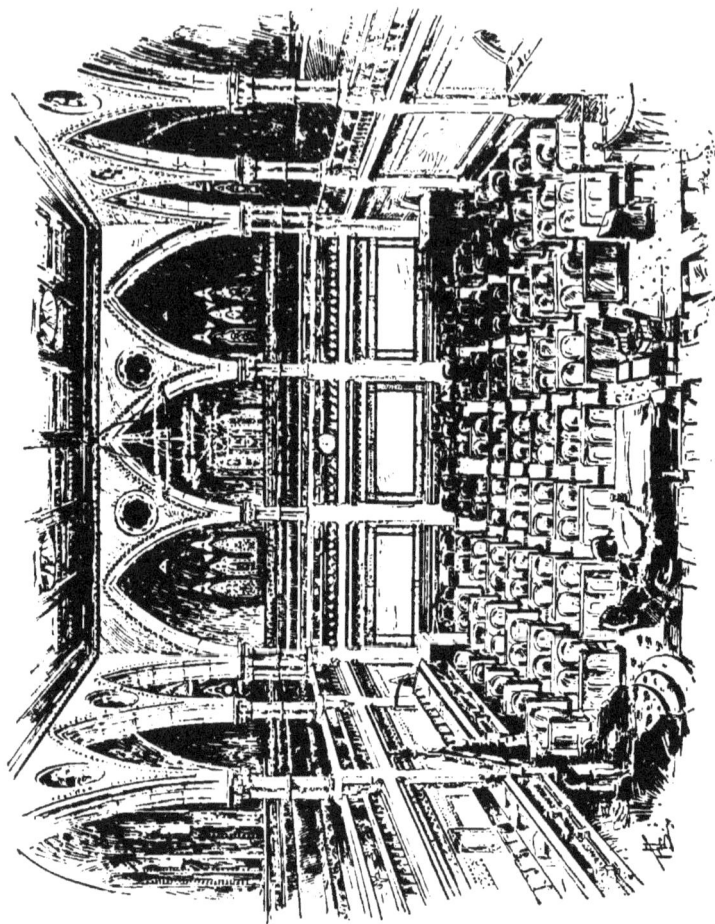

PART OF THE INTERIOR OF THE HOUSE OF COMMONS, OTTAWA.

as bears the same proportion to the number of its population as the number sixty-five bears to the population of Quebec when ascertained by the census. British Columbia, under the terms of union, cannot have her representation reduced below six. Under the census of 1891, one member has been given tó every 22,477 persons throughout the Dominion—in other words, that is the unit of representation until the next census in the year 1901.

No property qualification is now required from a member of the house of commons, but he must be a British subject by birth or naturalization—that is to say, he must have taken the oath of allegiance as a British subject after living in the country three years under the law. He must not be a person convicted of crime, as the house would in such cases expel him. If he becomes insane, his seat is vacant under the general political law. He need not reside in the district for which he is elected ⅄ to parliament. He receives, and so do senators, one thousand dollars as an indemnity or allowance if the session exceeds thirty days in length, and ten cents a mile each way for travelling expenses, computed by the shortest postal route.

3.—Speaker of the House.

The speaker of the commons, or the permanent chairman—an office of great dignity and responsibility—is elected by the members of the commons on the first day of a new parliament, or whenever a vacancy occurs by death or resignation. He is assisted by a deputy-speaker, also elected every new parliament or in case of

7

a vacancy, and who presides over what are called committees of the whole, *i.e.*, the house without the speaker in the chair.

4.—Officers of the Houses.

In each house there is a clerk or chief officer appointed by the governor-general in council, and having the assistance of a large number of officers and clerks who, under his direction, write the journals, attend committees, translate the public documents, and discharge the countless clerical duties of a legislative department.

French or English may be spoken in debate in either house, and must be used in all the laws and records. All the debates are reported by an official body of shorthand writers ; in the commons they appear daily in the two languages.

The serjeant-at-arms is the principal executive officer of the commons, who has charge of messengers and pages, looks after the furniture of the house and offices, arrests offenders against the privileges of the house, and carries the mace—a gilt emblem of the authority of the house—before the speaker on official occasions when parliament is sitting. In addition to a serjeant-at-arms, the senate has also a gentleman usher of the black rod, who is the officer commanded by the governor-general to summon the commons to attend him in the senate chamber at the beginning or end of a session of parliament.

CHAPTER III. ·

5. Dominion Franchise.—6. How Elections are Held.—7. Meeting of Parliament.—8. Elections after a General Election.—9. Oath of Allegiance.—10. Independence of Parliament and Corrupt Practices.

5.—Dominion Franchise or Voter's Qualifications.

Previous to 1885, the franchise for the several provincial legislatures was the franchise for the house of commons, but in that year, after a very protracted debate, an electoral franchise act was passed by parliament for the whole Dominion. The franchise, though somewhat complicated in its details and expensive in its machinery, is so broad as to be on the very border of universal franchise. All persons must be registered on a list of voters, prepared in accordance with the law, of which the following is a summary :

All qualified male persons, who are British subjects by birth or naturalization of the full age of twenty-one years, not insane, idiots or convicts in prisons, or otherwise disqualified by law, can vote on the following conditions :

1. When the owner of real property (that is land or buildings) to the actual value of

$300 in cities,
$200 in towns,
$150 in other districts.

When the actual occupant or tenant of real property valued in cities, towns, and other districts as above, and in possession of such property for one year before being placed on the list of voters. In the foregoing cases owner and occupant means a person who owns or occupies property in his own right or in right of his wife.

2. When a resident within an electoral district with an income or yearly earnings of at least $300 from some profession, office, trade or investment in Canada, provided he has been a resident for one year before being placed on the list, or before the date of the application for that purpose.

3. When in receipt of a *life annuity*, that is, an income paid him for every year of his life, secured on real estate in Canada, to the value of $100 in money or money's worth.

4. A farmer's son, who does not vote under the foregoing provisions, has a vote, if for one year before being placed on the list he has resided with his father or mother on a farm, or other real property, which, equally divided among the father or mother and one or more sons, is sufficient to give father, son or sons, each a vote under the values given above as owners or occupants of real property (see *above*, sections 1 and 2).

5. When sons of owners of real property, not a farm, on similar conditions as a farmer's son, just stated (see *above*, section 4).

6. When a tenant or occupant of real property, who has been in possession of the same one year before being placed on the list, and pays a rental of $2 monthly, $6 quarterly, $12 half-yearly, or $20 yearly.

7. When a fisherman, resident in the electoral district and owner of real property and boats, nets, fishing gear and tackle, or share or shares in a registered ship to the actual value of at least $150.

8. When an Indian (except in Manitoba, Keewatin, British Columbia or the Northwest Territories, where the Indians have no votes) in possession and occupation of a distinct tract of land in an Indian reserve, the improvements on which are valued at fully $150, or who is otherwise qualified under the law.

The judges of all courts, whose appointments rest with the governor-general, cannot vote—that is to say, all superior and county court judges. Revising officers, returning officers, and election clerks, all counsel, agents, attorneys and clerks of candidates who may be paid for their services, cannot vote in the electoral district in which they have been so engaged, but they may do so elsewhere. Deputy returning officers, poll clerks, constables and unpaid agents may vote. A returning officer, in case the votes are equal between two candidates at an election—in other words, in a tie—can vote. Mongolians or Chinese cannot vote (for Indians, see *above*, section 8). Voting throughout the Dominion is by ballot; electors can vote in more than one district when they are duly qualified to do so.

6.—How Elections are Held.

General elections are held on the same day throughout the Dominion; exception, however, is made in the case of such large, remote districts as Algoma and Nipissing in the province of Ontario, of Gaspé, Chicoutimi and Saguenay in the province of Quebec, and of Cariboo in the province of British Columbia, where the returning officers shall fix the day as the law provides—the object being to give all the electors in those constituencies full opportunity to record their votes.

When a general election has been decided on at a cabinet meeting, the premier so advises the governor-general, and if the latter sees no constitutional objection (see *above*, p. 76), parliament is dissolved by a proclamation in the name of the queen, the head of the executive authority, who alone can summon, prorogue, or dissolve the legislature. Another proclamation authorizes the issue of the writs of election, or order to the returning officer in each constituency or district that elects a member, fixing the date of the nomination of candidates. Any twenty-five *electors* (see franchise act, *above*, p. 99), may nominate a candidate for the house of commons by signing a paper in the form required by law, and depositing $200 with the returning officer, who shall return the same to the candidate in case of his election or of his obtaining at least one half of the votes polled in favour of the candidate elected, but otherwise the deposit goes into the public revenues. When there is no opposition to a candidate he is declared duly returned by the returning officer at the close of the time allowed for nominations. In case of an election, it takes place, except in the remote and thinly settled districts mentioned above (see p. 101), on the seventh day after nomination day, or on the following day when the seventh is Sunday or a statutory holiday. The places where the votes are taken are duly advertised under the law, and proper means taken to secure a full and correct poll. All votes are taken by ballot.

In each polling place or station there is a register of persons qualified to vote at the election, and when the name of a person presenting himself to vote is found therein, he receives a ballot paper from the deputy returning officer, on the back of which the latter has put his initials previously, so that they can be seen when the ballot is folded. On the counterfoil (see form of ballot *below*, p. 103) attached to each ballot there is placed a number corresponding with one placed opposite the voter's name in the poll book.

The following is now the legal form of a ballot paper for the dominion elections :

" *Dominion Ballot Paper.*

" Election for the electoral district of   18 .

1	DOE John Doe, Township of Nepean, County of Carleton, yeoman.	( )
2	ROE Richard Roe, of Town of Prescott, County of Grenville, Merchant.	X
3	STILES Geoffrey Stiles, of 10 Sparks Street, Ottawa, Physician.	( )
4	STILES John Stiles, of 3 Elgin Street, Ottawa, Barrister-at-law.	( )

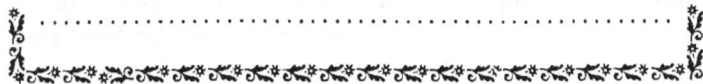

The names of the candidates in a ballot paper are as in the nomination paper. All portions of the ballot paper are coloured dark except the divisions containing the names of the candidates and the circular spaces opposite, which are to be white, as shown in the

above form.   The elector, as above, is supposed to have marked
his ballot paper in favour of Richard Roe.   The dotted line is a
line of perforations for easily detaching the counterfoil on which the
deputy returning officer has previously placed a number (see *above*,
p. 102).

The elector then proceeds alone into one of the com-
partments of the station, where he can *secretly* mark his
ballot paper.   He makes a cross with his pencil on the
white round part of the ballot paper opposite to the
division containing the name of the candidate for whom
he has decided to vote.   In case there are more than one
member to be returned for the district—as in the city of
Ottawa, for instance—he makes a mark opposite each
name of his chosen candidates.   He then folds up the
ballot paper so that the initials placed on the back by the
returning officer can be seen without opening it.   He
must hand the paper, so folded, to the returning officer,
who shall examine the initials and the number on the
counterfoil, so that he may ascertain if it is the same
paper he gave the elector.   If it be so, he shall tear off
and destroy the counterfoil, place the ballot paper in the
ballot box provided for that purpose, and always kept
locked during the voting, in the presence of the voter.

At the close of the poll or voting, which is fixed by
law from 9 o'clock in the morning, without interruption,
until 5 o'clock in the afternoon of election day, the
deputy returning officer in each polling place must
count the ballots in the manner prescribed by law, and
place his statement of the number of ballot papers and
all papers in his possession relating to the election, in the
ballot box, which will be locked and sealed and sent to
the chief returning officer.   The latter will open all the

boxes and sum up the votes for each candidate as given
in the statements of his deputies. He will declare the
candidate having the majority of votes duly elected ;
but in case of an equality or tie of votes, he shall give an
additional or casting vote to decide an election. Immediately after the sixth day after the final addition of votes
of the respective candidates, unless before that time he
receives notice there is to be a recount of votes by a
judge, as provided by the law, he must transmit his return
to the clerk of the crown in chancery at Ottawa, that a
certain candidate or candidates have been elected. The
clerk of the crown must publish the names of such members elect in the *Canada Gazette* or official paper of the
Dominion as soon as he receives them.

7.—Meeting of Parliament.

The proclamation of the governor-general ordering a
general election (see *above*, p. 101) sets forth the date
when all the writs of election must be returned by the
returning officers to whom they have been sent. Parliament is called together for the "despatch of business".
in another proclamation from the governor-general by
the advice of his council. The crown's action is guided
in this respect by the provision in the constitutional act
of 1867 that there must be a session of parliament once
at least in every year. In other words, twelve months
cannot pass between the close of one session and the
beginning of another session of parliament. The length
of a parliament, that is to say, of all its sessions—cannot exceed five years altogether. But the crown may
dissolve at any time during the five years when it

is deemed expedient to appeal to the people, but this power should not be rashly or indiscreetly exercised.

8.—Elections after a General Election.

In the foregoing paragraphs I have given some explanations as to the way a *general election* is conducted. In case a member, after a general election, resigns or dies, or his seat is declared vacant by a court of law (see *below*, p. 107), the crown does not issue a writ of election until the speaker of the commons, or other authority fixed by law, has issued a warrant—that is, an order to the clerk of the crown in chancery to issue a writ for an election. This writ goes to a returning officer appointed, as in all cases, by the governor-general in council. The proceedings with respect to nomination, election, voting by ballot, certificate of return of successful candidate, are the same in a special case as in that of a general election, described above.

9.—Oath of Allegiance.

All members elected to the house of commons, as well as senators appointed by the governor-general, are required by the law to take the following oath of allegiance before they can sit in either house of parliament :—

" I, A.B., do swear that I will be faithful and bear true allegiance to her majesty Queen Victoria."

Each new member of the senate and commons signs a roll with his name after taking the oath. The clerk and certain officers of the two houses are authorized by a commission from the governor-general to administer this oath.

10.—Laws Respecting Independence of Parliament and Corrupt Practices at Elections.

The laws for the preservation of the independence of parliament and the prevention of corrupt practices at elections are very strict, and practically in principle and details those in force in England.   The acceptance by a member of the house of commons of an office of emolument or profit from the crown shall thereby vacate his seat.   Members of that house, when called to the government as heads of departments, must at once resign their seats and be re-elected, though an exchange of offices can take place between ministers after their election under the conditions laid down in the law.   All officers of the public service and contractors with the government are forbidden to sit in parliament — an exception being made, as in England, of officers in the military service.   Since 1874 the house has given up its jurisdiction over the trial of controverted or disputed elections, which previously had been considered by committees exposed to all the insidious influences of purely political bodies.   The courts in the several provinces are now the tribunals for the trial of all such contested elections ; and the results have so far in Canada, as in England, been decidedly in the public interests.   The laws for the prevention of bribery and corruption are exceedingly strict ; and members are constantly unseated for the most trivial breaches of the law, often committed by their agents through ignorance or carelessness.   The expenses of candidates must be published by their legal agents after the election.   The whole intent of the law is to make elections as economical as possible, and diminish corruption. A candidate may be disqualified from sitting in the commons, or voting, or holding any office in the gift of the crown, for seven years, when he is proved personally guilty of bribery, and the voters in a constituency may be also severely punished when corruption is proved against them.

CHAPTER IV.

11. Methods of Conducting Business and Debate : Motions, Debate, Adjournment, Divisions, Petitions, Previous Question, Bills, Money Matters, The Budget, Going into Supply, Select Committees.—12. Prorogation.

11.—Methods of Conducting Business and Debate in Parliament.

The methods of business which the houses follow are intended to promote the despatch and efficiency of legislation. Their rules and usages are, in all essential particulars, derived from those of the English parliament. On the day parliament has been summoned by the crown to meet, the governor-general, either in person or by deputy—generally the chief justice of Canada, or other judge of the supreme court of Canada—proceeds to the upper chamber and there, seated on the throne, reads in the two languages the speech, in which his government set forth the principal measures which they purpose to present during the session. This speech, which is generally a concise and short document, is considered as soon as possible in the two houses. As soon as the formal answer to the address has been passed, the houses proceed to appoint the committees, and commence the regular business of the session. The proceedings commence every day with prayers, taken from the Church of England liturgy, and are read by the speaker of the commons in English or French according to his nationality, and by a paid chaplain in the senate. The rules of the two houses do not vary much with respect to the conduct of business.

THE FOLLOWING IS A SUMMARY OF THE LEADING RULES AND USAGES OF PARLIAMENT :—

Motions.—When a member wishes to obtain the opinion of the house on a question, he gives notice of a motion which appears after two days on the daily order of business. It must state clearly the nature of the question, and be seconded by another member. When it has been proposed, or in other words read, by the speaker from the chair, it is open to amendment and debate. An amendment is also a motion, but no notice need be given of it. Only two amendments to a motion can be under consideration at one time, but if one is rejected by the house another can be proposed, provided it is not the same as that on which the house has already expressed its opinion.

Debate.—The rules with respect to debate are neces-sarily strict. No member can speak except to a motion which is in regular form before the house—that is to say, read by the speaker from the chair, when it becomes a " question " for debate. A reply is only allowed, by courtesy, to the member who has proposed a distinct motion or question, and not to one who has made an amendment. But directly a new question has been proposed, as " that this house adjourn," "the previous question," or an amendment, members

are allowed to speak again, as the rule only applies — —
strictly to the prevention of more than one speech to
each separate question proposed. Members, as a rule,
sit with their hats on or off as they may please, but the
moment they rise to speak they must uncover and
address themselves to the chair. If any member should
inadvertently say "Gentlemen," instead of "Mr. Speaker,"
he will be called to order, though in the senate a speaker
addresses himself to " Honourable Gentlemen." Whilst
a member is speaking no one is allowed to interrupt
him, except with his own consent, or he has infringed a
point of order, and no one should pass between him and
the chair, because he is supposed to be addressing himself particularly to the speaker. Any offensive allusions
against the house, or any member thereof, are not per-
missible. No member must be referred to by name,
but every one disappears for the time being under the
title of "honourable member for Toronto," or whatever
the name of his constituency may be, and this rule, like
so many others, has for its objects the repression of per-
sonalities, and the temperate, calm conduct of debate.
No reflection must be cast on the upper house. Many
other rules exist, having for their object the keeping of
debate within moderate bounds, but it is not possible to
review them in a brief sketch of this character.

Adjournment of House or Debate.—The motion " *That
the house do now adjourn*" is always in order, and if carried
sets aside the question under discussion. The motion
" *That the debate be adjourned*" is also in order when a
"question" is under debate, and if it is carried the
"question" goes over until another day.

But if a motion for the adjournment of the house or of the debate is lost, then the debate on the question continues as if the former had never been made. But these motions can be renewed when a new question or motion is proposed at the same sitting of the house.

Putting the Question and Dividing the House.—When the debate on a motion or question is at an end, the speaker calls for the opinion of the house. He "puts" the question in this way : he will first read the motion and then say :

"Is it the pleasure of the house to adopt the motion (or amendment as the case may be)?" Those who are in favour of the motion (or amendment) will say "yea" ("content" in the senate); those who are of the contrary opinion will say "nay" ("non-content" in the senate). Members then call out "yea" or "nay" ("content" or "non-content" in the senate), and the speaker will decide from those voices—"I think that the 'yeas' ('contents') have it," or "I think that the 'nays' ('non-contents') have it." Or, if he is in doubt, he will say, "I cannot decide." Then a division takes place. Members are called in by the serjeant-at-arms and messengers, and when they are in their places the speaker again reads the question and says :

"Those who are in favour of the motion will stand up."

A clerk then calls the name of each member as he stands up in his place, and it is recorded by the chief clerk at the table on a printed list before him. When the "yeas" are all recorded in this way, the speaker calls upon the "nays" to rise, and when they are all duly entered, the chief clerk counts up the votes on both sides, and calls out the total number. The speaker then declares the question "lost" or "carried," according as the house has decided by the number of votes recorded.

If there is a main motion or first question, an amendment thereto, or second question, and also an amendment to that amendment, or third question, the speaker takes the opinion of the house, first on the amendment to the amendment, or third question; second, if that be lost, then on the amendment, or second question, and third, if that be lost, on the main motion or first question proposed to the house.

Petitions.—Every person has a right to petition parliament in respectful language on any question which comes within the right of parliament to deal with. Such petitions are presented by a member in his place, and must be signed by the person petitioning on the same sheet containing the prayer of the petition. If there are more than three petitioners then the names of three must appear on the sheet having the prayer. Every signature must be written by the person applying to parliament, but the petition itself may be printed in French or English. No appendices or papers can be attached thereto; no words can be rubbed out, or written between the lines.

Every petition to the two houses should commence with this form:

"To the honourable the senate (or house of commons, as the case may be) in parliament assembled.

"The petition of the undersigned humbly sheweth."

8

Then follows the nature of the petition. The conclusion should be a prayer, or a statement shortly summing up the previous part in these words :

"Wherefore your petitioners humbly pray that your honourable house will (here sum up object of petition). "And your petitioners as in duty bound will ever pray." Then come the signatures.

In case a petitioner requires a grant of money from the government he should send a petition, not to the house, which cannot receive such petitions, but

"To his excellency the governor-general in council," etc.

This memorial or petition should follow the foregoing form.

It should be sent to the member for the electoral district interested, to forward to "The honourable the secretary of state for Canada, Ottawa," or the petitioner can send it direct himself to the minister in question.

Petitions, however, framed in general terms, and not asking a money grant in *direct* terms, can be sent to the two houses through a member.

Previous Question.—This proceeding is an ingenious, though to many persons a perplexing, method of preventing an amendment being moved to a motion, and of coming to or avoiding a direct vote on that motion. It is proposed in the form, "That the question (*i.e.*, the motion under consideration) be *now* put." The debate then continues as before on the original or main question, and when it is concluded a vote is taken on the "previous question," as just stated. If the "previous question" is decided in the affirmative, a vote must be taken immediately on the original question. If the "previous" question" is decided in the negative, no vote can be taken on the original question, which disappears for the time being, since the house has decided by its vote that the question shall *not now* be put. The important distinction between the "previous question" in the Canadian parliament and the United States congress is that in the latter debate is closed when it is ordered, while in the former body discussion still continues on the question at issue.

Bills.—A mere resolution of the house only binds itself, and when it is necessary to make a law obligatory upon all the people of Canada, a bill must be introduced, and passed through several stages in the two chambers. Then it receives the assent of the queen, through the governor-general, and becomes a statute or legal enactment. A bill is, generally speaking, divided into several distinct parts : (1) the title ; (2) the preamble and statement of the enacting authority ; (3) the body of the act, consisting of one or more propositions, known as clauses or sections; (4) the schedules—the latter containing legal forms, documents, etc., mentioned in the body of the bill, and only necessary in certain cases. Bills are either *public*—that is to say, dealing with matters of a public or general nature ; or *private*—that is to say, relating to the affairs of corporations, companies, or individuals. The former class are introduced on motion in the ordinary way, "That leave be given to introduce a bill" (here follows title) ; but the latter must be brought up after a petition and a notice in the *Gazette* and local papers in accordance with strict rules, intended to give all persons interested in the scheme full knowledge of the proposed legislation. Private bills, when presented, must also be rigidly subject to the scrutiny of select committees for the reason just stated; and these committees consequently are clothed with a certain judicial character in cases of controversy. But all bills, public and private, must be read three times in each house, as well as considered in committee of the whole. The second reading is the stage when the principle or policy or necessity of the measure is discussed in the case of public bills—though not necessarily so as respects private bills—while the committee of the whole allows a free and full discussion of the clauses or provisions, without a limitation of the number of speeches on one question or motion. When a bill has passed the commons it is sent to the senate for its agreement, and as soon as that body has also subjected .it to the stages mentioned above, it is ready for the assent of the crown. In case of amendments by one house they must be agreed to by the other. If there is no such agreement, the bill drops for the session. As a rule, an interval of a day should elapse between the different stages of a bill, especially when it involves a tax or money vote. When it is finally passed and becomes law, it bears the signatures of the clerks of the two houses and of his excellency the governor-general on the back.

Money Matters.—The most important duties of the house are in connection with money matters. Here the constitution and the rules of parliament have imposed many guards and checks upon hasty expenditures or the imposition of taxes without due notice and consideration.

By the Union Act any measures for appropriating any part of the public revenue, or for imposing any tax or impost, must originate in the house of commons. The house itself is restrained by the same act. It cannot adopt or pass "any vote, resolution, address or bill for the appropriation of any part of the public revenue, or of any tax or impost, to any purpose that has not been first recommended to the house by a message of the governor-general." A rule of the house itself declares that if any motion be made in the house for any public aid or charge upon the people, " the consideration or debate thereof may not be presently (immediately) entered upon, but shall be adjourned until such further day as the house shall think fit to appoint ; and then it shall be referred to a committee of the whole house before any resolution or vote of the house do pass thereon." It follows from what precedes that no private member is permitted to propose a dominion tax upon the people, or to introduce a bill providing for a public grant ; such measures must be commenced by ministers of the crown in the shape of resolutions which are to be considered, in committee of the whole, and when adopted form the foundation of a bill.

The committees of supply and ways and means are the constitutional mode of providing for public expenditures. These committees are appointed at the beginning of every session, when an address has been passed in answer to the governor's speech. As soon as the committee of supply has been formed, and the government are ready, they bring down a message from his excellency with the estimates of the sums required for the

public service for the next financial year, which commences on the 1st of July and ends on the next 30th
June.

These estimates contain several hundred votes arranged
in the order of the various public services. For instance—
expenses of departments of government, militia, penitentiaries, administration of justice, immigration, Indians,
public works, railways and canals, quarantine and the numerous other subjects for which parliament votes annually large sums of the public money. These estimates
contain the expenditures for the current and the previous
year in parallel columns, for purposes of comparison, and
it is the duty of the minister responsible for a particular
expenditure to give full explanations on the subject
when they are demanded by the house. As every vote
is carefully considered a very considerable part of the
session is occupied by debates on this important committee, over which a permanent chairman, who is also
the deputy speaker, or another member in his absence,
presides.

The rules for proceeding in the committees of supply
and ways and means are precisely similar to those
observed in other committees of the whole house. Members are not confined to one speech, but may address the
committee as often as they please on a particular resolution. The chairman acts as speaker and decides all
questions of order. After the budget (see next page) is
formally before the house, and the leading members on
both sides have made their speeches on the commercial
and financial state of the country, the committee of
supply meets regularly and disposes of a large amount

of money at every session ; but every vote is very carefully scrutinized and the fullest explanations are demanded from the government, who, on such occasions, have
to perform the most difficult and wearisome part of their
legislative duties. Resolutions agreed to in committee
are reported to the house, but they are not received until
a later day. When the committee of supply has finished
its labours, and all the money votes have been adopted
by the house, the committee of ways and means passes
certain resolutions which provide for the grants shown
to be necessary by the first-mentioned committee ; and
then a bill, called the supply or appropriation bill, is
introduced by the government to carry out the resolutions. When this important bill has passed the usual
stages, it is sent up to the senate, where, however, it is
never altered, in accordance with constitutional usage.
On its return to the commons, it is carried up by the
speaker to the senate chamber. When his excellency
has assented to the bills passed by parliament during the
session (always in the queen's name), the speaker of the
commons addresses his excellency, and asks for an
assent to the supply bill, and this assent is granted
with the usual formula : " In her majesty's name, his
excellency the governor-general thanks her loyal subjects, accepts their benevolence, and assents to this bill."

The Budget.—When the estimates have been brought
in it is the duty of the finance minister to make his
financial statement, or, in parliamentary phrase, present
the " budget." This familiar word is derived from the
French and means "a bag;" in making his statement,
the finance minister *opens* the money bag of the people,

as it were, and shows them its contents, and what is most important *how best* to fill it. He will on this occasion review the expenditure of the past, and esti-mate that for the following year, give his opinion on the financial situation, and lay before the house a statement of any scheme of taxation that the government may have decided on, or of any changes that may be deemed necessary in the existing tariff. One of the most important and interesting debates of the session generally takes place after the delivery of this speech.

Questions and Motions on going into Supply.—From the beginning of the session, members ask questions of the government on every imaginable public topic, and make formal motions for papers relating to matters of general or local interest. All such motions and inquiries are made after two days' notice ; for the rules are very properly framed so as to prevent surprises, and give the house due information of the business to come daily before it. But in the Canadian house there are certain methods which enable members to move motions or ask questions without number, and even without notice. It is always open to a member to bring up an important question immediately—except, of course, when there is a subject under consideration—and debate it at any length on a motion for the adjournment of the house. Then, as soon as committee of supply is moved on any day, a member may make a motion on any question he wishes, unless it refers to the votes to be discussed in supply. As the rules do not permit any amendment to be made to a motion at such a stage, "the previous question," in the English parliamentary sense, is practically in force and it is possible to get a direct vote on an issue, without the evasions that amendments offer on other occasions. While in the case of all bills and other motions, amendments must be relevant to the question, members can here bring up any subject they please. This is a practice which has its historical origin in the fact that in old times, when the English parliamentary system was developing itself, the people's representatives laid down the principle that the king must redress their grievances before they should grant him the supply he asked from the nation. Those times have long since passed away and the people now fully control all taxes and expenditures, but the crown still asks for money through the ministers, and the commons grant it in due form. It is no longer necessary to threaten the crown with a refusal of supplies unless the people's grievances are redressed ; but still they can refuse it to an unfaithful government should the necessity arise. As a matter of fact, should the government be defeated in a session before supply is voted, the house would pass only such votes as are necessary to meet the actual wants of the public service, and leave the whole question of supply open until the crisis is over and there is in office a ministry which has the confidence of the house and country.

Select Committees.—Much of the business of the two houses is first discussed and deliberately considered in small bodies of members, varying in number, and chosen on a motion duly made and seconded. Bills, public and private, are sent to these committees, which must report for or against them in all cases. In these select bodies, no bill or question can be considered except it is referred to them by the house. Members can speak as often as they like, but otherwise the rules of debate in the house itself prevail. Questions are put as in the house, and the chairman, who is always elected at the first meeting, only votes in case of a tie, or equality of votes. In private bill (see *above*, p. 115) committees, however, the chairman can vote as a member, and give a casting vote when there is a tie. All committees must report to the house the result of their conclusions on a bill or other subject. Witnesses can be examined under oath when necessary.

12.—Prorogation.

When the business of parliament is closed, the governor-general comes down and assents to the bills as stated above (p. 116). He then reads a speech shortly reviewing the business of the session, and when he has finished, the speaker of the senate rises and says :

" It is his excellency the governor-general's will and pleasure that this parliament be prorogued until *(date)*, to be then here holden ; and this parliament is accordingly prorogued *(date)*."

The commons then retire, and the session is at end according to law.

If parliament is not called together " for the despatch of business " by the date mentioned in the foregoing speech—a very unlikely event under ordinary circumstances—a royal proclamation is issued from time to time in the *Canada Gazette,* further proroguing the legislature. The legal effect of a prorogation is to put an end to all bills and other proceedings of parliament in whatever state they are in at the time, and they must be commenced anew, in the next session, exactly as if they had never been begun.

CHAPTER V.

13. Distribution of Legislative Powers under a Federal Union.—
14. Subjects of Dominion Legislation.

13.—Distribution of Legislative Powers.

An essential characteristic of a federal union is the division or distribution of legislative powers between the government of the union as a whole, and the several countries that compose that union. Accordingly, the British North America Act or constitution of Canada gives to the dominion or central government at Ottawa the control of certain matters of a general or national character, and to the provincial governments the control of certain matters of a provincial or local importance. When we come to consider the nature of the provincial governments (see *below*, p. 158) I shall set forth the subjects under their control. At present we have under consideration the duties and powers of the dominion government.

14.—Subjects of Dominion Legislation.

The 91st clause of the constitution gives to the parliament of Canada the sole or exclusive right of making laws on the following subjects:

1. The public debt and property.
2. The regulation of trade and commerce.

[123]

3. The raising of money by any mode or system of taxation.

4. The borrowing of money on the public credit.

5. Postal service.

6. The census and statistics.

7. Militia, military and naval service and defence.

8. The fixing and providing for the salaries and allowances of civil and other officers of the government of Canada.

9. Beacons, buoys, lighthouses and Sable Island.

10. Navigation and shipping.

11. Quarantine and the establishment and maintenance of marine hospitals.

12. Sea-coast and inland fisheries.

13. Ferries between a province and a British or foreign country, or between two provinces.

14. Currency and coinage.

15. Banking, incorporation of banks and the issue of paper money.

16. Savings-banks.

17. Weights and measures.

18. Bills of exchange and promissory notes.

19. Interest.

20. Legal tender.

21. Bankruptcy and insolvency.

22. Patents of invention and discovery.

23. Copyrights.

24. Indians and lands reserved for the Indians.

25. Naturalization and aliens.

26. Marriage and divorce. [But the provincial governments control the solemnization or celebration of marriage, see *below*, p. 159].

27. The criminal law, except the constitution of the courts of criminal jurisdiction, but including the procedure in criminal matters [see *below*, p. 166].

28. The establishment, maintenance, and management of penitentiaries.

29. Such classes of subjects as are expressly excepted in the. _ _
enumeration of the classes of subjects by this act assigned exclusively to the legislatures of the provinces.

The subjects just mentioned in sub-section 29 are
(see *below*, p. 159) lines of steam or other ships, railways,
canals, telegraphs and other works and undertakings extending beyond the limits of a province, or declared to
be "for the general advantage of Canada," or of more
than one province, by the Canadian parliament.   A
steamer running from Montreal to Pictou, in Nova
Scotia, a railway between Nova Scotia and New Brunswick, a bridge over the Ottawa river, which divides the
two provinces of Ontario and Quebec, are among the
works that come under this clause.

In order to lessen doubts, the constitution also provides that any of the foregoing subjects shall not come
within the class of matters of a local or private character
over which the provincial governments have sole legislative power (see *below*, p. 158).   In the case of other
matters not coming within the class of subjects belonging to the provinces, the parliament of Canada has alone
power to make laws for the peace, order and good
government of the Dominion.

In short, the respective powers of the parliament of
the Dominion and the legislatures of the provinces are
stated in express terms in the constitution ; any subject
that does not fall within the powers of the provincial
governments belongs to the Dominion. This is intended
to prevent disputes, as far as possible, as respects the
powers of the separate governments.

The subject of education belongs exclusively to the
provinces, but in case certain rights enjoyed by religious

minorities in the provinces are prejudicially affected by the laws of those provinces, the parliament of Canada may interpose and pass such legislation as will remedy an act of injustice that the provincial governments refuse to repeal. This is, however, a subject which falls properly to a later page (see *below*, p. 160).

The dominion and local governments also exercise certain rights in common. The dominion parliament may make laws on the subjects of agriculture and immigration for any and all of the provinces, and each legislature may do the same for the province over which it has jurisdiction, provided no provincial act is in conflict with any dominion act. Both these authorities are equally interested in the promotion of matters so deeply affecting the development of the natural resources of all sections. The provinces, excepting Manitoba, have the control of their lands and mines, while the Dominion is interested in the opening up of the vast territorial area which it has in the Northwest.

The dominion government have, by the constitution, a general power of vetoing or disallowing any act of a legislature within one year after its receipt from the government of a province. The conditions under which this important power should be exercised are explained on another page (see *below*, p. 162).

The constitutional law, as I have shown, has been framed with the object of setting forth, as clearly as possible, the powers given to the dominion and provincial governments, but the experience of twenty-seven years shows no written law, however carefully framed, can prevent differences of opinion as to its meaning.   The dominion government may read the language of a section in one way, and the provincial government, or the person whose rights are in question, another way.   Language, at best, is imperfect when it comes to define rights.

In the following section I shall explain the methods provided by the constitution for the removing of doubts as to the meaning of its provisions, preventing conflicts between the dominion and provincial authorities, and at the same time doing justice, as far as possible, in all cases where rights are affected.

CHAPTER VI.

1. Methods of Interpreting the Written Constitution.—2. Supreme Court.—3. Exchequer Court.—4. Admiralty Court.—5. Judicial Tenure of Office.

1.—Methods of Interpreting or Explaining the Written Constitution.

· The federal union of Canada derives its existence from a constitution, known as the British North America Act, just as a municipal body, or any incorporated company, obtains its powers from the law bringing it into existence. Consequently every power, executive, legislative or judicial, exercised by the dominion or provincial governments, is subject to the constitution. This constitution comes under the conditions applied to all statutes or laws. Its meaning must be construed or explained by the judges who are its authorized interpreters.

The judges of the courts of the provinces, from the lowest to the highest courts, can and do constantly decide on the constitutionality of statutes passed by the legislative authorities of the Dominion. They do so, in their capacity as judges and interpreters of the law, and not because they have any special commission to that effect, or are invested with any political duties or powers by the constitution. The judges of the provinces are appointed and paid by the dominion government, but the constitution, maintenance and organization of their courts are placed under the provincial governments. The judges decide on cases that arise under the laws governing their respective provinces. Such cases frequently relate to the constitutional rights of the Dominion and of a province. The decision of provincial judges is not final, for the constitution has provided for the establishment of a supreme court of the Dominion, to whom appeals can be taken from the inferior courts of the provinces.

2.—The Supreme Court of Canada.

In 1875 it was deemed advisable to pass an act providing for the establishment of a supreme court of Canada. But this court is only a general court of appeal for Canada in a limited sense, since the existing right of appeal in the various provinces to the privy council has been left untouched. Nor can it be called a final court of appeal for Canada, since the privy council of England entertains appeals from its judgments (see *above*, p. 65). This court consists of a chief justice and five "puisne judges,"—puisne meaning simply inferior in rank—two of whom, at least, must be appointed from the bench or bar of the province of Quebec—a provision intended to give the court the assistance of men specially acquainted with French Canadian law. Under the conditions set forth in the act, an appeal can be taken to this court from the highest court of final resort in a province in civil and criminal cases. The decisions of the superior courts of the provinces in cases of controverted elections may also be reviewed by the court. In Quebec cases the appeal must always come from the court of

9

queen's bench or the superior court in review (see p. 190); and the question at issue must involve $2,000, unless it affects the validity of a statute and other specified matters. The governor-general in council may also refer to the supreme court, for hearing or consideration, important questions relating to legislation of the provinces, or of the Dominion, education, or any other matter of a constitutional nature on which it is necessary to obtain a judicial opinion. Constitutional controversies between the Dominion and any province, and between the provinces themselves, can be referred to the court when the legislature of a province has passed an act providing for such useful references—useful, because they help to prevent friction in the working of the federal machinery. This court is intended to be, as far as practicable, a court for the settlement of controversies that arise in the working of the constitutional system of Canada. The judicial committee of the privy council entertains appeals from the supreme court only when the case is of gravity, involving questions of public interest or some important point of law, or is of a very substantial character.

3.—The Exchequer Court of Canada.

Another court having authority throughout the Dominion is the exchequer, which originally formed part of the supreme court of Canada. The two courts were separated in 1887, and a judge especially appointed by the governor-general in council to preside over the exchequer court. The name of this court carries us back to early English times. The king's treasury was in charge of an important officer, called "hoarder," or treasurer, because he took care of the "hoard" or royal

supply of money. As the king's revenues increased in
amount, and disputes grew up in connection with their
collection and management, it was necessary to divide
the duties between two departments, one administrative
and the other judicial. The chancellor of the exchequer
—the finance minister—is still the most important member of the cabinet of England. When the English
courts of justice were formed out of the great council or
supreme court of the king (see *above*, p. 57), questions
affecting the revenue were referred to a committee or
court called the exchequer, which derived its name
originally from a *chequered* cloth which covered the table
at which the accounts were considered, and suggested to
the looker-on the idea of a game of chess between the
taxpayer and the royal officials. The duties of the
court grew in importance, and were extended to all suits
or actions in which the crown was interested. The
Canadian court has authority to hear and decide those
cases in which the revenues or property, or other interests
of the crown are involved. It hears claims against the
dominion government when any person suffers injury
from the construction or operation of a public work, and
can award damages to such persons.

4.—Admiralty Court of Canada.

The dominion government have also, under the
authority of an imperial statute, conferred on the
exchequer court the powers of an admiralty court to
hear and determine all civil questions relating to contracts or claims in respect of necessaries and wages, and
other matters arising out of navigation, shipping, trade
and commerce, in Canadian waters, tidal and non-

tidal. The governor-general may appoint a judge of
a superior court, or of a county court, or any barrister of
not less than seven years' standing, to be a "local judge
in admiralty" of the exchequer court in such districts as
may be necessary for the purposes of the act. The
provinces of Quebec, Nova Scotia, New Brunswick,
Prince Edward Island and British Columbia constitute
such districts. The maritime court of Ontario has been
abolished, and the admiralty jurisdiction of the exchequer
court is exercised in what is known as the Toronto
admiralty district.

5.—Judicial Tenure of Office.

The judges of the supreme and exchequer courts, and
any other dominion courts, hereafter established, hold
office, like all the judges of the superior courts in the
provinces, during good behaviour, and can only be
removed on an address passed by the senate and house
of commons to the governor-general, after full investigation into any charges that may be made against them.
In this way the judiciary is practically independent of
political or popular caprice or passion, and able to discharge their high functions with fidelity and partiality.
The judges of these supreme and exchequer courts are
appointed from the superior courts of the provinces or
from barristers or advocates of distinction and of at
least ten years' standing at the bar.

CHAPTER VII.

THE DOMINION GOVERNMENT: REVENUE AND EXPENDITURE.

*1. Duties of Customs and Excise.—2. Cost of Government.—
3. Consolidated Revenue Fund.—4. Canadian Currency.*

1.—Duties of Customs and Excise.

I have now given my readers a summary of the
principal duties of the executive, legislative and judicial
departments of the Canadian government. The question
will now occur to every one who has followed me so far,
How does this government meet its expenses? The
answer is, chiefly by a system of taxation, presented and
carried in the parliament of the Dominion in the manner described above (p. 116). The system is not *direct*
taxation—that is to say, it is not a certain amount taxed,
as in cities and other municipal divisions, on everyone's
property and collected from the great body of the
people individually. It is *indirect* taxation—that is to
say, imposed on the goods brought into the country by
merchants and traders, who alone pay the duties directly
and add such charges to their expenses and necessary
profits. These taxes are called "customs duties," from
an old Norman French word, *coustume*, meaning a
customary or usual tax of the country, which has come
to be generally applied to any duty on foreign goods.
The people in the end, who are consumers of such goods,
pay these duties to a greater or less extent. Competition
among merchants tends to keep prices to the lowest

point compatible with the profit which every merchant must make. In addition to the duties imposed on goods brought or imported from other countries, like spirits, tobacco, woollens, cottons, silks, hardware, furniture, pianos and the countless articles purchased by the people which make up the great proportion of dominion taxation, there is a large sum collected directly from persons engaged in the manufacture of beer, whiskey, tobacco, and cigars, known as "excise duties"—the word excise coming from an old French word meaning an assessment or tax. Customs duties may be either *ad valorem* or *specific;* the first meaning the levying of a certain percentage of duty on the marketable value (*ad valorem*) of the goods at the original place of shipment, as sworn to by the owner or importer, and verified by the customs appraisers or valuators; "specific" meaning a definite or fixed duty collected on goods of a particular kind, or upon a specified quantity of a commodity, entered at the custom-house. In 1894 the duties collected on imports used in the country were $19,198,114 altogether ; the amount of excise duties was $8,381,088; other revenues, from the sale of public lands, tolls on canals and other works, post office and other sources, amounted to $8,795,489. The total revenue consequently in that year was $36,374,691, mostly from customs and excise duties. I cite these figures simply to show the importance of such taxes in the government of a country.

2.—Cost of Dominion Government.

These taxes and revenues are necessary to meet :

1. The charge on the public debt which was on the 30th June, 1894, $308,348,023. This is, however, the

gross debt, and from which are generally deducted certain assets or interest-bearing investments, loans, cash and banking accounts, which bring the net debt down to $246,183,029 at the same date. The debt has been principally created by the construction of public works, canals and railways ; subsidies to railways, assumption of provincial debts under the terms of confederation.

2. Legislation, senate and house of commons, franchise act, election expenses, etc.

3. Civil government, or salaries of governor-general lieutenant-governors, the departments of the public service, Northwest government, etc.

4. Public works, including buildings of all kinds, piers and harbours, experimental farms, etc.

5. Railways and canals.

6. Administration of justice, mounted police, lighthouse and coast service, militia and defence, immigration and quarantine, geological survey, superannuation, fisheries, Indians, ocean and river steam service, penitentiaries, mail subsidies, post office, and a great variety of other services necessary for the government of the Dominion.

The total ordinary expenditure in 1894 was $37,585,-025, as against $13,486,092 in 1868, in the infancy of the development of the confederation and before the construction of public works of national importance.

3.—The Consolidated Fund of Canada.

All taxes and other revenues of Canada are paid into the treasury in accordance with the law, and form what is generally known as "the consolidated fund of Canada," out of which are paid all the charges and expenses incident to the collection and management of this fund, and all the expenses of government. These expenses are annually voted by parliament in the mode explained above (see p. 117).

While certain sums are authorized annually by the appropriation act—which comprises the annual grants voted every session in supply—other payments are made under the sanction of statutes. These statutes, which are permanent and can only be repealed or amended by another act of parliament, provide for salaries of the governor-general, lieutenant-governors, ministers of the crown, judges, and other high functionaries, whose compensation, it is agreed, should not depend on annual votes, though it is always competent for any member to move to reduce them in the shape of a bill, which may become an act or law if the two houses agree to pass it.

All moneys are paid out of the treasury under certain forms required by statute. A thorough system of audit by a public officer, the auditor-general, who can only be removed on an address of the senate and house of commons to the governor-general, has the effect of preventing any public expenditure not authorized by parliament. Large sums are borrowed from time to time by the government on terms which must be approved by parliament.

4.—The Currency of Canada.

The treasury also issues notes to the value of 25 cents, $1, $2, $4, $50, $100, $500, and $1,000 ; but the dominion issue in any one year may not exceed four million dollars, and the total amount issued and outstanding, at any time, may now exceed twenty millions, secured for redemption by gold and Canadian guaranteed securities.

The banks of Canada may also issue notes—five dollars being the value of the lowest—the payment of which is secured, as far as possible, by making the payment of the notes a first charge on the assets of a bank, and by other provisions of a well devised general banking act intended to guard the monetary interests of the public. Canada has no "mint" or establishment to coin gold, silver and copper money. The Canadian silver and copper coin in general circulation has been "minted" in England for the use of this country. The silver coin in use are of the value of fifty, twenty-five, twenty (very few now), ten and five cents. Canada has no gold coin of her own. The large notes of $500 and $1,000, issued by the government, are principally held by the chartered banks as part of their cash reserves, and for purposes of settlement between banks.

CHAPTER VIII.

The British North America Act places under the control of the dominion government the militia, naval service, and defence of Canada. The command-in-chief of the land and naval forces of and in Canada, however, continues to be vested in the queen. A department of the dominion government, called the department of militia and defence (see *above*, p. 80), has the superintendence of this important part of the public service. Since confederation English troops have been removed from all places in Canada except Halifax, which is a strongly fortified military post, and the headquarters of the North American squadron, under the command of a vice or rear admiral. On the Pacific side Esquimalt, on the island of Vancouver, is also being fortified, and will be garrisoned by imperial troops.

The withdrawal of English troops to so great an extent from Canada has necessarily thrown large responsibilities upon the Canadian government since 1867 for the protection of a confederation extending over so immense a territory between two oceans. Canada has attempted to fulfil her obligations in this respect by the expenditure of a large sum of money during twenty-seven years for the drill, instruction and arming of an effective militia, drawn from the great body of the people. In this way a spirit of self-reliance has been stimulated

[138]

from one end of Canada to the other, and on more than one emergency the national forces have proved their capacity to secure peace and order and put down rebellion.

By the law of Canada the militia consists of all the male inhabitants of Canada of the age of eighteen years or upwards and under sixty, not exempted or disqualified by law; the population being divided into four classes, as follows :

The first class comprises those aged eighteen or upwards and under thirty, being unmarried or widowers without children.

The second class comprises those between the ages of thirty and forty-five, being unmarried or widowers without children.

The third class comprises those between eighteen and forty-five, being married or widowers with children.

The fourth class comprises those between forty-five and sixty.

And those liable to serve shall be called upon in the foregoing order.

The following persons are exempt from enrolment and actual service at any time : judges, clergymen and ministers of all religious denominations, professors in colleges and teachers in religious orders, persons engaged in the collection or management of the revenue, the wardens and officials of all penitentiaries and lunatic asylums, persons physically disabled, and any person being the only son of a widow and her only support. Half-pay and retired officers of the imperial forces. sailors actually employed in their calling, pilots during the season of navigation, and masters of schools are exempt from service, except in case of war. Quakers, Mennonites and others may be exempted altogether under regulations prescribed by the governor-general in council.

The militia is divided into active and reserve, land and marine forces. The land force is composed of corps raised either by voluntary enlistment or ballot. The active marine force shall be raised in the same way, and composed of seamen, sailors and persons whose occupation is on vessels navigating the waters of Canada, and the reserve force, land and marine, consists of the whole of the men not serving in the active militia for the time being.

The period of service in the militia is three years. The number of men to be trained and drilled annually is limited to forty-five thousand, except as specially authorized, and the period of drill is to be sixteen days, and not less than eight days each year.

The Dominion is divided into twelve military districts, in each of which a permanent military staff is maintained, under command of a deputy adjutant-general. The permanent corps and schools of instruction consist of royal Canadian dragoons, royal Canadian artillery, garrison artillery and a royal regiment of Canadian infantry. The total strength of these permanent corps is limited by the militia law to a thousand men.

The royal military college at Kingston, which is under the control of the militia department, was founded in 1875, and has proved on the whole a most successful institution. Of the total number of cadets who have graduated, a large number have been gazetted to commissions in the imperial army. Four commissions are annually offered by the imperial government, and in 1888 six others were offered.

Heretofore an imperial officer has been chosen from the regular English military force and given the rank of a major-general in Canada, to command the militia and supervise their instruction and equipment, under the control of the minister of militia, who is responsible to parliament for the efficiency of this department. So far no active marine militia has been organized in the Dominion, but the naval defences continue exclusively under the care of the imperial government. In the Northwest Territories peace and order have been secured for years by the employment of a most efficient body of mounted police (see *Seventh Part*).

BIBLIOGRAPHICAL NOTE.

My readers should consult the following books on the nature and working of dominion government : Bourinot's *Manual of Constitutional History* (Montreal, 1884) ; his *Canadian Studies in Comparative-Politics* (Montreal, 1890), and in the "Transactions of the Royal Society of Canada," 1892, section 2 ; his *Parliamentary Government in Canada*, in the "Papers of the American Historical Association" (Washington, 1892) ; his *Federal Government in Canada*, in "Johns Hopkins' University Studies" (Baltimore, 1889). Dr. Todd's *Parliamentary Government in the Colonies*, 2nd ed. (London, 1894), should be studied by advanced students. The works mentioned in the bibliographical note at end of the Second Part of this book (see *above*, p. 68) with reference to the cabinet and parliamentary government in England also apply to the dominion government. For a clear explanation of the rules, usages and understandings which govern the practice of parliamentary government, see Professor Dicey's *Law of the Constitution*, chap. xiv, 3rd ed. (London and New York, 1889). For rules and usages governing proceedings of legislative bodies, see Bourinot's *Procedure of Public Meetings* (Toronto, 1894), pp. 26-57. More ambitious students can consult his largest work on *Parliamentary Procedure*, 2nd ed. (Montreal, 1892), which also reproduces the author's short constitutional history mentioned above (p. 42), with additions to end of 1891. The last chapter of this work should be read by students, since it is devoted to *General Observations on the Practical Operation of Parliamentary Government in Canada*. Bagehot's work on the English constitution (see *above*, p. 69) is very valuable in this connection. The author may also refer to a paper of his own, published by the American Historical Association (Washington, 1891), on *Canada and the United States : a Study in Comparative Politics*. It shows the advantages which Canadians contend that their cabinet and parliamentary system of government possesses over the irresponsible system of their neighbours in the United States. The best work that shows the inferiority of the congressional government of the republic compared with parliamentary government is that by Professor Woodrow Wilson, on *Congressional Government* (Boston, 1887).

In the *Canadian Almanac* for 1891 (Toronto) there is an article by Mr. C. Campbell on the *Flags and Arms* of the Dominion and provinces, which will be interesting to those who wish to study the subject intelligently. In the same publication for 1895, there is additional information in an article on *Imperial and Canadian Flags*.

For full information on Revenue and Expenditure, Trade and Commerce, Militia and Defence, Customs and Excise, Public Debt, Currency and other matters relating to the government of Canada, reference must be made to the official "blue books," known as Public Accounts, Trade and Navigation Returns, Report of Minister of Militia, etc., and to the Statistical Year Book of Canada, all of which are published yearly at Ottawa by the Queen's Printer.

FOURTH PART

THE PROVINCIAL GOVERNMENTS

CHAPTER I.

1. Introduction.—2. Lieutenant-Governor.—3. Executive or Advisory Council.—4. List of Executive Councils in the Provinces. —5. Provincial Arms.—6. Flags of Lieutenant-Governors.

1.—Introduction.

The provinces of Nova Scotia, New Brunswick, Prince Edward Island, Quebec, Ontario, Manitoba and British Columbia, are so many political divisions, all enjoying extensive powers of local government and forming parts of a Dominion whose government possesses certain national attributes essential to the security, successful working, and permanence of the federal union, established by the British North America Act of 1867.

In all the provinces at the present time, there is a very complete system of local self-government, administered under the authority of the British North America Act, by means of the following machinery :

A lieutenant-governor appointed by the governor-general in council ;

An executive or advisory council, responsible to the legislature ;

A legislature, consisting of an elective house in all cases, with the addition of an upper chamber appointed by the crown in two provinces only ;

ONTARIO LEGISLATIVE BUILDINGS, TORONTO.

A judiciary, composed of several courts in each province, the judges of which are appointed and paid by
the dominion government ;

A civil service, with officers appointed by the provincial government, holding office during good behaviour,
and not removed for political reasons ;

A municipal system of councils, composed of mayors,
wardens, reeves and councillors, to provide for the
purely local requirements of the cities, towns, townships, parishes and counties of every province ;

A complete system of local self-government in every
municipality of a province, to provide for the management and support of free schools for all classes of the
people.

2.—The Lieutenant-Governor.

The lieutenant-governor, who holds his office in practice for five years, is appointed by the governor-general
in council, by whom he can be dismissed for "cause
assigned," which, under the constitution, must be communicated to parliament. He is therefore an officer of
the Dominion, as well as the head of the executive
government of a province, and possesses, within his
constitutional sphere, all the authority of a lieutenant-
governor before 1867. He acts in accordance with the
rules, usages and conventions that govern the relations
between the governor-general and his privy council (see
above, p. 82). He appoints his executive council and is
guided by their advice so long as they retain the confidence of the legislature. In the discharge of all the
executive and administrative functions that devolve
constitutionally upon him and require the action of the

crown in a province, the lieutenant-governor has all the
necessary authority. He can summon, prorogue and
dissolve the legislature, make appointments to office,
and perform all those executive acts by the advice of
his advisory council which are necessary for the government of the province. The remarks given above with
respect to the governor-general in council apply with
equal force to the lieutenant-governor in council (see
above, p. 83).

3.—The Executive or Advisory Council.

The executive council, which is the name now given
to the body of men composing the administration of
each province, a name borrowed from the old provincial
systems of government, varies from eight members in
Ontario to five in British Columbia, holding, as a rule,
various provincial offices as heads of departments. Their
titles vary in some cases, but generally there is in every
executive council an attorney-general, whose duties are
to act as law adviser of the government and its departments, enforce the law by prosecution in the criminal
courts, and perform other acts in connection with the
administration of justice in a province. All the mines
and minerals, public lands and forests thereon, except in
Manitoba, belong to the provincial governments, which
derive from them—especially in Ontario and Quebec—a
large revenue. In each province, consequently, there is
a commissioner of crown lands, whose duty it is to look
after their sale, lease "limits" for the cutting of timber,
supervise mining lands under special regulations, and
exercise general authority over the public domain. In
Nova Scotia and British Columbia, where the mines and

minerals are very valuable, there is a department specially entrusted with the management of those sources of
provincial wealth.

In every province there is a minister generally called
treasurer, whose special function it is to administer its
financial affairs ; a commissioner to look after its
public works ; a secretary and registrar to manage
the correspondence of the government, register all commissions under the provincial seal, as well as bonds and
securities given by public officers. In some of the
provinces there is also a minister who collects useful
information relating to the agricultural, mechanical and
manufacturing interests of the province, has control of
model farms and agricultural colleges—wherever established, as in Ontario—and encourages all societies and
exhibitions connected with the interests of agriculture,
horticulture, fruit raising and dairying, and other indus-
tries of the same class. In the Ontario cabinet there is
also a minister of education, since that branch of the
public service is of exceptional importance in that
province in view of the great expenditure and large
number of common and grammar schools, collegiate
institutes, normal and model schools, besides the provincial university in Toronto.

All the members of the executive council, who hold
departmental and salaried offices, must vacate their seats
and be re-elected as in the case of the dominion
ministry. The principle of ministerial responsibility to
the lieutenant-governor and to the legislature is observed
in the fullest sense. All the conventions and understandings that govern the relations between the governor-

LEGISLATIVE BUILDINGS, QUEBEC.

general and his ministers apply with equal force to the relations between a lieutenant-governor of a province and his councillors (see *above*, p. 82).

3.—List of the Executive Councils in 1895.

In British Columbia :—
President of Council.
Attorney-General (Premier).
Chief Commissioner of Lands and Works.
Minister of Finance and Agriculture.
{ Minister of Education and Immigration.
{ Provincial Secretary and Minister of Mines.

In Manitoba :—
} President of Council and Minister of Agriculture (**Premier**).
} Railway Commissioner.
Attorney-General and Land Commissioner.
Minister of Public Works.
Provincial Secretary.
Provincial Treasurer.

In Ontario :—
Attorney-General (Premier).
Secretary and Registrar.
Treasurer.
Commissioner of Crown Lands.
Commissioner of Agriculture.
Commissioner of Public Works.
Minister of Education.
One member of Council without a department or office.

In Quebec :—
President of the Council (Premier).
Commissioner of Crown Lands.
Commissioner of Agriculture and Colonization.
Attorney-General.
Commissioner of Public Works.
Treasurer.
Secretary and Registrar.
One member of Council without office.

In New Brunswick :—

> Attorney-General (Premier).
> Provincial Secretary.
> Surveyor-General.
> Chief Commissioner of Public Works.
> Solicitor-General.
> Two members of Council without office.

In Nova Scotia :—

> President of Council and Provincial Secretary (Premier).
> Attorney-General.
> Commissioner of Works and Mines.
> Four members of Council without office.

In Prince Edward Island :—

> Attorney-General (Premier).
> Commissioner of Public Works.
> Provincial Secretary and Treasurer.
> Five members of Council without office.

This list shows that the premier generally chooses the attorney-generalship when he belongs to the legal profession, but there is no rule on the subject, and he may select any position he prefers. In five of the provinces there are councillors who have no departmental office, and consequently receive no special salary, their expenses while attending meetings of the council being alone paid. The crown has always the right to summon whom it pleases to the cabinet. Not unfrequently, as it will be seen by reference to the offices bracketed in the foregoing list, a member of the council will be entrusted with the responsibilities of more than one department of the government. Executive councillors are called "honourable," but only while they are members of the council.

4.—Provincial Seals and Coats of Arms.

All the provinces have arms of their own, which appear on their great seals, or on any ensigns they have a right to use. Each provincial seal is composed as follows :

In the centre the royal arms, without supporters, but surmounted by the crown ; surrounding the shield, the motto "Dieu et mon droit." Below this shield a somewhat smaller one, containing the provincial coat of arms. Surrounding the whole : "The seal of the province of Ontario" (or whatever the province may be).

On the following page we give a sketch of all the arms of the provinces as they are composed at present.

5.—Flags of the Lieutenant-Governors.

The lieutenant-governors of the provinces have each a flag, displaying the provincial arms (see p. 154) surrounded by a wreath of maple leaves—but without the crown—on the white ground of a union jack (see *above*, p. 91).

FLAG OF THE LIEUTENANT-GOVERNOR OF ONTARIO.

ARMS OF ONTARIO.

ARMS OF QUEBEC.

ARMS OF NEW BRUNSWICK.

ARMS OF NOVA SCOTIA.

ARMS OF
MANITOBA.

ARMS OF
BRITISH COLUMBIA.

ARMS OF
P.E. ISLAND.

PARVA SUB INGENTI

CHAPTER II.

*1. Legislatures. — 2. Number of Members therein. — 3. Voters'
Qualifications in all the Provinces.*

1.—The Legislatures.

The legislatures of the provinces are composed of a
lieutenant-governor, a legislative council and a legislative
assembly in the provinces of Nova Scotia and Quebec ;
of a lieutenant-governor and a legislative assembly only
in the other five provinces. In Prince Edward Island,
however, there is an assembly elected on a basis different
from the other provinces. The legislative council,
elected for many years on a property qualification, was
abolished as a separate house in 1893 and united with
the assembly. The fifteen constituencies now return
each a councillor elected on a real estate qualification, to the value of $325 ; and a member elected
on the general franchise (see *below*, p. 161) for the
province. The legislative councillors in Quebec and
Nova Scotia are appointed by the crown, and must have
a property qualification. The president or speaker is
also appointed by the lieutenant-governor in council and
holds office during pleasure. Members of the council
retain their positions during life, unless they become
bankrupt, convicted of crime, absent for two sessions
consecutively (in Quebec only), or otherwise disqualified

[155]

by law. The council of Quebec consists of twenty-four members; that of Nova Scotia of about twenty. Their legislative rights are similar to those of the senate of Canada. They can commence or amend all classes of legislation except money or taxation bills (see *above*, 94). While they may reject such bills as a whole, they cannot amend them.

The legislative assemblies of the provinces are elected by the people on a very liberal franchise—manhood suffrage in Ontario, New Brunswick, Manitoba and British Columbia, and practically so in Prince Edward Island. A property basis still prevails in Nova Scotia and Quebec (see *below*, pp. 160, 161). The number of members varies from ninety-four in Ontario to thirty in Prince Edward Island. They do not require any property qualification, but must be British born or naturalized subjects of the queen, and male citizens of the age of twenty-one years not disqualified by law. They are paid a certain compensation during a session, varying from $800 in Quebec to $160 in Prince Edward Island, with the addition of a small sum or a mileage rate, ten cents each way in some cases, to pay travelling expenses. Members are nominated and elected on the same day in the provinces, and the vote is by ballot, except in Prince Edward Island. The methods of conducting elections, from the time of a dissolution until the return of writs for a new legislature, are practically the same as those for the dominion parliament. The lieutenant-governor, by the advice of his council, issues a proclamation duly dissolving the old legislature and appointing the day for the return of writs, and calling the new legislature together. Returning officers receive the writs and fix

the day for nomination and voting according to law.
Voters mark and deposit their ballots in the same
secrecy as at a dominion election (see *above*, p. 104).

The provincial laws providing for the independence of
the legislature, like those of the Dominion, prevent
contractors and persons who receive salaries and
emoluments from the dominion or provincial governments from sitting in the assemblies. The statutes
against bribery and corruption are as strict as those for
the Dominion. In all cases the provincial judges try
cases of disputed elections, with the same satisfactory
experience that has been the result of a similar system
in the dominion elections.

The legislatures of the provinces have a duration of
four years—in Quebec, of five—unless sooner dissolved
by the lieutenant-governor. They are governed by the
constitutional principles that obtain at Ottawa. The
lieutenant-governor opens and prorogues the assembly,
as in Ontario, New Brunswick, Prince Edward Island,
Manitoba and British Columbia, or the assembly and
the legislative council in Nova Scotia and Quebec,
with the usual formality of a speech. A speaker
is elected by the majority in each assembly, or is
appointed by the crown in the upper chamber. The
rules and usages that govern their proceedings are
derived from those of England, and do not differ in any
material respect from the procedure in the dominion
parliament (see *above*, p. 110). The rules with respect
to private bill legislation are also equally restrictive.
The British North America Act requires that the
legislatures of Ontario and Quebec must sit once in
every twelve months, like the dominion parliament (see

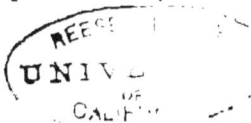

MANITOBA LEGISLATIVE BUILDINGS, WINNIPEG.

above, p. 105), but even without this constitutional direction the fact that supplies for the public service must be voted every year before a fixed day—either the first of July or the first of January in the different provinces—forces the several legislative bodies to meet before the expiration of a financial year. If they did not meet to pass a new supply or appropriation bill (see *above*, p. 119) before the end of that year, the province would be without money to meet the payment of the majority of public salaries, and expenditure on public works or other matters of provincial necessity.

2.—Number of Members in the Legislatures of Canada.

The legislative assemblies of the provinces have the following number of members, all of whom are required to take the oath of allegiance required for members of the senate and house of commons of the dominion parliament (see *above*, p. 106).

PROVINCES.	MEMBERS.
British Columbia	33
Manitoba	40
Ontario	94
Quebec	73
New Brunswick	46
Nova Scotia	38
Prince Edward Island	30
Total number in provincial assemblies	354
Legislative councillors in Quebec and Nova Scotia	44
Legal maximum of senators and members in the dominion parliament in 1895	293
Northwest assembly	26
Total number of members in the legislative bodies of Canada	717

or one representative for about every 7,000 souls of the population of the Dominion.

3.—Voting Qualifications or Electoral Franchise in the Provinces.

In the provinces every native-born Canadian, or subject of her majesty by birth or naturalization, who is a male person of the age of twenty-one years, not insane, not convicted of crime, nor otherwise disqualified by any law, and who is duly entered on the official list of voters, can vote at legislative elections within their respective provinces on the following conditions :

In British Columbia. — Residents in the province for twelve months, and in an electoral district for two months of that time. Chinese and Indians have no vote. The system is consequently manhood suffrage.

In Manitoba.—Residents in the province for six months, and in the electoral division for one month before the issue of proclamation appointing the registration clerk therein. The system here is also manhood suffrage. Indians and persons of Indian blood receiving an annuity or treaty money from the crown, and all persons receiving salaries or fees from the dominion or provincial governments to amount of $350 a year and upwards, have no votes.

In Ontario.—Residents in the province for nine months before the time fixed by law for beginning to make the assessment roll in which they should be entered as qualified to vote, providing they are at the time actually residing in the municipal district in which they vote. The system here, too, is manhood suffrage. Enfranchised Indians—those who have obtained by law all the privileges of citizens—can vote on the same conditions as other voters ; unenfranchised Indians, not residing on an Indian reserve, or among Indians, can vote on a property qualification.

In Quebec.—Owners or occupants of real estate valued in cities at $300, or $200 in other municipalities, or which yields a value of $20 a year. Tenants paying an annual rental for real estate of at least $30 in a city, and $20 in any other municipal division. Also teachers under the control of school commissioners or trustees ;

rentiers, or retired farmers, with a rental of at least $100 yearly; farmers' sons working on their parents' farms, if divided equally between them as co-proprietors ; sons of owners of real property residing with parents, on similar conditions as last ; fishermen, owners or occupants of real property and boats, fishing gear, or of shares in a ship of actual value of at least $150. The system is consequently based on property, and is more restrictive than in any of the provinces, except Nova Scotia, whose franchise is very much the same.

In New Brunswick.—Residents in a district for twelve months before the making up of voters' lists. Persons assessed for the year on real estate to the value of $100, or on personal and real property together to the amount of $400, whether residents or not. Priests or other christian ministers, or school teachers, or professors in colleges. The system is manhood suffrage.

In Nova Scotia.—Persons assessed on real property valued at $150, or on personal, or on personal and real property together, valued at $300. Persons exempted from taxation, when in possession of the property just stated. Tenants, yearly, of similar property. Sons of foregoing persons, or of widows, in possession of enough property to qualify as stated above, and actually residing on such property. Persons having an annual income of $250. Fishermen with fishing gear, boats, and real estate, assessed at an actual value of $150, provided that such property is within the county where the vote is given. Dominion officials generally, and some provincial employees, cannot vote at provincial elections.

In Prince Edward Island.—Residents in an electoral division who have performed statute labour for twelve months before an election. Owners or occupants of real estate, within the electoral district, of the clear yearly value of $6, provided they have occupied such property six months before election. Residents in Charlottetown and Summerside who have paid a provincial poll tax, or twenty-five cents on such civic poll tax for year preceding election. Owners or occupants of at least eight acres of certain reserved land for six months in Georgetown. The system is manhood suffrage to all intents and purposes. Certain dominion officials cannot vote at provincial elections.

11

BRITISH COLUMBIA LEGISLATIVE BUILDINGS, UNDER CONSTRUCTION.

CHAPTER III.

*1. Legal Enumeration of Subjects of Provincial Legislation.—
2. Education.—3. Dominion Power of Disallowance.*

---

1. — Legal Enumeration of Subjects of Provincial Legislation.

The subjects that fall within the legislative authority of the provincial governments are very numerous and affect immediately every man, woman and child in a province. Comfort and convenience, liberty and life, all the rights of citizens with respect to property, the endless matters that daily affect a community, are under the control of the provincial authorities.

The legislature may, in each province, " exclusively make laws " in relation to the classes of subjects enumerated as follows:

1. The amendment, from time to time, notwithstanding anything in the British North America Act, of the constitution of the province, except as regards the office of lieutenant-governor.

2. Direct taxation within the province in order to the raising of a revenue for provincial purposes.

3. The borrowing of money on the sole credit of the province.

4. The establishment and tenure of provincial offices, and the appointment and payment of provincial officers.

5. The management and sale of the public lands belonging to the province, and of the timber and wood thereon. [In the case of Manitoba, which was made a province after 1867, the public lands,

as well as those of the Northwest generally, belong to the dominion government.]

6. The establishment, maintenance and management of public and reformatory prisons in and for the province.

7. The establishment, maintenance and management of hospitals, asylums, charities and eleemosynary institutions in and for the province, other than marine hospitals.

8. Municipal institutions in the province.

9. Shop, saloon, tavern, and auctioneer and other licenses, in order to the raising of a revenue for provincial, local or municipal purposes.

10. Local works and undertakings other than such as are of the following classes :

a. Lines of steam or other ships, railways, canals, telegraphs and other works and undertakings connecting the province with any other or others of the provinces, or extending beyond the limits of the province ;

b. Lines of steamships between the province and any British or foreign country ;

c. Such works as, although wholly situate within the province, are before or after their execution declared by the parliament of Canada to be for the general advantage of Canada, or for the advantage of two or more of the provinces (see *above*, p. 125, for explanations).

11. The incorporation of companies with provincial objects.

12. Solemnization of marriage in the province.   Marriage and divorce, however, belong to the dominion government (see *above*, p. 124).

13. Property and civil rights in the province.

14. The administration of justice in the province, including the constitution, maintenance and organization of provincial courts, both of civil and of criminal jurisdiction, and including procedure in civil matters in those courts.

15. The imposition of punishment by fine, penalty or imprisonment for enforcing any law of the province made in relation to any matter coming within any of the classes of subjects enumerated in this section.

16. Generally all matters of a merely local or private nature in the province.

A careful consideration of the foregoing subjects will show how large and important a measure of local self-government is given to all the provincial members of the confederation. Provincial legislation in every way more nearly affects the daily life and interests of the people of a province than the more general and national legislation of the Dominion. For instance, indirect taxation on imports does not come home to all classes in every day life like those taxes which are imposed by municipalities on the authority of provincial statutes.

2.—Education.

It will be seen above, however, that the all-important question of education does not fall within the enumeration of matters belonging to provincial legislation, but that it was considered necessary to devote a special clause to this subject in the constitutional act of 1867. The reason for this must be sought in the political history of the question.

While the different provinces before confedera.ion were perfecting their respective systems of education, the question of separate schools attained much prominence. The Protestant minority in Lower Canada, and the Roman Catholic minority in Upper Canada, earnestly contended for such an educational system as would give the Protestants in the former, and the Roman Catholics in

LEGISLATIVE BUILDINGS, NEW BRUNSWICK.

the latter province, control of their own schools. Finally, in those two provinces, separate schools obtained at the time of the union, and it accordingly became necessary to give the minorities in question guarantees for the continuance of those schools, as far as such could be given in the constitution. The British North America Act now provides that while the legislature of a province may exclusively make laws on the subject of education, nothing therein shall prejudicially affect any of the denominational schools in existence before July, 1867. Where in any province a system of separate schools existed by law at the time of the union, or was thereafter established by the legislature, an appeal lies to the governor-general in council from any act of a provincial authority "affecting any right or privilege" of a Protestant or Roman Catholic minority. In case the provincial authorities refuse to act for the due protection of the rights of minorities, in accordance with the provisions of the constitution, then the parliament of Canada may provide a remedy for the due execution of the same. In the constitution given to Manitoba in 1870 there are similar provisions, and an appeal can be made to the governor-general in council when a provincial law or decision affects any right or privilege of the Protestant or Roman Catholic minority in relation to education. Parliament can only within its own discretion intervene to provide a remedy when the provincial authority does not pass such legislation as seems necessary to the governor-general in council under the provisions of the constitution.

3.—Dominion Power of Disallowance.

The British North America Act gives to the dominion government a direct control over the legislation of each province. While the imperial government can disallow (reject) an act of the Canadian parliament at variance with the interests of the empire (see *above*, p. 68), the governor in council can within one year from its receipt, disallow any act of a provincial legislature, and consequently prevent it becoming the law. Previous to 1867 the imperial government could disallow any act of a provincial legislature within the limits of British North America. The power over the provinces in this respect has now been transferred to the central government of ·Canada since 1867. This political power is one to be exercised with great discretion and judgment, as other- wise it may involve consequences fatal to the harmony and integrity of the confederation. It may be laid down in general terms that this "veto" can be properly exer- cised when the act under consideration is beyond the, constitutional power of the legislature, or when it is hostile to the rights enjoyed by a minority under the constitution, or when clearly dangerous to the peace and unity of the Dominion generally. The danger arises from the exercise of the power, on the grounds of public policy, in the case of a question clearly within the con- stitutional powers of a legislature. The principle that should prevail, as a rule, is to leave to their operation all acts that fall within the powers of the provincial legis- lature, which within its legal sphere has as absolute a right of legislation as the dominion parliament itself; and if the dominion authorities, at any time, for suffi-

cient reasons, consider it necessary to interfere in pro-　—
vincial affairs, they must be prepared to justify their
action before parliament and the country so deeply
interested in the preservation of the union.　As a rule,
it is the wiser policy to obtain an opinion from the
courts in all cases of doubt, involving nice and delicate
points of law, rather than to use a political power which
is regarded with suspicion by the provinces.　Fortunately
the law allows such references to the supreme court of
Canada (see *above*, p. 130).

CHAPTER IV.

1. Judicial Appointments.—2. Constitution and Organization of the Provincial Courts.—3. Civil Law of French Canada.—4. English Common Law.—5. Statutory Law.

1.—Judicial Appointments.

The written constitution provides that the government of the Dominion shall alone appoint and pay the judges of the superior, district and county courts of the provinces, except those of the probate courts in Nova Scotia. Justices of the peace, police and stipendiary magistrates are, however, appointed by the provincial governments. The judges of all the superior courts can only be removed on an address of the two houses of the dominion parliament to the governor-general, and an inquiry before a committee of the commons or senate into any charges that may be made against them. Judges of the supreme or superior courts must be barristers or advocates of at least ten years' standing at the bar of a province ; county court judges, barristers of ten or seven years' such standing. Stipendiary and police magistrates must be, generally, of at least three years' standing. All justices of the peace must have a certain property qualification in the majority of the provinces. All judicial appointments are made on the recommendation of the dominion minister of justice, whose duty it

[170]

is to inquire into any charges made against judges, and
to advise the houses of the proper course to pursue in
such cases. When judges wish to obtain leave of
absence from their duties, or to retire from the public
service, it is through the department of justice all the
necessary measures are taken.

2.—Constitution and Organization of the Provincial Courts.

The constitution provides also that the governments
of the provinces shall have sole control of the constitution,
organization, and procedure of all their own courts,
having civil and criminal jurisdiction. At any time
they may make changes in the constitution of those
courts, abolish any one of them, add a new court, or
impose additional duties on existing courts. But whenever a new judge of a superior, or district, or county
court is required by a provincial act, it is the Dominion
that provides the salary and makes the appointment.
But while the dominion parliament has no right to
abolish, or interfere with the constitution of the provincial courts within their provincial powers, it is quite
competent for that body to assign to those courts
duties in connection with matters which fall within the
undoubted powers of the central government—the trial
of disputed dominion elections, for instance. In short,
the dominion government can call upon the provincial
judiciary to carry out their legislation.

The constitution gives to the provinces exclusive
control over all matters affecting property and civil
rights. and consequently the provincial courts have to
deal with subjects that affect immediately all classes of

persons.   The provincial legislature can alone pass
legislation touching these matters.   On the other hand,
the dominion parliament can alone make laws relating
to crime and criminals ; that is to say, define the nature
of those numerous offences against public order, religion,
morals, persons, rights of property, and the administration
of law and justice, that fall under the criminal law, and
may be punished by death, or imprisonment, or fines.
Treason, murder, manslaughter, forgery, fraud, breach of
trust, libel, burglary, receiving of stolen goods, robbery
and theft, conspiracies, are among these offences against
public order, persons and the rights of property.   The
regulation of the procedure or the formal steps in the
trial of such offences is also entrusted to the dominion
parliament.   On the other hand the trial of such offences
must take place in the courts of the province which alone
have authority to administer justice in such cases under
the rules laid down by the criminal code of Canada, and
in the absence of such rules in accordance with the
common law that governs every province in the absence
of statutory enactment.

From the preceding paragraphs it will consequently be
seen that the provincial courts have conclusive powers to
try and determine all civil and criminal suits and
actions at law, affecting the lives, liberties and property
of the people within their provincial limits ; that they
regulate both the law and procedure in matters of
personal or private rights, and that the dominion
government alone makes rules of law and procedure in
criminal matters.   The reason of this division of
legislative authority must be sought in the historical
fact that in all the English provinces, which had so long

enjoyed local self-government before 1867, there were differences both in the laws and procedure relating to civil rights and property, though based on the general principles of English jurisprudence, while in one great province there was a distinct system or code of law to which the people had been attached for more than two centuries and a half.

3.—The Civil Law of French Canada.

The criminal law of England has prevailed in all the provinces since it was formally introduced by the proclamation of 1763, and the Quebec Act of 1774. The French Canadians never objected to this system of law, since it gave them the advantage of trial by jury, unknown to French law. The civil law, however, that prevailed in Canada under the French rule, has continued to be the legal system in the province of Quebec since the cession, and has obtained a hold now in that section, which ensures its permanency as an institution closely allied with the dearest rights of the people. Its principles have been carefully collected and enacted in a code which is based on the famous code prepared by the orders of the Emperor Napoleon in the beginning of this century. The rules of procedure relating to the civil law have also been laid down in a distinct code. The civil law of French Canada had its origin, like all similar systems, in the Roman law, on which were engrafted, in the course of centuries, those customs and usages which were adapted to the social condition of France. The various civil divisions or departments of France had their special usages which governed each, but all of them rested on the original foundation of the Roman code of 527–534 before Christ. The customary law of Paris became the fundamental law of Canada during the French rule. The law has been materially modified since 1763 by contact with English laws and customs, and by the necessities and circumstances of a new country ; but still, despite all the amendments and modifications it has undergone in order to make it more in keeping with the conditions of modern life and the needs of commerce and enterprise, it contains all those important principles which have the sanction of ages in all those countries where a similar system prevails, and which affect the civil rights of individuals, the purchase and transfer of property, marriage and inheritance, and many other matters of direct interest to all persons in a community.

4.—The English Common Law.

In the other provinces the common law of England forms the foundation of their jurisprudence. Its general principles were brought into this country, as into the United States, by the early English colonists, but they never adopted those parts of the law which were not suited to the new condition of things in America. It is composed of rules, principles and customs, long established in England, and found in judicial decisions and the records of the courts. It has been called, with much force, "judge-made law." It is a system replete with the principles of individual liberty and self government. Magna Charta (see *above*, p. 58) and the bill of rights (see *above*, p. 58) only asserted principles of this ancient law. It is founded on the actual experiences of life, and not on mere theory or speculation.

5.—The Statutory Law.

In addition to the body of the common law, Canada has also availed itself of those statutes which have been passed by parliament in England from time to time to meet a condition of things to which the old maxims of the law could not apply. The establishment of legislatures in the provinces, we have seen, was only a little later than the entrance of the large British population, and it was therefore in their power to adapt English statutes to the circumstances of this country at the very commencement of our history, or to pass such enactments as were better suited to the country. Thus it happens that gradually a large body of Canadian statutory law has been built upon the common law foundation of the legal structure, and with a view of making the law more intelligible it has consequently been wisely ordered, at different times, that all these statutes should be revised and consolidated—that is, all the statutes on one subject combined into one—by commissions composed of learned lawyers and judges. The people of the Dominion and of all the provinces, except Prince Edward Island, have now easy access to the statutory law that governs them. It is also found convenient in the intervals between the consolidations of the statutory law to collect together, from time to time, all the enactments on a particular subject and incorporate them, with such amendments as are found necessary, in one statute. This has been found especially useful in the case of laws affecting railways, insurance, banking, and other matters of public import. The criminal law has been consolidated in this way and forms a distinct code, or systematic arrangement of the criminal rules of law to be applied by the courts.

CHAPTER V.

When we come to review the judicial system of the provinces we find in each of them several courts of superior and inferior jurisdiction; that is to say whose powers vary very much in importance and are duly set forth in the statutes giving them legal existence and authority. These courts may be conveniently classified as follows—commencing at the foot of the judicial structure—before I proceed to give a summary of their constitution and functions in every province:—

1. Inferior courts of civil jurisdiction, for the recovery of debts, and the settlement of civil actions of limited amount.

2. Inferior courts of criminal jurisdiction, for the summary and speedy trial of offenders against the criminal law, for the preservation of the peace in every community, for the preliminary examination of charges of crime, and the committal of the accused to prison for trial before a higher court.

3. Superior courts, for the trial of civil and criminal cases, not limited in amount or nature, before a judge and jury in each judicial district.

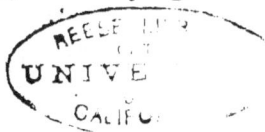

12 [177]

4. Special courts for the dissolution of marriage—only in some provinces—the proving of wills, the trial of disputed provincial and dominion elections, the revision of voters' lists and of assessment rolls in municipalities, etc.

5. The highest or supreme court in each province, the court of appeal, to which cases are brought as the law provides, from the courts of inferior jurisdiction classified above.

By means of this machinery there is in each province most elaborate provision made for the settlement of controversies of every kind, for the prevention and punishment of crime, the preservation of law and order. The nature of this machinery is more fully explained below.

1.—Courts for the Collection of Small Debts.

In the provinces the following courts try actions for the recovery of small debts :—

In Ontario.—The division courts whose jurisdiction does not extend beyond $200 in actions for debt or contract. In no case can the sum of the amount to be gone into exceed $400. Their jurisdiction does not cover in any shape gambling debts, liquor drunk in a tavern, or notes of hand given therefor, titles to land, will or settlement, tolls, customs or franchise, slander, seduction, wills or testaments, or actions against a justice of the peace for anything done in the execution of his office. Appeals lie under certain conditions to a divisional court of appeal (see *below*, p. 189). As a rule the presiding judges are judges of the county courts, but any barrister may be appointed to hold the same.

In Quebec.—The circuit court (see *below*, p. 179), recorders' courts in cities (in cases of wages and actions between lessors and lessees), commissioners' courts established in certain parts of the country, and magistrates' courts.

In New Brunswick.—Stipendiary* or police magistrates, parish commissioners, and justices of the peace, where the debt does not exceed $80.

In Nova Scotia.—One or two justices, according to the amount of the debt, which cannot exceed $80 in any case.

In Prince Edward Island.—The city court at Charlottetown, and the small debt court at Summerside, where the amount does not exceed $80 and $50 respectively.

In British Columbia.—Stipendiary and police magistrates, where the debt does not exceed $100.

In Manitoba.—The county courts are the courts for the collection of small debts (see next paragraph).

2.—County Courts.

Higher in the legal structure are the county courts, which have larger powers in civil actions than those just named. The judges in these courts are appointed, paid and removed only by the dominion government. The following statement shows the powers of these judicial bodies :

In Ontario, to the amount of $200 for debt or damages, or on notes of hand or, where the amount is ascertained by the defendant's signature, to $400. In Nova Scotia, to $400 but not less than $20. In New Brunswick, to $400. In Prince Edward Island, to $150. In Manitoba, to $250. In British Columbia, to $1,000.

The superior courts of Quebec are in some respects county courts, since a judicial district includes one or more counties, but their jurisdiction in civil cases is not limited. Below them are the circuit courts, which have exclusive jurisdiction where the sum is not less than $100 : also in all suits for school taxes and school fees, and church dues, without reference to the amount ; and from their

---

* Stipendiary comes from the Latin *stipendiarius*, and means one who receives a fixed salary by the year for regular service as distinguished from an ordinary justice of the peace who is not so paid or employed.

decision in such cases there is no appeal.   In actions which do not arise in the chief town (chef-lieu) of a district, the court has jurisdiction (except at Quebec and Montreal) to the extent of $200, and over all suits to which the crown is a party.   In these cases there is an appeal to the superior court.   The circuit court is presided over by a judge of the superior court.   The "circuit court of the district of Montreal" is held by one of two judges called "circuit judges of the district of Montreal," but judges of the superior court can hold it, and are vested with the same powers as the circuit judges.

In Montreal, and other cities in the province of Quebec, the recorders are civic judges, having jurisdiction to decide actions for taxes and assessments due to the city, market dues, water rates, recovery of fines and penalties imposed by the city charter or by-laws of the city.

The county courts, properly so called, have no jurisdiction in cases involving any title to land, the validity of wills (except in British Columbia), libel, slander, breach of promise of marriage, or in actions against a justice of the peace for anything done by him in the execution of his office.

3.—Jurisdiction of Inferior Courts in Criminal Cases.

In criminal cases the law gives to the lower courts a certain limited jurisdiction.   In all the cities of Canada —and also in every large town of Ontario—there are police or stipendiary magistrates who try offenders and punish them summarily for drunkenness, disturbances, breaches of the peace, and other minor offences, or send for trial at the superior courts those persons who are charged with criminal offences and cannot or do not wish to be tried in these courts of mere summary jurisdiction (see *below*, p. 182).   Justices of the peace have also power to convict persons charged with a criminal offence, where the services of police or stipendiary magistrates are not available.   In the province of Quebec the recorders have the powers of police magistrates or of two or more justices for the preservation of the peace. In all cases of criminal charge it is simply the duty of the presiding magistrate, or justices, as the law of a province may provide, to see whether the evidence brought before him is sufficient on the face of it to authorize him to send the accused person to a higher court for trial. In trivial matters the magistrate simply issues a summons or order to the offender to appear before him on a certain day. In serious offences, like charges of murder, forgery, breach of trust, robbery, arson, and so forth, he issues his warrant, which is a command to a constable or policeman to arrest the accused and bring him before the court immediately. When a person disobeys a summons the magistrate will issue a warrant for his arrest. The· justice can commit a person to jail who refuses to be sworn or to give evidence in a case. Prisoners may be "remanded," that is to say, their case may be postponed until another day for adequate reason. Bail may be taken for their appearance in such cases according to the circumstances of the case and the nature of the offence. Witnesses are called for the prosecution, and counsel may be heard on both sides. The accused may be heard in answer to the charge, after the examination of the witnesses for the prosecution, and whatever he says is taken down in writing—and as the justice warns him—can be given in evidence against him at the trial. Every witness called by the accused to testify to any fact relevant to the case must be heard. The information—that is the written statement, of the charge or charges generally on oath, on which the justice issues his warrant—the evidence, and

all other papers relating to the inquiry must be forwarded by the magistrate to the clerk or other proper officer
of the court by which the accused is to be tried. In
cases where the accused is not charged with treason, or
an offence punishable by death, or offences against the
queen's government or person, bail may be taken for his
appearance before the trial court by two justices or by a
judge of any superior or county court in the district
where he may be confined. In the other cases mentioned above, bail can only be allowed by order of a superior
court of criminal jurisdiction for the province, the high
court of justice in Ontario, the queen's bench in Quebec
and Manitoba, or the superior courts in other provinces.

The following judicial functionaries may at once—*summarily*, as it is legally called—dispose of cases of persons
accused of theft, assault, gambling, or minor criminal
offences, who may choose to be tried without a jury in
preference to being committed to jail for trial before a
higher court :

In Ontario, Quebec and Manitoba.—Judges of county courts,
recorders, commissioner of police, judge of the sessions of the
peace, police and district magistrates, or other judicial officers who
can alone, under a provincial law, perform such acts as are usually
done by two or more justices of the peace.

In Nova Scotia and New Brunswick.—Recorder,* county court
judge, police or stipendiary magistrate, commissioner of police.

In Prince Edward Island and British Columbia.—Any two
justices of the peace.

---

* The recorders of the maritime provinces appear now to be nothing
more, as a rule, than solicitors or advisers for municipal corporations.
The towns' incorporation act of Nova Scotia allows the stipendiary magistrate of a town to hold the office, and this is accordingly done very
generally in the province. In the province of Quebec the recorders are
judicial officers and can act as judges of sessions (see *above*, pp. 180, 181).
The office is a survival of old English judicial practice.

4.—Courts of Superior Jurisdiction.

In the provinces there are above all the inferior courts just named, what are in practice high courts of justice, having unlimited jurisdiction in all civil and criminal cases.

The separate courts that long existed in Canada as in England—known as queen's bench, common pleas and chancery—have been now practically abolished, and one court can try and determine any case of law or equity that comes before it in due process of law. For instance, the queen's bench, chancery and common pleas divisions of the high court of justice in Ontario no longer sit or give judgments as such divisions, but all are qualified to deal with any subject or point of law. In Prince Edward Island, however, the chancery court is still in existence as a distinct tribunal, though its procedure has now been much simplified. The following paragraphs show the constitution of these superior courts in each province :

In Ontario.—One of the two divisions of the supreme court of judicature called the high court of justice, composed of three divisions, queen's bench, chancery, and common pleas, which have equal jurisdiction in all matters, civil and criminal, not specially confined to the county, surrogate and division courts. The queen's bench is composed of a chief justice or president and two justices ; chancery, of a chancellor or president and three justices ; common pleas, of a chief justice or president and two justices.

In Quebec.—The queen's bench for the trial of criminal cases, in Montreal and Quebec—and elsewhere when necessary—composed of a chief justice and five justices. A single judge holds the criminal court. The superior court, composed of a chief justice and an acting chief justice (who resides in Montreal or Quebec according as the chief justice lives in the one or other city), and of twenty-eight justices who live in the chief towns of the judicial districts of the province. It has full jurisdiction in all civil cases not within the exclusive powers of the circuit or other· courts of limited jurisdiction. A judge of this court has criminal jurisdiction in the districts outside of Montreal and Quebec.

In New Brunswick.—The supreme court, composed of a chief justice and five judges, each of whom acts as a trial judge throughout the province. One of the judges of this court sits as a judge in equity. The supreme court has original jurisdiction in all matters not belonging to the divorce, admiralty, probate and county courts, whose functions are defined by law.

In Nova Scotia.—A supreme court, composed of a chief justice and six justices, each of whom sits as a trial judge throughout the province. It has original jurisdiction in all matters not specially delegated to the lower courts, but it cannot hear and determine actions for debt under $80, except by way of appeal to the court *in banco,* that is to say, to the whole *bench* or court. Any one of the judges can exercise the powers previously vested in a judge of equity.

In Prince Edward Island.—The supreme court, composed of a chief justice and two justices, having original jurisdiction in all civil and criminal cases. In civil cases, of debt, the action must be for an amount above $32. All causes beyond the jurisdiction of the county court can be tried before a judge of this court. A court of chancery still exists as a separate court in this province. Two assistant judges of the supreme court are vice-chancellor and master of the rolls, who preside over two courts having equal power and jurisdiction in such matters as now in Ontario are given to the high court of justice. The lieutenant-governor is nominally chancellor—simply a survival of the old judicial system.

In Manitoba.—The court of queen's bench, composed of a chief justice and three justices, possessing all the powers of the superior courts of the other provinces.

In British Columbia.—The supreme court, composed of a chief justice and four justices, having full jurisdiction in civil and criminal cases as in other provinces.

CHAPTER VI.

5.—Probate and Surrogate Courts.

Besides the courts of superior and inferior jurisdiction mentioned above, there are others of a special nature. The probate courts of the provinces of Nova Scotia, New Brunswick and Prince Edward Island, known also as surrogate* in Ontario and Manitoba, are presided over by one judge, and have power to deal with all matters relating to the will or testament of deceased persons, or the administration of the effects of persons who leave no such will or testament. The word "probate" shows the character of the duties of this court; its principal function is to prove—the Latin word "*probare*" having that meaning—that a will is legally executed, and can be carried out according to the last wishes of the testator. But its jurisdiction extends over

---

* Surrogate comes from a Latin word, meaning to put in another's place, and was formerly applied in English law to a deputy or substitute of an ecclesiastical judge, a bishop or his chancellor, who, until recent years, had authority in cases of wills,

OSGOODE HALL (SUPERIOR LAW COURTS), TORONTO.

all testamentary matters and causes, subject to the revision of the superior courts—the chancery division of the high court of justice in Ontario. In Quebec the jurisdiction in probate rests with the superior court. In British Columbia the county courts have jurisdiction up to matters involving $2,500, and the supreme court beyond that amount. In Ontario and Manitoba the county judges are surrogate judges.

6.—Heir and Devisee Court in Ontario.

This court has power to determine claims to land in the province where the crown has issued no patent in favour of the proper claimants. Commissions under the great seal are issued, when necessary, to commissioners, the judges of the superior courts or other persons, to deal with such cases as they arise.

7.—Courts for Trial of Controverted Elections.

In the case of controverted or disputed elections for the dominion parliament or the provincial legislatures, the statutory law of the Dominion and of each province gives jurisdiction to the judges of the superior courts to try and determine them. In provincial contested elections one judge is sufficient; but the dominion law requires that two judges preside at a trial of every election petition. Appeals lie to the supreme court of appeal of a province in case of a provincial, and to the supreme court of Canada in case of a dominion election.

8.—Courts of Revision of Assessment Rolls and Voters' Lists.

The county or district judges in Ontario and other provinces also act as a court of appeal from the first court of revision held by a municipality in matters of disputed assessment (see *Fifth Part*, sec. 10). They also act for the revision of voters' lists for provincial elections. Revising officers of the lists of voters for dominion elections are, in all the provinces except Quebec and British Columbia, a county or district judge or a barrister of five years' standing at the bar, as the governor-general in council may choose to appoint. In Quebec he must be a judge of the superior court or an advocate of five years' standing ; in British Columbia, a judge of a superior or county or district court, or a stipendiary magistrate or a barrister of five years' standing. This revising court can compel the attendance of witnesses, the production of papers and books, and exercise all the powers of the superior courts of a province necessary to enable it to carry out the provisions of the franchise law.

9.—Courts of Divorce.

In the provinces of Nova Scotia, New Brunswick, and Prince Edward Island there are courts with power to dissolve a marriage between parties for such causes as the law allows. In the case of British Columbia, the supreme court of that province holds that it possesses all the jurisdiction conferred on the court of divorce in England. By the British North America Act the parliament of Canada has sole power to deal with the subject of marriage and divorce, and can alone grant divorce by special legislation on each case that comes before it from Quebec, Ontario, Manitoba, and the Northwest Territories, where no courts have been established by its authority. The courts in the maritime provinces existed before 1867, and continue to exercise their powers in the absence of dominion legislation. The senate, where bills of divorce are first presented by usage (see *above*, p. 94), has a special committee and special rules on the subject.

10.—Supreme Courts of Appeal in the Provinces.

In all the provinces there are the following courts of highest jurisdiction, to which appeals can be made from the judgment of a court, presided over by one or more judges:

In Ontario.—One of the divisions of the supreme court of judicature, called the court of appeal, composed of a chief justice and three justices.   It hears appeals from the three divisions of the high court of justice, queen's bench, common pleas and chancery, within the limitations fixed by the judicature act.   In cases of an appeal from a divisional court of the high court of justice, four members must sit as a court; from a single judge three are a quorum.   In case of illness or unavoidable absence of a judge, the vacancy may be filled by a judge of the high court, so as to make a quorum.   The court of appeal may sit in two divisions at the same time, with the assistance of such number of judges of the high court as may be necessary at the time.

Below the court of appeal are the divisional courts of the high court of justice of Ontario.   Appeals are allowed to one of those divisional courts—each of which is composed of three judges—but limitations are imposed on the right of subsequent appeal to the chief court of appeal.   An act of 1895 provides that there shall not be more than one appeal in the province from any judgment or order made in any action or matter save at the instance of the crown, or in a case in which the crown is concerned, or in such cases as are specified in the statute.   Appeal upon special leave from a divisional court to the chief court of appeal shall not be allowed unless the matter in controversy exceeds the sum or value of $1,000, exclusive of costs, or involves indirectly or otherwise that sum or value; or involves the validity of a patent; or where the judgment or order involves a question of law or practice on which there have been conflicting decisions or opinions by the high court of justice, or by judges thereof; or where a judgment or order is in regard to a matter of practice, but affects the ultimate rights of parties to the action to the extent of the said sum or value ; or where there are other sufficient special reasons for treating the case as exceptional and allowing a further appeal.   In case a party appeals to a divisional court of the high court in a case in which an appeal lies to the court of appeal, the party so appealing shall not be entitled to afterwards appeal from the said divisional court to the court of appeal, but any other party to the action or matter may appeal to the court of appeal from the judgment or order of the divisional court.   No judge shall sit as a judge on the hearing of an appeal from any judgment or order made by himself.

In Quebec.—The court of queen's bench which hears appeals from the superior court in civil cases.   It also hears appeals on points of law under the criminal code (see *above*, p. 172).   As a court of appeal, four judges constitute a competent court, though five, and no more, can sit.   A minor court of appeal is the court of review, consisting of three judges of the superior court, and reviewing judgments given by a single judge of that tribunal.   If this court of review confirm the first judgment, an appeal can be made only to the supreme court of Canada, or to the judicial committee of the privy council.   If the judgment is reversed by the court of review, an appeal is allowed to the queen's bench, appeal side.

In New Brunswick.—The supreme court sitting as a full court, but of whom four justices form a quorum.

In Nova Scotia.—The supreme court, sitting *in banco*, or a full court, of whom four—or three in case of illness—form a quorum.

In Prince Edward Island.—The supreme court sitting as a full court, and having jurisdiction in appealed chancery cases.

In Manitoba.—The court of queen's bench, sitting as a full court, of whom three form a quorum.

In British Columbia.—The supreme court, sitting as a full court, of whom three shall be a quorum.

From the judgments of the foregoing provincial courts of appeal there are appeals to the supreme court of Canada (see *above*, p. 129) and finally to the judicial committee of the privy council under the limitations and conditions laid down for such an appeal (see *above*, p. 66).

Appeals are allowed to the supreme court of Canada in criminal cases only when the court of appeal in a province is not unanimous. No appeal can be brought in any criminal case from any judgment or order of any court of Canada to the judicial committee of the privy council (see *above*, p. 66).

11.—Process.

Every court gives effect to its powers by forms of proceeding (process) set forth in the statute defining its jurisdiction and in its rules of practice. In civil actions, process is of various kinds: 1. A writ of summons to compel a defendant to appear before a court. 2. Subpœna, or summons to witnesses to appear and give evidence in a suit or be subject to a penalty or punishment (which is the translation of *subpœna*). 3. Summons to jurors to appear at a trial. 4. Execution of a judgment or order of a court, besides other proceedings not necessary to mention here. A warrant is a guarantee or protection (the original meaning of an old French word *warant*) to the person executing it that he has authority for so doing. It is by warrants that persons charged with crime are brought before a magistrate and committed to prison, and other processes necessary in civil and criminal cases executed.

12.—Sheriff and Officers of the Courts.

The most important officer in the execution of process of law is the sheriff, who is appointed by the lieutenant-governor in council in the provinces, and by the governor-general in the territories. One sheriff is appointed for every county or judicial district in a province. Here again we have another example of our close adherence to old English names. The sheriff was in Saxon times the judicial president of the *scir-gemot*, or assembly *(gemot)* of the shire *(scir)*, one of the divisions of the English kingdoms. He was the " reeve " or headman of the shire, the *scir-gerefa*, which has in the course of centuries been softened to sheriff. In Norman times the shire became a county, and its government, judicial, military, and financial, was practically executed by the sheriff, who was directly responsible to the king. In the course of time he was deprived of his large powers, and became a purely civil officer. He is now in Canada an officer of dignity, connected with the superior courts, whose orders, sentences and judgments are carried out under his direction, even to the execution of a criminal. He summons juries, has charge of the jails and their keepers. He appoints his own deputies and officers, and is responsible for their misconduct and negligence in executing the process of the courts. He gives security for the proper performance of his onerous duties.

In connection with the courts there is also a large body of officers, known as county attorneys, clerks of the peace, deputy clerks of the crown, county court clerks, registrars of high or surrogate courts, and others, all of whom are appointed by the government of a province to perform special duties in connection with the administration of justice. Every process of a court is duly issued, and registered in the records of the court, by the proper officer. The prothonotaries* in Quebec and elsewhere are the clerks of the superior courts, who issue writs, keep the archives and records, and enter judgments. In Quebec they have the right to appoint tutors and render judgments in certain uncontested commercial cases.

The name of constable, now the lowest in the judicial machinery, goes back to early Norman times, when it represented an office of high dignity, which nobles were proud to hold. The constables of the superior court are generally known as bailiffs. All constables are "peace officers" who serve the summons and warrants of the proper courts. In cities they are known as policemen. They can arrest persons who break the law in their presence, and bring them before the proper court at the earliest possible moment. Otherwise they act only under an order from a magistrate, sheriff, or court. In times of threatened riot or disturbance, special constables are appointed by justices to preserve the peace. Constables are appointed by the judges of sessions or magistrates, or municipal councils, or police commissioners, as the law provides in each case in a province.

13.—Office of Coroner.

The office of coroner goes also back to early English times, when he was a royal officer specially appointed to

---

* From two Greek words, meaning a first notary or clerk.

13

look after the peace and interests of the crown (Latin *corona*, thence *coroner*) in a special district allotted to him. It is now his duty to inquire into the cause of the death of a person who is killed or dies suddenly, or in prison. When the circumstances of the case require an investigation, he summons a jury, calls witnesses, and holds an "inquest" on view of the body at the place where it was found. Upon the facts disclosed a verdict is given by the jury. Persons may be charged with murder, manslaughter, or culpable negligence, according to the nature of the death. When a coroner's "inquisition" (inquiry or investigation) charges a person with manslaughter or murder, he must issue his warrant to bring the accused immediately before a magistrate or justice, who will proceed to make inquiry into the case as the law provides. Coroners can also investigate the origin of fires, when the circumstances point to incendiarism or criminal design.

14.—The Legal Profession.

In each of the provinces there is a law society, incorporated by statute, for the promotion of the interests of the legal profession, and the regulation of the study necessary before admission to the practice of law. In nearly all the provinces every person must be entered as a student-at-law, according to the rules of the several law societies, for five years before he can be admitted to the bar. But an exception is made in the case of one who has taken a degree in arts or law in a recognized university. In Ontario, Manitoba and British Columbia, the term of studies for a barrister is then reduced to three years. In Quebec, only one year is taken off for admission as "an advocate"—the general designation of a lawyer in this province—when a student has received a degree in law in a university. In Nova Scotia and New Brunswick, four years' study is required for admission as an attorney, but one year is taken off in the case of a university graduate. Then a man can be admitted as a barrister one year after becoming an attorney. In Prince Edward Island, five years' study is necessary for an attorney and one year later he can be admitted as a barrister, but two years are taken off for a university graduate. An attorney is one who does not plead in court, but prepares "the brief," or case for the barrister, who can alone plead and argue before the judge. In Ontario, attorneys are now called solicitors, and they must study as clerks in the office of a practising solicitor for five years, but two years are also taken off in case of a graduate of a university. In all the provinces examinations are necessary before a man can be admitted to the study and practice of law, under the regulations of the different law societies. The universities of the provinces now, generally speaking, have regular courses of lectures and examinations in law, and confer degrees of bachelor and doctor of laws.

The attorney-general of a province has precedence at the bar over all other members, but he ranks below the minister of justice as attorney-general of the Dominion. Both the dominion and provincial governments appoint queen's counsel, who have a certain precedence at the bar, and ought to be always men of high legal standing.

15.—Notaries.

In Quebec, notaries form a distinct profession, and are incorporated. They are public officers, whose special duty it is to draw up and execute legal deeds, assure the date thereof, preserve the same in safe keeping, and deliver copies and extracts of the same, for certain fees regulated by law. No advocate or physician can hold the position. A course of five years' study is required before admission. In the other provinces, notaries are generally lawyers, appointed for that special purpose by the lieutenant-governor in council. Other persons, not members of the legal profession, can be appointed when they have the qualifications required by law. A notary —generally called "notary public,"—as in Quebec, certifies deeds and other writings, or copies of the same, and his seal and certificate give them validity at home and abroad. Their most common duty is in the "protesting" of notes and bills of exchange—in other words, a legal declaration necessary when such commercial paper or liability is not paid at the time and place required under the law governing these matters.

CHAPTER VII.

1.—Origin of Courts of Assize, Nisi Prius, Oyer and Terminer, etc.

The judges of the high courts of justice, whether called supreme or superior, or high courts, make what are called " circuits " of a province at least twice a year, and hold courts for the trial of civil and criminal cases not limited in their nature. These are the courts in which life and property are most deeply involved. Here we see in full operation that system of trial by jury which has always been the distinguishing feature of English law and justice, as compared with the methods of France and other nations. These courts have long been known as courts of assize, nisi prius, of oyer and terminer, of general jail delivery. In their origin and methods of procedure we see the example of England as in all our institutions of government. When it became necessary to separate the original king's court (*curia regis*) of early Norman days into branches to meet the increasing demands of the people for justice, three divisions were formed : (1) The exchequer attended to revenue and fiscal matters ; (2) common pleas, to all matters of a civil nature ; (3) the king's bench, to criminal and all other business not given to the other courts.   In the course of time another court arose, known as the chancery, to provide redress for petitioners who could not readily obtain it under the rules of law and procedure that obtained in the common law courts.   Justices also were sent on the circuit of the kingdom to administer justice in counties.   It seems to have been always a fundamental principle of the administration of law in England that cases, whether civil or criminal, should be tried in local courts or in the presence of the county and people where the suitors or accused lived, and not in a distant or unknown tribunal.   It was as an expansion of this principle that trial by jury arose in the judicial system of England.   In olden times, for a long while after the Norman conquest, it was customary to summon twelve persons who lived in the immediate neighbourhood where a dispute had arisen, and to swear them to tell the truth according to their knowledge of the facts, or by their " recognition," as it was called.   In fact, they were simply witnesses who acted to the best of their knowledge and belief, and represented the opinions of the district where they lived.   Eventually there arose out of this primitive method of coming to a conclusion on a disputed case, the practice of calling witnesses, and of summoning twelve men of the neighbourhood to decide on the facts as set forth in the evidence.

In the words jury, assize, nisi prius, oyer and terminer, we see the evidences of Norman influence in the courts of England and her colonial possessions.   " Jury " comes from an old French word meaning to " swear," and was applied to the body, because the ordinance or "assize"- that first summoned them required each member to take an oath. "Assize" is also derived from the Norman French, and was used originally to designate the sittings or sessions of a judicial or even legislative body, and subsequently even to the ordinance or law of such an assembly. "Nisi prius" is also a phrase of old legal proceedings. Formerly the sheriff of a county was commanded to bring a jury to Westminster—the central tribunal of the kingdom—on a certain day *unless before* (the translation of "nisi prius") that time the justices of assizes came into the district. Now a trial at nisi prius means simply when an action is tried before a judge and jury. The words "oyer and terminer" (hear and determine) are also relics of the days when English statutes and the proceedings of the courts were in Norman French. Consequently when we hear of the judges holding such courts we know that it means that they come clothed with authority to hold sittings at which they will hear and judge all cases brought before them. Then there is a general jail delivery. The jails then must deliver up their prisoners for trial before a jury of sworn men chosen from the neighbourhood, as in old English times. Below I explain the method of choosing a jury on a criminal trial (p. 205).

Persons on bail must come forward and surrender themselves for trial, or else their securities will have to pay the penalties the law has required.

2.—Trial by Jury in Canada.

Trial by jury, which never existed under French rule, was established in Canada in 1785 in matters of commerce and personal wrong. Of course the system formed part of the criminal law which was introduced into Canada after the cession in 1763, and the king instructed the governor-general, Murray, to pass an ordinance to permit French as well as English to sit as jurymen. Gradually it came very generally into operation, even in matters under the civil law. At present, jurymen in all the provinces except Manitoba and British Columbia require to be British subjects who are on the assessment roll of a county or other district where they serve, and to possess a certain amount of real or personal property. In Manitoba and British Columbia they need only be actual residents and electors in a district. In Quebec and Nova Scotia grand jurors need a higher qualification than petty jurymen. Jurymen are chosen by ballot by selectors — certain officials of a county—in Ontario and some of the other provinces, but the process is too complicated to explain it here intelligently. The complete list of jurors chosen for a sitting of a court or assize is called a " panel," from the fact that originally the list was written on a little slip or piece (*panel* in old French) of parchment. The men selected for particular trials are said to be "impannelled," entered or enrolled on the list.

In civil cases of disputed facts juries are still required in the majority of the provinces, but of late years the tendency has been to allow the judge himself to decide on the evidence in matters where there are nice and complicated points of law at issue, and juries are now becoming less common. As a general principle, however, in the determination of actions at law the judge decides the law, and the jury the facts of the case. . In all criminal cases before the court an accused has a right to a jury of twelve men, and the verdict must be unanimous for conviction. It is optional for him to be summarily tried by a county judge or justice (see *above*, p. 176) in certain cases.

In the trial of issues of fact in civil actions it is no longer necessary to have a jury of twelve or to have their unanimous verdict. In Ontario, the number of a jury is twelve, or eleven under certain circumstances, and the number required for a verdict is ten. In the other provinces the respective numbers are as follows : Quebec, twelve in all and nine for a verdict ; Nova Scotia, nine in all and seven for a verdict after four hours' deliberation ; in New Brunswick, seven in all and five for a verdict in the supreme court, but five in all and four for a verdict in the county court ; in Prince Edward Island, seven in all and five for a verdict ; in Manitoba, twelve in all but nine for a verdict, though parties may agree to a jury of nine ; in British Columbia, eight in all in the supreme court, with three-fourths for a verdict in the same court, but five in all and three-fourths for a verdict in the county court, when in either case they have been in deliberation for three hours and are not unanimous in all respects.

3.—Trial of Civil Actions.

In actions between persons for the settlement of a dispute, the one who commences the suit for redress is called the plaintiff (from the French word meaning *one who complains*), and the other who is asked to give that redress or to defend his refusal is the defendant (from a French and Latin word meaning *to ward off*, or *contest*). The plaintiff obtains from an officer of a court a writ of summons containing a statement of the claim, and this is served on the defendant, who has to put his defence in the form required by law. The case is placed before the court in a *pleading*, the object of which is to get from both parties a full statement of the claim and defence. When the case is ready for trial, and is called by the officer of the court, the counsel for the plaintiff opens the pleadings, or explains the nature of the claim at issue. He then calls upon his witnesses, who are examined one after the other by himself under the rules of evidence, and cross-examined by the defendant's counsel to break down their testimony, if possible, or bring out some points in favour of the defendant's side. Then, when the evidence for the plaintiff is all in, the defendant may call and examine his witnesses, who are cross-examined in turn by the plaintiff's counsel. If there are no witnesses for the defence the plaintiff's counsel sums up his evidence, and the defendant's counsel replies. Sometimes the judge may order a "nonsuit"; *i.e.*, on the ground that the plaintiff has failed to make out his case. But when evidence is given on both sides, the counsel for the defendant sums up, and the counsel for the plaintiff replies. If the case is one for a jury, the judge reads the evidence and makes such observations as law and usage allow him, and instructs the jury as to the law of the case. The jury then retire to their room to consider their verdict, which will be based on the facts, the law of the case they must take from the judge. If they have decided (see *above*, p. 201) for the plaintiff or defendant they return, and through their foreman state its nature. If they cannot agree, and the judge is of opinion that there is no probability of their coming to an agreement, they are discharged from attendance, and the case has to be tried at another time before a new jury. Speaking generally, the costs are paid by the person who has lost his suit. These are, however, matters of detail to be decided by the court according to its discretion and the circumstances of the case. The law gives suitors in civil cases every possible opportunity of appeal to the court above (see *above*, p. 182). A plaintiff or defendant may conduct his own case, but when neither is a lawyer the wise course is to employ a professional man. A person charged with a criminal offence has also the right to defend himself.

4.—Trial of Criminal Offences.

In criminal cases, involving life and liberty, justice proceeds with great deliberation. It is the duty of the crown prosecutor—a county crown attorney in Ontario— to take all the steps that the law requires for the trial of a prisoner committed to jail by a magistrate (see *above*, p. 175) on a criminal offence. Before the person can be tried before the court of assizes he must be indicted—that is, the court must have before it a statement showing in strictly legal form, but in explicit and popular language, the nature of the offence for which he is to be tried. This indictment must be prepared by the crown counsel or attorney authorized by the attorney-general of a province to look after the preliminaries of crown cases. It is his duty to submit the " information " (see *above*, p. 175) and all other papers setting forth the cause of commitment before what is called a grand jury, which is composed of, in the provinces, not less than twelve and not more than twenty-four persons chosen specially from a carefully selected panel or list of jurymen (see *above*, p. 200). The grand jury do not "try" an accused. No witnesses in support of the prisoner are examined, but the jury simply come to a conclusion whether there is sufficient evidence before them to put the prisoner on his trial. If the jury decide that there is a case against the prisoner, then their foreman writes a "true bill" on the bill of indictment or the information laid before them. If there is no such case, he writes "no case," and the accused is entitled to his liberty unless there is another bill of indictment in his case to be considered. A dominion law now provides that seven grand jurors may find a true bill in any province where the "panel" is not more than thirteen, but the governor must first proclaim or officially announce the day when this provision comes into force, and this has been done in Ontario. A Manitoba statute requires the assent of at least eight jurors out of the fifteen summoned on the panel. In Manitoba two-thirds of the jury must speak English and one-third French ; in Quebec and Montreal one-half must speak English and the other half French.

In the case of a "true bill," the accused is put on his trial before a petty (from the French *petit*) or common jury, chosen from the panel for that sitting of the court (see *above*, p. 200).

The counsel for the crown is always a prominent barrister and queen's counsel learned in the law, chosen to conduct the prosecution by the attorney-general of the province. In all criminal cases the crown, or the reigning king or queen, is the prosecutor, and in his or her name all actions are brought against those who commit a criminal offence. Her representative in a province is the attorney-general, whose duty it is to protect the interests of the crown and people in all criminal cases affecting life, liberty and property. When the prisoner is standing in the dock,* in the presence of the court, the indictment must be read to him, and he is called upon to plead " guilty," or " not guilty " as it most invariably happens. The next step is to choose twelve jurors from the panel. Each juryman is called by name and address, but before he is sworn, both crown and accused, acting through their respective counsel, can "challenge " (or object to) a juryman serving on the trial. This objection may be without cause assigned ("peremptory") or for some special cause, as that he has expressed or is known to have an opinion on the case, that he is a particular friend of the accused, or is otherwise likely to be influenced one way or the other, The number of "challenges " are regulated by the law. chiefly with respect to the gravity of the offence.

The following is the procedure in calling a jury to try a prisoner : The name and number of each juror on the panel, and the place of his abode, are written on separate pieces of card, each of equal size. These cards are handed to the proper officer of the court by the sheriff or his deputy, or other person having the panel in his charge, placed in a box provided for that purpose, and then well shaken together. The officer of the court draws one card at a time, and calls out the name and number on the same, until such a number of persons

---

* Probably from an old Dutch word, meaning a cage. A prisoner is placed in the dock for felonious offences, or in other words for grave crimes.

have answered to their names as will probably be sufficient to provide a full jury of twelve, after allowing for challenges. The officer then proceeds to swear each juror in the order in which his name is called, provided he is not challenged or obliged to stand by. Provision is made for mixed juries of English and French speaking persons in Quebec and Manitoba, when necessary.

The twelve men at last selected and sworn in this way compose the jury to try the prisoner on the indictment presented by the crown. Then the crown counsel states the case against the accused, and points out the nature of the evidence to be produced. Witnesses for the crown are called, and when each has sworn or "affirmed" to tell "the truth, the whole truth, and nothing but the truth," he or she is duly examined by the crown counsel. Sometimes the court orders, in important cases and under special circumstances, that witnesses be kept out of the court room and separately examined. Counsel for the defence can cross-examine the witnesses. At the close of the case for the prosecution the defence must declare whether it intends to present evidence, and if the reply is in the negative the crown's counsel may sum up, and the defence follows. The attorney or solicitor-general, or counsel acting in behalf of either, may reply, but this is reserved for special occasions, or he may reply instead of summing up. When the defence has evidence to adduce, it has the right to open, and then examine witnesses. Any person on trial may give evidence on his or her own behalf. When the evidence for the defence is closed the counsel can sum up. The crown's counsel replies, and the judge finally reviews the evidence with strict impartiality and explains the law as in civil suits (see *above*, p. 202). The jury then retire in charge of an officer of the court to consider their verdict. When they have decided they come into court, and after each has answered to his name, the foreman declares whether the prisoner is "guilty," or "not guilty." When they cannot agree, and the court is satisfied that it is useless to keep them longer, they are discharged from attendance, and a new jury may be drawn from the panel or the trial postponed on such conditions as justice may require. Sometimes in giving a verdict of guilty on a case of capital punishment the jury may consider some circumstances justify them in adding a recommendation of mercy, but this fact cannot prevent the passing of the sentence, though the judge must report the recommendation to the crown. Sometimes the judge has it in his discretion not to impose the highest penalty of the law, but to lessen its severity. But in cases of high treason or murder he has no such discretion.

5.—Appeals in Criminal Cases.

The law allows appeals to a higher court in criminal cases under special circumstances, and on the conditions laid down in the code. Points of law may be taken to the court of appeal. If that court gives a final decision on the question submitted, it is final; but if any of the judges dissent, the case may go to the supreme court of Canada. Sentence may be postponed until the point at issue has been decided. A new trial may be allowed, or other order given in the interests of justice. The court of appeal or the minister of justice may also order a new jury when the court before which the trial took place gives leave to the prisoner's counsel to apply to the appeal court on the ground that the verdict was against the weight of evidence, or when the minister of justice himself entertains a doubt as to the justice of the conviction.

If no appeal is allowed, or no new trial ordered, the verdict and sentence of the first court hold good, and the convicted person must suffer the punishment that the law has awarded him, unless indeed at the last moment the governor-general is advised under extraordinary and exceptional circumstances, that cannot well be defined here, to exercise the royal prerogative of mercy, and modify the sentence, or pardon the prisoner.

6.—Speedy Trial of Criminal Offences.

In the case of persons committed to jail for trial for certain minor criminal offences, they may elect—state their preference—to be tried at once without a jury by the following judicial functionaries out of the regular term or sittings of the court, at which they would be tried in the due course of law.

In Ontario, county judges. *In Quebec,* judges of sessions, or district magistrates, or sheriff where there are no such magistrates. *In Nova Scotia* and *Prince Edward Island,* county judges. *In Manitoba,* judges of the queen's bench or county courts. *In British Columbia,* judges of the supreme or county courts.

7.—Extradition of Criminals.

Treaties exist between England and several foreign countries—the United States being one—for the extradition (surrender) of persons who have fled to Canada after committing certain criminal offences in those countries. A judge may issue his warrant for the arrest of a fugitive on a foreign warrant, or on an information or complaint laid before him. The judge may hear the case in the same manner, as nearly as may be, as if the fugitive were brought before a justice of the peace, (see *above*, p. 175) charged with committing a criminal offence in Canada. When he commits a fugitive to prison he shall transmit all the papers in the case to the minister of justice, who, after inquiry, may order his surrender to the officer authorized by a foreign state to receive him. He cannot be surrendered until the end of fifteen days after committal, and he can in the meantime apply for a writ of *habeas corpus* (see *below*). The crimes for which a person may be surrendered are of a grave character: murder, forgery, larceny, embezzlement, abduction, arson, robbery, perjury, obtaining goods by false pretenses, and many others ; but no person can be given up for a purely political offence.

8.—Writs of Habeas Corpus.

This famous writ, like so many proceedings in old English times, was written in Latin, and is now recognized by words that appeared therein, meaning "you have the body to answer" (*habeas corpus ad subjiciendum*). It is closely associated with the liberties of Englishmen, and its origin must be sought in the principles of the common law, which forbade the commitment of any person to prison without sufficient cause. This principle was embodied in *Magna Charta* (see *above*, p. 58), but it was not until the reign of King Charles II. that power was given to any court to issue the writ in cases of persons imprisoned on a criminal charge in England, or the colonies, or other countries, and not until 1816—or

14

nearly 140 years later—was it extended to commitment on civil charges. In French Canada no such law was ever in force, and it was only after the cession of Canada to England that it was introduced as a part of the English criminal law, and incorporated into an ordinance to prevent doubts as to its operation. Now the law permits any person who is in prison on a criminal charge, and believes he has a right to his personal liberty, to obtain a writ or command of a superior court to the jailer to bring him before that court, when his case may be fully argued on the points raised ; and if he can show that he is unlawfully detained the court will order him to be discharged from custody. It is now chiefly useful in proceedings for the surrender of a criminal fugitive to the authorities of another country (see *above*, p. 208).

CHAPTER VIII.

1.—Sources of Revenue.

The revenues of the provinces are chiefly derived from the proceeds of royalties from mines (very valuable in Nova Scotia), the sales of crown lands, timber and minerals, and the subsidies or annual allowances made by the dominion government under the authority of the British North America Act, for the purpose of enabling them to carry on their government (see *below*, p. 213). The ninety-second section authorizes the legislatures to impose direct taxation on the province in order to raise a revenue for provincial purposes, to borrow money on the sole credit of the province, and to raise money from shop, saloon, tavern and auctioneer licenses, in order to the raising of a revenue for provincial, local, or municipal purposes. When the Quebec convention sat, this question of provincial revenue was one that gave the delegates greatest difficulty. In all the provinces the sources of revenue were chiefly customs and excise duties which had to be set apart for the general government. Some of the delegates from Ontario, where there had been for many years an admirable system of municipal government in existence which provided funds for education and local improvements, saw many advantages in direct taxation ; but the representatives of the other provinces could not consent to such a proposition, especially in the case of Nova Scotia, New Brunswick and Prince Edward Island, where there was no municipal system, and the people depended almost exclusively on the annual grants of the legislature for the means to meet their local necessities. All of the delegates, in fact, felt that to force the provinces to resort to direct taxation as the only method of carrying on their government, would be probably fatal to the success of the scheme, and it was finally decided that the central government should grant annual subsidies, based on population, the relative debts, the financial position, and such other facts as should be brought fairly into the consideration of the case. These financial arrangements were incorporated with the act of union, and necessarily entail a heavy expense annually on the exchequer of the Dominion. In consequence of the demand that arose in Nova Scotia for " better terms," previous to and after the union, the parliament of the Dominion, in the session of 1869, legislated so as to meet the difficulty that had arisen, and it was accordingly decided to grant additional allowances to the provinces, calculated on increased amounts of debt as compared with what they were allowed in the British North America Act of 1867 to enter the union. Manitoba, British Columbia, and Prince Edward Island also obtained annual subsidies in accordance with the general basis laid down in the constitution. It is from these subsidies that all the provinces derive the greater part of their annual revenues. Nova Scotia has a considerable fund from the proceeds of " royalty," or a tax levied on the quantity of coal and other minerals raised at the mines. Ontario is in the most favourable position from the very considerable revenue raised from lands and timber dues, and from the admirable system of municipal government, which has during half a century given such a stimulus to local improvements. In none of the provinces has there been a general system of direct taxation adopted for provincial purposes. In the maritime provinces the extension of a system of municipal government, within a few years, will probably in the course of time relieve the provincial governments of some local expenditures that have been defrayed out of the general funds.

2.—Provincial Subsidies.

The subsidies and allowances paid in 1893-4 by the dominion government to the several provincial authorities in accordance with law are as follows :—

Ontario	$1,339,287
Quebec	1,086,713
Nova Scotia	432,814
New Brunswick	483,569
Manitoba	437,600
British Columbia	243,585
Prince Edward Island	221,051
Total	$4,244,619

3.—Crown Lands in the Provinces.

In all the provinces there are large tracts of public, unsettled lands, called crown lands. By the British North America Act all the lands, mines and minerals

that belonged to Canada, Nova Scotia and New Brunswick at the union remained in possession of the governments of those provinces. The terms of union with
Prince Edward Island in 1873 enabled its government to
purchase the claims of the proprietors to whom all the
lands of the province had been granted by the imperial
authorities in 1767. In this way the government of the
island became at last owners of a small tract of crown
lands not occupied by the inhabitants who, for the most
part, had been only tenants before the purchase in
question. The British Columbia government, on entering the federation in 1871, retained their public lands
with the exception of what is known as the "railway
belt," which they conveyed to the Dominion for the construction of the Canadian Pacific railway. In Manitoba
and the Northwest Territories the public lands remain
under the control of the dominion government. All
these dominion and provincial lands can be granted
only by the crown; that is to say, by the governments of Canada and of each province. The history
of tenure of land in England and her colonial possessions goes back to many centuries ago. In earliest
English times, all land that was not held by individuals
belonged to the nation, and was called "folk-land." It
could be disposed of only by consent of the people's
council, the witenagemot, or assembly of the wisemen.
Gradually as the king's power increased, and he came to
be regarded as the nation's representative, the public
land was looked upon as his own. At first, he asked the
assent of the council before granting it, but eventually he
dispensed with that form altogether. With the coming
of Norman William the principles of feudalism—from

"feod," an estate—which had so long prevailed in France
and Germany, were established in England.   Feudalism
was based on the principle of a lord giving protection to
an inferior, or vassal or tenant, for a certain service.
This tenant or vassal received land from his lord in return
for personal military service, or money or men.   The
absolute proprietorship in the soil, however, rested in the
lord who could resume it on a failure of the tenant or
vassal to perform his obligations.   The king gave land to
nobles or lords for a certain service ; they again divided
those lands among their own retainers also on certain
conditions of homage or. service.   But the king of
England from William's time was the supreme lord to
whom the barons and nobles, as well as the tenants under
them, alone owed allegiance and service.   " Folk-land "
became now " crown land."   The whole soil of England,
except the ecclesiastical domain, fell into the king's
possession as a result of the conquest, and he granted
it to those whom he chose.   No land henceforth could
be held as a grant except from him.   In the course
of centuries all the military conditions of land tenure
and other aids which the king claimed as lord paramount
of the kingdom were swept away, and the public or crown
lands became a portion of the national revenue.   The
sovereign has given up his ancient hereditary revenues,
of which the crown lands were a part, in return for a
" civil list," or a fixed sum of money granted by parliament for the support of government and the maintenance
of the dignity of the crown.   In this way the crown land
has again become practically the folk-land.   The conveyance of land in England is still remarkably encumbered
by the conditions of old feudal tenure, but Canada as

a new country is free from all such difficulties. The seigniorial tenure of French Canada was a simple form of feudalism, but it was abolished forty years ago, and every man can now hold his land as the sole proprietor (see *above*, p. 25). In the present mode of granting the public domain, however, we see a relic of feudalism. The crown is still theoretically the owner, and in its name alone can the public land be granted away. The crown, however, now means the government of the Dominion, or the government of a province, according as the lands lie in the one or the other, and they convey and grant land by a legal document called a "patent." In all the provinces, and in the Dominion (see *above*, pp. 80, 144), some member of the government has the supervision and management of this branch of the public service. Throughout Canada there are registry offices under the charge of officials whose special duty it is, in return for a small fixed fee, to record all grants, titles and mortgages, and all other matters touching the sale, conveyance, and encumbrances of real estate, and to supply every information that may be required at any time on such matters.

BIBLIOGRAPHICAL NOTE.

The references in the bibliographical note at end of Part Three (see *above*, p. 141) apply to this Part; especially Bourinot's *Constitutional Works*, and Todd's *Parliamentary Government in the Colonies*, where a review is given of the constitutional systems of the different provinces. In all these books comments are made on the operation of the dominion veto of provincial legislation, and the great usefulness of the decisions of the courts in cases of constitutional doubt and difficulty. All the books on the cabinet system of England, mentioned in the previous bibliographical notes (see *above*, pp. 68, 141) can be consulted in connection with provincial government.

FIFTH PART.

MUNICIPAL GOVERNMENT

IN THE PROVINCES.

---

[217]

CHAPTER I.

NATURE OF THE MUNICIPAL SYSTEMS OF THE PROVINCES.

1. Growth of Local Self-Government.—2. Statutory Law Governing Municipal Institutions.—3. Municipal Divisions.—4. Constitution of Councils.

1.—Growth of Local Self-Government.

We have now to consider the important place occupied by local self-government in the provincial structure. In the days of French rule, as my readers have already been told (see *above*, p. 15) the most insignificant matters of local concern were kept under the direct control of the council and especially of the intendant at Quebec. Until 1841 the legislature of Quebec was practically a municipal council for the whole province, and the objection of the *habitants* to any measure of local taxation prevented the adoption of a workable municipal system. In Upper Canada, however, the legislature was gradually relieved of many works and matters of local interest by measures of local government which infused a spirit of energy and enterprise in the various counties, towns and cities. The union of 1841 led to the introduction of municipal institutions in both the provinces, in conformity with the political and material development of the country. By 1867 there was a liberal system in operation in Upper and Lower Canada, but the same cannot be said of the maritime

[219]

provinces. It has been only within a few years that the legislatures of Nova Scotia and New Brunswick have organized a municipal system on the basis of that so successfully adopted in the larger provinces. In Prince Edward Island, however, matters remain much as they were half a century ago, and the legislature is practically a municipal council for the whole island. Charlottetown and Summerside have special acts of incorporation giving them elected mayors and councils, with the right of taxation for municipal purposes as in other provinces. At the present time all the provinces, with this one exception, have an excellent municipal code, which enables every defined district, large or small, to carry on efficiently all those public improvements essential to the comfort, convenience, and general necessities of its inhabitants. Even in the territories of the Northwest every facility is given to the people in every populous district, or town, to organize a system equal to all their local requirements (see *Seventh Part*).

2.—Statutory Law Governing Municipal Institutions.

The ninety-second section of the British North America Act (see *above*, p. 159), gives to the legislature of every province full control over municipal institutions. The legislature can consequently establish, amend, and even abolish a municipal system within the provincial territory. While every province has a general law regulating its municipal divisions and their councils, there are also numerous special statutes relating to the corporations or municipal councils of cities and towns. All councils exercise their powers in accordance with statutory enactment, and when they exceed them at any time

CITY AND COUNTY BUILDINGS (UNDER CONSTRUCTION), TORONTO.

they can be restrained by the courts, should the matter be brought before them, by legal process.

3.—The Municipal Divisions.

While there are many differences in the details of the machinery, all the municipal systems of the provinces are distinguished by certain leading characteristics. The municipal divisions common to all provinces are county, city, town, township and village. In Quebec the parish, which is first an ecclesiastical or church district, can also be formed by the civil authority at the request of the inhabitants into a municipality. In New Brunswick, the parish dates back to the closing days of the last century and still remains a civil division, but it is also now applied in statutes to incorporated towns and cities. The county in all the provinces is the largest municipal division, and is really made up of the townships (or parishes as in Quebec and New Brunswick) within its territorial limits.

4.—Constitution of Councils in the Provinces.

In Ontario the county councils are composed of reeves and deputy reeves of the townships and villages within the county, and of any towns which have not withdrawn from its jurisdiction. The reeves and deputy reeves annually elect from among themselves a warden as head of the council. In township and village councils there are a reeve or head, and four councillors ; but when there are five hundred electors within any such division then each receives a reeve, deputy reeve and three councillors; and for every five hundred additional names another deputy reeve takes the place of a councillor. In this way a village or a township receives larger representation in the county council. Reeves, deputy reeves and councillors are yearly elected by a general vote in villages and townships when such divisions are not divided into wards like cities; in case of such a division, councillors elect deputy reeves or reeves. The council of every town consists of a mayor or head of the same (annually elected by general vote), and three councillors annually elected for every ward where there are less than five wards, and of two councillors for every ward where there are five or more wards, and if a town has not withdrawn from the jurisdiction of the council of the county in which it lies, then a reeve is added; and if a town has the names of five hundred persons entitled to vote at municipal elections on the last revised voters' list then a deputy reeve is added, and for every five hundred additional names of persons so entitled to vote on such list there must be elected an additional deputy reeve. But the law also provides for a reduction of councillors in towns when the electors pass a bylaw to that effect. The council of every city is composed of a mayor, who is the head of the same, and of three aldermen for each ward. Mayors are annually elected by a general vote of the ratepayers in the city, and the aldermen by the ratepayers of the respective wards. The law also makes arrangements for the formation of a "provisional council" whenever a junior county of a union of counties wishes to form a distinct municipal division. In such a case a temporary council is formed of the reeves and deputy reeves within the county until a permanent organization is effected under the law. The council elect a provisional warden for one year under these circumstances.

In Quebec the county councils are composed of all the mayors in the " local municipalities ". in the county. These mayors are called " county councillors " in the county council and choose the head or warden every year from among their number. The " local municipalities " comprise parishes, townships, towns and villages, which are governed by councils, each of which is composed of seven councillors elected by the ratepayers in each municipal district, or appointed by the lieutenant-governor of the province in case of a failure to elect. A councillor remains in office for three years, but subject to the condition that two councillors must be elected or appointed two years consecutively and three every three years. The mayor or head of council is elected by a majority—a quorum—of the whole council and holds office for a year. Cities and many of the towns have special acts of incorporation, and aldermen and councillors are in all cases elected by a general vote of ratepayers. In the majority of cities the mayors are elected by a general vote ; in some, by the board of aldermen.

In Nova Scotia the county councils consist of councillors annually elected by the ratepayers—one for each polling division of a county electing a member to the house of assembly—and of a head or warden, appointed by the council every year. Town councils are composed of a mayor and not less than six councillors, elected by the ratepayers. Many of the towns have special acts of incorporation but all are now subject to a general act. The mayor is elected annually, and a councillor for two years. In Halifax, which has a special charter, the mayor is elected annually, the eighteen aldermen for three years, one-third being elected every year.

In New Brunswick the county councils consist of two councillors elected annually for every parish—except in special cases provided for by law—and of a warden appointed annually by the council. Cities have special acts of incorporation, and elect their mayor and aldermen.

In Manitoba the city councils consist of a mayor or head, and of two aldermen for each ward. The town council, of a mayor and two councillors for each ward. The village council, of a mayor and four councillors. A council in a rural municipality consists of the reeve (or head) and of such a number of councillors—not exceeding six, and not less than four—as the bylaw of the district may fix. Mayors, aldermen, reeves and councillors are annually elected by the ratepayers. One alderman for each city ward is elected for two years.

In British Columbia the city councils consist of a mayor, and of not more than twelve and not less than seven aldermen, except in the cities of Nanaimo and New Westminster, which may increase the number to thirteen, including the mayor. Mayors and aldermen are elected annually. Township and district councils consist of not more than seven, and not less than four councillors, and a reeve (or head), all elected annually. The number may be increased to eight in all, including the reeve, by a unanimous vote of the council.

15

CHAPTER II.

5. How a Council Exercises its Powers.—6. Election of Councils. — 7. Heads and Officers. — 8. Meetings. — 9. Bylaws. — 10. Municipal Assessment or Taxation. — 11. Borrowing Powers of Councils.—12. Historic Origin of Names of Municipal Divisions, etc.

5.—How a Council Exercises its Powers.

After this short summary of the municipal councils in each province we may now continue a review of the features common to the systems of all the provinces. The inhabitants of each of the municipalities described in the foregoing chapter, form a "body corporate" whose powers are exercised by their respective councils under the municipal law. The name of such corporate bodies is "the corporation of the county, city, town, etc.," or, as in Quebec, "the municipality of the county," or "parish," or "town," as the case may be. This legal name should be used on all occasions and in all documents affecting the corporation. The council—generally known as "the council of the city of Ottawa," or "the county of Carleton," as the case may be—has powers only within the limits of its municipal district, except in special cases where the law extends its authority. Its orders within its legal powers must be obeyed by all

[226]

CITY HALL, MONTREAL.

persons subject to its jurisdiction. It can acquire real and personal property by purchase, sell or lease the same, enter into contracts, and sue and be sued in any cause and before any court like any private and incorporated company or individual.

6.—Election of Councils.

All councils are elected by the ratepayers in their respective municipal divisions ; that is to say, by electors rated on real or personal property on the assessment roll. In Ontario, Manitoba and British Columbia, farmers' sons resident with their parents can vote. In Manitoba and British Columbia, persons holding "homesteads" under the dominion law (see *below*, p. 277) can also vote. In the majority of the provinces, all taxes must be paid before an elector can vote. In all cases, an elector must be a British subject, of the age of twenty-one, and not a criminal or insane. Widows and unmarried women, rated on the assessment roll, can vote in Ontario ; in Manitoba and British Columbia, all women who are taxed in their own right can vote. Wardens, mayors, aldermen, reeves and councillors must in all cases be British subjects and possess a certain amount of real property, varying in the provinces. They must take an oath or make a declaration of office and qualification before assuming their seats. The elections are held at such times as the law provides in each province—generally in the first part of January in each year. Nominations of candidates are made by a certain number of electors on a day fixed by the law before such elections. In all the provinces, except Quebec, the voting is by ballot. The laws of the provinces generally — those of Ontario being most complete—provide for the contestation of any municipal election on the ground of violence, fraud or corruption, or incapacity, or informality in the proceedings. Corrupt practices can be severely punished. Judges, police or stipendiary magistrates, sheriff and sheriff's officers, jailers, constables, officers of the courts, officers of the councils, persons having contracts with a council, solicitor or attorney of the corporation, cannot sit in any municipal council of the provinces. In Ontario, Quebec, and some other provinces the disqualification extends to tavern-keepers and persons engaged in the sale of liquors by retail. In Quebec no priest or clergyman can sit in the council; in the other provinces it is optional for them. All persons over sixty years of age, members of parliament, members of government, all persons in the civil service of the crown, professors of universities, and teachers in schools, firemen and fire companies, are exempted in Ontario and other provinces from being appointed to a council or any other municipal office. In all these cases of exemptions and disqualifications the law in each province must be consulted as it is impossible to give here more than those common to all the provinces.

7.—Heads and Officers of Councils.

The head of a council, as shown above, (pp. 222, 223) is a warden, or mayor, or reeve. He is chief executive officer of the corporation. He presides over the meetings of the council, signs, seals, and executes, in the name of the council, all debentures, contracts, agreements or deeds made and passed by the corporation, unless the council otherwise provides. It is his duty to be vigilant in executing the laws for the government of the municipality;

to supervise the conduct of all subordinate officers as far as lies in his power ; to cause all positive neglect of duty to be punished ; to recommend to the council such measures as may conduce to the improvement of the finances, health, security, cleanliness, comfort and ornament of the municipality.   All heads of councils, as well as aldermen in cities are, by virtue of their office, justices of.the peace within their respective municipal divisions as long as they are in office, for purposes arising under the municipal law.   Connected with every municipal corporation is a large body of officials, appointed in all cases by the councils, and holding their offices during pleasure. Such officers as clerks, and treasurers, are permanent in their nature, but the majority of others, like assessors, valuators, auditors, road commissioners, or surveyors, pathmasters, poundkeepers, are, as a rule, appointed from year to year.   The practice is to continue efficient men in office as long as they are willing to serve.   The most important officer of every council is the clerk, whose duty it is to record the proceedings of the council, keep all the books, publish bylaws, and perform numerous other duties regulated by law or the bylaws or resolutions of the appointing body.   The treasurer receives and keeps all corporation moneys, and pays out the same as the law or the regulations of the council direct.   In Quebec and some other provinces the duties of clerk and treasurer are practically combined in an official called secretary-treasurer.   One or more auditors, from time to time, review the accounts of all receipts and payments of the officials of the municipality, and report to the council. Other important officers of councils are these: solicitors, to advise councils in all matters of legal doubt or controversy—called recorders in Nova Scotia*; engineers, in cities to look after public works like waterworks, sewage, and other matters of public necessity and convenience ; assessors, or valuators, or commissioners (in cities), to make annual lists of all the ratable property, on which the councils can fix the yearly rates levied on the tax-payers of a municipality; collectors, to collect these taxes or rates and pay them to the treasurer ; fire wardens and firemen, for the prevention of fires ; fence viewers, or inspectors to regulate boundary and other fences; pound-keepers, to receive and retain in safe keeping all stray animals, which may be restored to the owners on pay-ment of expenses, or else sold by auction after a proper delay ; pathmasters, or road surveyors, or overseers of highways, to look after the condition of public roads, enforce statute labour, and perform other services in connection with the public roads and bridges. The council of any municipality may at any time by bylaw appoint other officers to carry out the provisions of any act of the legislature, or enforce a bylaw of the corpora-tion. The law provides for the establishment of health officers and the taking of proper measures to prevent the spread of contagious or infectious diseases. Provision is made by the existing statutes for the appointment of constables in rural districts and policemen in cities for the preservation of peace and order, and the due execution of the law. In Ontario there is ample pro-vision made for the establishment in cities and towns of courts presided over by police magistrates (see *above*, p. 174). The councils must first establish police offices,

---

* See *above*, p. 176 note.

and affirm the expediency of appointing salaried police magistrates, and provide for the whole or part of their salary. The lieutenant-governor in council appoints such officers in all provinces except Nova Scotia, where cities and town councils appoint. Councils throughout Canada also make provision for the establishment and maintenance of jails, lock-ups, city or town halls in their respective municipal divisions, as the law in such cases provides.

8.—Meetings of Councils.

The time for the first meeting of a new council is fixed by the municipal law of each province—generally some time in the first month of the year—but all subsequent meetings can be held in accordance with the regulations of each council unless otherwise provided. All meetings are held openly, except under special circumstances as defined by the regulations. The head of the council presides over a meeting, and in his absence some member of the council, as the law or regulations order. He maintains order and decorum, but an appeal may be made to the council against his rulings. A quorum or a majority of the whole council is necessary for a meeting for the transaction of business, but a majority of such a quorum can pass any order, resolution or bylaw, or perform any other act within the powers of the council. As a rule open voting prevails, but in British Columbia the election of officers is by ballot. The regulations generally provide that no member can vote on a question in which he has a direct personal pecuniary interest—the common parliamentary law in such cases. Minutes of proceedings of a meeting must

be always read, confirmed, and signed by the chairman
at a subsequent meeting. In the provinces of Ontario,
British Columbia, Nova Scotia and New Brunswick the
head of the council votes as a member, and when there
is a tie or equality of votes the matter or question under
discussion is lost or negatived. In Quebec he can vote
on every question, and has also a casting vote in case of
a tie. In Manitoba he votes only when there is a tie.
Select committees are appointed, as in parliament, for
the consideration of special matters of municipal business, and they must report their results to the council.
All the rules of councils are based on those of the house
of commons and legislative assemblies of Canada. In
all matters of doubt reference is made to the regulations
and usages of parliament, directing the conduct of debate, divisions, and other matters of order and procedure
(see *above*, p. 109).

9.—Bylaws of Councils.

The legislative powers of all councils are exercised by
bylaws when not otherwise authorized by statute. A
bylaw is a special law of a corporation or municipality,
which it has a right to pass in a certain form for a local
or municipal purpose defined by the general statutory
law establishing municipalities.

Every council may also make regulations for governing
the proceedings of the council, the conduct of its members, the appointing or calling of special meetings, and
generally all such other regulations as the good of the
inhabitants of the municipality requires, and may repeal,
alter or amend its bylaws. Every such bylaw, to have
legal force, must be under the seal of the corporation,

signed by the head, or by the presiding officer of the meeting at which it was passed, and by the clerk or secretary-treasurer of the corporation.

The power of passing bylaws gives to the various municipal councils of the provinces a decided legislative character. The subjects embraced within their jurisdiction are set forth with more or less distinctness in the municipal acts of the majority of the provinces, especialiy of Ontario and Quebec—those of Nova Scotia and New Brunswick being less perfectly defined. The council of every city, town or incorporated village may pass bylaws for the construction and maintenance of waterworks, the amounts required to be collected under local improvement bylaws, licensing and regulating transient traders, the purchase of real property for the erection of public school-houses thereon, cemeteries, their improvement and protection, cruelty to animals, fences, exhibitions and places of amusement, planting and preservation of trees, gas and water companies, shows, exhibitions, tavern and shop licenses, public morals, giving intoxicating liquor to minors, nuisances, sewage and drainage, inspection of meat and milk, the weight of bread, contagious diseases, fevers, prevention of accidents by fire, aiding schools, endowing fellowships, markets, police, industrial farms, parks, bathing houses, cab stands, telegraph poles, prevention of fires, construction of buildings, public libraries, charities and numerous other subjects immediately connected with the security and comfort of the people in every community.

All bylaws must be printed and advertised in one or more newspapers, and posted in public places. In case of aid to railways or waterworks, or the pledge of the

CITY HALL, WINNIPEG.

municipal credit for certain other public purposes, defined in the municipal law of Ontario, Quebec and other provinces, a vote of the ratepayers and property holders must be taken.   In Ontario, where the law is very clear and explicit, the assent of one-third of all the taxpayers of a municipal division is required to give legal force to a bylaw giving aid in any shape to a railway or other company, or raising upon the credit of the municipality any money not required for its ordinary expenditures, and not payable within the same municipal year.   In Ontario, British Columbia and Manitoba, the vote is always by ballot, and any resident or other person interested in a bylaw, order or resolution of a council may take proceedings in the courts to quash the same for illegality.   The reference of bylaws of municipalities to the ratepayers of a municipal division for their acceptance or refusal is the only example which our system of government offers of what is known in Switzerland as the *referendum* (reference) of laws to the vote of the whole people before they can come into operation.

10.—Municipal Assessment or Taxation.

The most important duty of every municipal council is the raising of money for local purposes by direct taxation.   The burden of taxation is on real property— that is to say, on buildings, land, machinery, trees on lands, mines and minerals, except where they belong to the crown.   In British Columbia, improvements on land are exempted up to a certain amount.   Incomes are taxable in the majority of the provinces, and so are bonds, securities, and other personal property within the limitations fixed by the law in each case.   The following

classes of property are free from municipal taxation in
the provinces generally: imperial, dominion, provincial
and municipal property; Indian lands, churches, par-
sonages, and lands immediately connected therewith
(except in Manitoba); educational, charitable, scientific
and literary institutions; agricultural and horticultural
societies; incomes of the governor-general and lieutenant-governors; household effects and tools in use. In
Ontario, also, incomes up to $7co when derived from
personal earnings, those up to $4co when not so derived,
and those of farmers from his farm, are all free of taxes.
In British Columbia, also, incomes up to $1,500 are
exempt; in Quebec and Nova Scotia to $400. In some
of the provinces special interests are protected. For
instance, in Ontario, British Columbia and Manitoba,
the produce of the farm in store or warehouse on the
way to sale, live stock and implements in use; in Nova
Scotia and New Brunswick, fishermen's boats, nets and
outfit to $200. But in all these matters of taxation
there are so many differences in the provinces that it is
impossible to do more here than refer generally to the
subject. Reference must be had to the assessment laws
of the provinces in all cases.

All municipal, local or direct taxes are raised and
levied upon the real or personal taxable property according to the value given in the roll of the assessors,
or valuators, or assessment commissioners appointed by
each municipality in the different provinces for such
purposes. The council of a municipality assesses and
levies upon this taxable property a sufficient sum in
each year to pay all debts and meet all legal expendi-

tures. The laws of the provinces restrain, as far as practicable, the powers of the corporations in this particular, and any person can ascertain by referring to the general law governing municipal bodies, or to a special charter of a city or town, the extent of authority of a council in levying a rate and creating debt. In case a person considers he is rated too high on an assessment, or is treated 'exceptionally or unjustly, he can have an appeal to a court of revision, composed of members of the council as a rule, and finally to the courts—the county court in Ontario, Manitoba and British Columbia, and the circuit court in Quebec. In New Brunswick there is a board of valuators to whom an appeal can be made, and leave is also given under exceptional circumstances to have recourse to the supreme court. In Nova Scotia there is an assessment court of appeal in towns, and thence to the council under certain conditions.

11.—Borrowing Powers of Councils.

All councils have power under the formalities required by the law of each province to borrow money, and to levy special rates for the payment of such debts on the ratable property of the municipality. All bylaws for borrowing money must receive the assent of the ratepayers before they can be enforced. Municipal debentures—or legal certificates of a debt due by the municipality—can be issued to secure the repayment of sums borrowed in accordance with the strict provisions of the law governing such cases. All municipal property is liable for the redemption of such debentures and the payment of municipal liabilities.

12.—Historic Origin of Names of Municipal Divisions and of their Officers.

In the names of the municipal divisions and of the machinery of municipal administration, we see again some examples of the closeness with which Canadians cling to the names and usages of primitive times of English government. The "township" carries us back to the early days when our English forefathers lived in their village communities, of which the "tun" or rough fence or hedge that surrounded them was a feature. The chief officer or headman of this township was the reeve, who as an "active" or "excellent" member of his community took part in the various assemblies (moots) of the people. The "alderman"—from "ealdorman" or elder man—is a link connecting us with the early government of shires (for *shire*, see *above*, p. 192), and was an office of high dignity, still represented by the English lord-lieutenant of present times. In Ontario there remains in the legislative electoral divisions a district known as the "riding," which is a changed form of "thriding" or "triding," or a local district made and named by the Danes in English Yorkshire. The ancient English shire, which was under an "ealdorman" for civil and military purposes, became a "county" in Norman times because a count (comte) or earl replaced the former functionary. Our representative body for the local government of a county is no longer called the "folk moot" but the "council," which comes to us from the Normans, who again adopted it from the Latin *concilium* (or a "collection" of people). The mayor was an important officer connected with the royal palace of

France and has also come to us from Norman times—
its original meaning of "greater" *(major)* having been
gradually applied to the principal officer of a local community or municipality. The "parish" has its origin in
a Greek word, first applied in early English and French
times to a "circuit" or district, presided over by a priest
or vicar, and which for convenience sake was formed into
a civil division. Bylaw means simply the law made for
the government of a "bye," which was a name given by
the Danes to the old English "tun" or township.

BIBLIOGRAPHICAL NOTE.

The reader may consult Bourinot's *Local Government in Canada*, in
Johns Hopkins' University Studies, (Baltimore, 1887), and "Transactions
of the Royal Society of Canada," 1887, section 2, for a short account of the
origin and development of municipal institutions in the Dominion. A
useful book is that by Mr. J. M. McEvoy, on *The Ontario Township*,
(Toronto, 1889), with an introduction by Professor Ashley. The report
of the Ontario Commission on Municipal Institutions, (Toronto, 1888, 1889,
and 1893), is too diffuse and badly arranged to be of much practical use
to an ordinary student, though it is useful for purposes of consultation on
points of the practical operation of municipal institutions in Canada and
elsewhere. In Bourinot's large edition of *Procedure of Public Meetings
and Municipal Councils*, (Toronto, 1894), there is a section giving a
summary of the statutory law of Ontario respecting municipal councils and
their meetings, and also some notes on the systems of the other provinces.
A student who wishes full information on such subjects will be obliged to
study the statutes of his own province in every case, since there are no
special books treating the question in a popular form. Fitness for citizenship means not only study but practical observation of the working of
municipal government.

SIXTH PART.

SCHOOL GOVERNMENT

IN THE PROVINCES.

---

16   [241]

CHAPTER I.

1. Introduction.—2. Public Schools in Ontario.—3. Public Schools in Quebec.

1.—Introduction.

Such a review of the institutions of Canada as I have attempted in this work would be imperfect if it did not include a summary, however short, of the leading features of the machinery that regulates and governs the educational system of each province. Education is necessarily the foundation of active citizenship and good government.

From the following summary of the machinery of school government in all the provinces it will be seen that it is based on the following principles : a general supervision of education in every province by a department of education, and contributions from the provincial funds for the support of public schools free to all classes of the people ; this supervision is exercised by means of government superintendents and inspectors, appointed by the provincial government to visit and report on the condition of the schools of every county ; the provincial grant is supplemented by such contributions from the inhabitants of every school district as the law provides in each case ; assessments for this purpose are levied, generally speaking, in connection with the municipalities in each province ; every school district

UPPER CANADA COLLEGE, TORONTO.

manages its schools and funds through trustees elected — — by the ratepayers. In this way the government of a province and every municipal district are directly identified and co-operate with each other for the support and development of the education of the people.

2.—The Public Schools in Ontario.

In this province there is a department of education, composed of a minister as a head, and members of the executive government (see *above*, p. 151) as a committee of council, and entrusted with the administration of a most excellent school system. That system comprises three main features of elementary, secondary and higher education : the kindergarten, public and separate schools, high schools and collegiate institutes, and the university, all representing a complete organization. A child enters the kindergarten or children's garden*—German in its origin—at perhaps four years of age, the public school at six, and the high school at thirteen. After four or five years' close study at the high school or collegiate institute he passes after examination into the university, where he attains his degree of bachelor of arts, and honours according to his ability and proficiency at the end of four years. The public and high schools and the university are undenominational, but the law (see *above*, p. 165) enables Roman Catholics to establish under certain conditions common schools for themselves. Separate high schools are not provided for in the school law. The term "separate schools" applies also to

---

* The name of this pleasant method of imparting education to very young children was given by Friedrich Froebel, a German teacher, who introduced the system in rooms opening on a garden.

Protestants and coloured persons, but as a matter of practice the exception to the general principle of the common school system is confined chiefly to Roman Catholics.

In addition to the schools mentioned above, there are also under the direction of the department : kindergartens, county model schools, provincial normal schools, and the school of " pedagogy," in which the highest class of teachers receive a thorough professional training. The educational association, and teachers' institutes perform a useful work in the same direction. Provision is also made for the establishment of art schools. Children who may be vicious or immoral can be sent to industrial schools.

By the law all children between eight and fourteen are obliged to attend school for the full term during which the school is open. The minister of education, with the aid of a large staff, has the general direction of all the educational forces of the country. Inspectors of high schools, separate schools, and county model schools are appointed by the government. County inspectors are appointed by the county councils, and city inspectors by the public school boards, from persons having high qualifications as teachers.

Provision is made for the support of education by the government and the municipalities. Counties are under obligation to make grants of money to high schools, and both counties and townships must aid public schools. Each township is divided into sections, each of which is provided with a public school, managed by a board of three trustees who hold office for three years—one going out of office annually, when a successor is appointed. A grant is given by the government to each school accord ing to the average attendance of pupils, and the county council is required to give an equal amount. In addition, the township council must vote a grant of $100 (or $150 if two teachers are employed) to each school. Cities, towns and incorporated villages also receive a legislative grant, and the municipal councils raise the balance at the request of the board of trustees, which consists of six or more elected members, two from each ward, of whom one retires annually. If the board so decides, the elections may be by ballot, and on the same day as the municipal elections. The trustees select the teachers— all of whom must have certificates of qualification,—determine the amounts to be expended for school sites, buildings, equipments and salaries, and supervise the school affairs generally of their special division. The separate schools are all under government inspection, and are generally conducted under the same regulations as the public schools. All public schools are free. High schools are established by the county and city municipalities, with the approval of the lieutenant-governor in council. High schools may be formed by the government into collegiate institutes if they can come up to higher conditions imposed by the law. Government grants to these institutions of superior education are mainly based on the efforts of the locality. The county council must vote a grant at least equal to that of the legislature. After the county and legislative grants have been received, any further amount required in addition to the fees paid up to meet the cost of maintenance must be made up by the municipality or district where the high school is situated on the requisition of the board of trustees. Each board consists of at least six trustees and, except in the case of cities and towns separated from the county, three of these are appointed by the county council, and three by the council of the town or village where the high school is situated. If the district is composed of more than one municipality, then each is represented on the high school board. In towns separate from the county, all the trustees are appointed by the town council. In cities, the council also appoints the trustees, and if two high schools are established, twelve trustees are appointed, and if more than two the council appoints eighteen trustees. Each trustee holds office generally for three years; two other trustees holding office for one year may be added, one by the public school board and the other by the separate school board of the city, town or incorporated village where the high school or collegiate institute is placed.

High school trustees and members of boards of education cannot hold positions in the municipal councils of the municipality or county in which those schools are situated.

Church doctrines are not taught in the public schools, but the principles of christianity form an essential feature of the daily exercises. Every public and high school is opened and closed with prayer and the reading of the scriptures, but without comment or explanation. The trustees and clergy, however, of all denominations are empowered to make special arrangements for religious instruction to the pupils of their own particular church at least once a week, after the close of the school

ENTRANCE TO TORONTO UNIVERSITY.

in the afternoon. No pupil is required to take part in any religious exercise objected to by his parents or guardians.

The highest institution of learning controlled by the provincial government is the university of Toronto, whose property is vested in the crown, and administered by an officer appointed by the government. All appointments are made by the lieutenant-governor in council, and all statutes of the senate regulating the institution must receive the approval of the same. The management and administration of the affairs of the university are placed in a board of trustees, a senate and a council, each composed as the law provides. A number of universities and colleges in the province—at present twelve in all—are " federated " with the university. All colleges so federated participate in all the advantages that the university offers. A university so federated ceases to exercise its own powers of conferring degrees except in divinity. The university confers degrees in arts, agriculture, law, medicine, dentistry, and science, and civil engineering. The degrees conferred give all students the standing of *alumni* (graduates) of the provincial university.

3.—The Public Schools in Quebec.

In the province of Quebec there is a department of education composed of a superintendent and a council of public instruction with two secretaries. The superintendent is a non-political head, appointed by the lieutenant-governor in council. He is a member of the council, and its chairman by virtue of his office. The council is made up of Roman Catholic and Protestant members, and divided into two committees in the same way for the purpose of supervising the educational affairs of those denominations. Each of the two committees meets separately and exercises independent action in reference to all matters which concern the educational work under their respective control. Each appoints its own chairman and secretary. One of the two secretaries of the department is a Protestant. The superintendent is a member of each committee, but he votes only in the one to which by religion he belongs. The schools are Roman Catholic and Protestant—the separate schools being known as "dissentient" (see *above*, p. 165)—and religion is considered as the basis of education. The clergy of the Roman Catholic church and of other denominations consequently take a leading part in the management of education, and are largely represented on the two committees of the council. School inspectors, of qualifications defined by the law, are appointed for one or more counties of the province by the government on the recommendation of either committee of the council. Roman Catholic and Protestant boards of examiners examine and grant certificates or diplomas of qualification to inspectors and teachers.

The educational institutions of the province are divided into elementary schools, model schools, academies or high schools, and normal schools. In each municipality, village, town and city, there are public schools for the elementary education of youth, under the control of school commissioners, or trustees in the case of dissentient schools—elected by the proprietors of real estate paying taxes or monthly fees. Each municipality is divided into school districts. Each municipality elects five commissioners, or three trustees, who hold office generally for three years, and form a body corporate for the administration of school affairs. No school teacher can be a commissioner or trustee in his own municipality or a contractor for a corporation of which he is a member. These commissioners and trustees appoint teachers, acquire and sell property for school purposes, and cause to be levied by taxation the sums necessary for the support of schools. In all places where a valuation of property has been made by the municipal authorities, it serves as the basis of the taxes to be imposed on the authority of the school law. Otherwise three valuators are appointed by the commissioners or trustees. Each school board has a secretary-treasurer appointed by the same to act as clerk and treasurer. He collects and pays all moneys due to and payable by the corporation. Trustees of dissentient schools have the same powers and duties as commissioners of Roman Catholic schools. They alone have the right of imposing and collecting the taxes upon the dissentient inhabitants.

To entitle a municipality to a share of the legislative grant — the " common school fund "—made for the support of education, a sum equal to that grant must be raised by the municipality, except in the case of poor and thinly settled districts, to which special conditions apply. The superintendent pays the respective shares of the common or provincial school fund to the several boards of commissioners or trustees in two semi-annual payments. He may retain eighty dollars to support a model (or superior) school in each municipality.

The government provide for the establishment of Roman Catholic and Protestant normal schools, and appoint their principals and teachers on the recommendation of the respective committees of the council. Roman Catholic and Protestant academies, model or superior schools managed by trustees, also receive government aid on the recommendation of the same committees, and with the approval of the lieutenant-governor in council. In the same way grants are also made to universities, colleges, seminaries, and educational institutions other than elementary schools. Such institutions receive aid in the relative proportions of the respective Roman Catholic and Protestant populations of the province according to the last census.

CHAPTER II.

*1. Public Schools in Nova Scotia.—2. In New Brunswick.—
3. In Prince Edward Island.* ˥

1.—The Public Schools in Nova Scotia.

In this province the members of the executive council
(see *above*, p. 152) form a council of public instruction
with extensive powers of general direction and administration. A superintendent of education is also appointed
by the government to have a supervision of educational
matters and to act as secretary of the council. A provincial board of examiners inquires into and reports on
the qualifications of candidates for licenses to teach.
Inspectors of schools are also appointed by the council
of public instruction on the recommendation of the
superintendent. Normal and model schools are supported by the government, and the council appoints the
principals and their assistants. All the public schools
of the province are undenominational. The public
school system provides for the free education of all
persons from the age of five years upwards, in a prescribed course of study extending from the kindergarten
or primary grade of the common or elementary schools
to the end of the superior course of the academy and
high school. The high school system is virtually a

provincial university of a high school grade, and every
academy and high school an affiliated college, the
diplomas being granted on the report of the provincial
board of examiners.

The province is divided into districts, with a board of
seven or more commissioners for each, appointed by the
council. These commissioners determine the boundaries
of school sections—the smallest territorial division—
establish new ones with the approval of the council, and
adjudicate on matters specially connected with the same
over a district which, on the average, is perhaps equal to
half a county of the province. Each school section in
a county has an executive board of three school trustees,
whose duties are the same as in Ontario and other provinces. They are elected by the ratepayers of their respective divisions. Each year one trustee retires and a
new officer is elected. Each board has a secretary-treasurer to collect and disburse all school moneys. Teachers, duly licensed by the council of public instruction, are
employed by the board, and receive aid from the public
treasury out of the sum annually voted by the legislature for schools. They are graded into four classes
and paid according to their qualifications and to the
number of days the schools have been in session. Municipalities must annually vote a certain amount as provided in the law for the support of schools. When any
sum is required by a section above the provincial grant
and the annual rates raised by the municipality, it must
be determined by the majority of the ratepayers of the
section at a school meeting regularly called for that
purpose. Each academy (or high school) established in
a county receives from the government a sum based on

HARBORD STREET COLLEGIATE INSTITUTE, TORONTO.

the attendance, the number of qualified teachers and the salaries paid them by the municipality in which the academy is situated. Ratepayers at a public meeting, as provided by law, decide the amount to be raised by the section to supplement the sum granted by the province and county. Inspectors visit each school and county academy at least yearly. The attendance at school is stimulated by making the greater part of the county fund payable in proportion to the attendance. There is also a local option law by which two-thirds of the qualified voters at an annual school meeting may make the attendance of all children between seven and twelve compulsory within certain limits.

An incorporated town forms a separate school section, and the control and management of public schools are vested in a board of five commissioners, three of whom are appointed from the members of the council, and two by the government. The former are elected annually, but at every annual selection at least one of the three persons previously chosen shall, if there be one remaining in the council, be appointed. The government commissioners remain in office for three years. The town clerk is secretary and treasurer of the board. Attendance between the ages of seven and fourteen is compulsory in towns, but exemptions are made under certain conditions in cases of children above twelve and thirteen years of age.

In the city of Halifax there are twelve commissioners, six chosen by the lieutenant-governor in council, and six by the city council.

The regulations are well calculated to secure to every child a free education.

17

A provincial school of agriculture, mining schools at coal mining centres, schools for the deaf, dumb and blind, also add to the effectiveness of the public free school system of Nova Scotia.

2.—The Public Schools in New Brunswick.

In this province the lieutenant-governor, the members of the executive council (see *above*, p. 152), the chancellor of the university of New Brunswick and a chief superintendent of education, constitute a board of education for the administration of the education of the province. The superintendent is appointed by the lieutenant-governor in council, and acts as secretary to the board. Duly qualified inspectors are appointed by the board. All public schools are undenominational and free. The law provides for primary, advanced, high, superior and grammar schools wherever practicable. The government also support a normal school with model departments, and appoint the principal, who selects his assistants with the approval of the board.

Each school district in a county has a board of three trustees and an auditor, elected by the ratepayers—the former for three years. The schools are supported (1) from the provincial treasury; (2) from a county school fund; (3) from district assessment. Teachers are duly licensed, graded in three classes, and paid a proportion of the provincial grant according to their grade of qualifications. Any further sums required for school purposes beyond that ordinarily voted must be determined by a meeting duly called for that purpose in the district. Loans may be raised for seven years in special cases. The government grant to any superior or grammar school established in a county or parish, or district, is equivalent to that raised by the district for the support of teachers. The schools in St. John are managed by a board of nine trustees, of whom the government appoint four and the city council five. In Fredericton the government appoint three and the city council four members of a board of trustees. In the case of incorporated towns the board of trustees are seven, appointed as in Fredericton.

The university of New Brunswick, which is a provincial institution, is open to all persons irrespective of creed, and forms a corporation of twelve members, nine of whom are appointed by the lieutenant-governor in council—one being the chancellor—and two by the associated *alumni*. The superintendent is by virtue of his office always a member. Members of the corporation constitute the senate or governing body. It confers degrees under the law regulating its functions. A certain number of students are admitted into the undergraduate course from each county, free of fees for education, upon the condition of passing the regular matriculation or preliminary examination.

3.—The Public Schools in Prince Edward Island.

The general supervision of education is given by the law to a provincial board, composed of the members of the executive council (see *above*, p. 152), the principal of the Prince of Wales college, and the chief superintendent of education, who acts as secretary. The superintendent is appointed by the lieutenant-governor in council, and duly qualified inspectors, who have to visit each district half-yearly, by the board of education. A normal school is now amalgamated with Prince of Wales college, which was established for the higher education of the young. The principal and assistants of the college and normal school are appointed by the board of education. The grades are primary, advanced and high schools. They are free to all children between five and sixteen years, and non-sectarian. Teachers are required to open the schools with the reading of the holy scriptures by children without comment or explanation, but no children are required to attend if their parents or guardians object to this reading. Teachers must hold a license from the board of education—attendance at one term of the provincial training school being one of the qualifications. The salaries are provided for by a provincial grant, and by district assessment when it is necessary to increase the former allowance. All other expenditures are met by local or district assessment, and loans for seven years may be raised to pay cost of new school-houses. At the annual school meeting of a district three trustees are elected for three years—one member retiring each year. No teacher in active employment can act as trustee. In the city of Charlottetown, and town of Summerside, the board of trustees consists of seven members, of whom the lieutenant-governor in council appoints four, and the council of each place appoints three—all of whom hold office during pleasure. All the boards of trustees appoint a clerk or secretary, who acts also as treasurer or accountant. All accounts and payments are duly audited—two auditors being appointed by councils of Charlottetown and Summerside, and one elected by a school district in other cases. The duties of trustees are the same as those in Ontario and other provinces.

CHAPTER III.

1. The Public Schools in Manitoba.—2. In British Columbia.

1.—Public Schools in Manitoba.

In this province there is a department of education composed of the executive council (see *above*, p. 151) or a committee thereof. It appoints and fixes salaries of inspectors, teachers of provincial, normal and model schools, and directors of teachers' institutes. An advisory board of seven members—four appointed by the department for two years, two elected by public and high school teachers, and one chosen by the council of the university of Manitoba — determine qualifications of teachers and inspectors, prescribe forms of religious exercises, classify and organize normal, model and high schools, appoint examiners and perform other important duties. Inspectors cannot be teachers or trustees of a public or high school.

All education is now free and undenominational by the provincial legislation of 1890—the Roman Catholics having previously enjoyed denominational schools under the law. All persons in rural municipalities between five and sixteen, and in cities between six and sixteen, are required to attend. Religious exercises are conducted according to the regulations of the advisory board, but pupils whose parents object need not remain. In any

THE RYERSON PUBLIC SCHOOL, HAMILTON.

case religious exercises are entirely at the option of the trustees of a school. Three trustees are elected for three years after the first election in a rural district. A secretary-treasurer receives and disburses all moneys at the order of the board. In cities, towns and villages two trustees are elected for each ward. One trustee for each ward, as determined by ballot, retires annually; the other continues one year longer. In every village, not divided into wards, there are three trustees.

The schools are supported by grants from the legislature, from the proceeds of the sale of public lands granted for that purpose by the dominion government, and taxes levied on the ratepayers of the municipalities under the conditions provided in the law. The taxes are levied by the municipal council on the requisition of the trustees. Collegiate departments for more advanced education are connected with the public schools at Winnipeg and Brandon, and larger towns whenever practicable. A normal school has been established. All teachers must hold certificates of the first, second or third class as issued under the regulations of the department of education or advisory board.

The university of Manitoba is a provincial institution, under the direction of a council, named by the provincial colleges with which it is affiliated, by the convocation, and by the board of education. It is only an examining and degree-conferring body.

2.—The Public Schools in British Columbia.

In this province the minister of education and other members of the executive council (see *above*, p. 151) constitute a council of public instruction. The government appoint a superintendent of education, who is also secretary of the council. The schools are free and undenominational, but "the highest morality shall be inculcated and the Lord's prayer may be used at the opening or closing." A provincial board of examiners grant certificates to teachers, which must always be signed by the superintendent. The council appoint one or more qualified inspectors. Schools are divided into common, graded, and high schools. The law contemplates the establishment of a normal school. In each rural district there is a board of three trustees elected by the householders and freeholders, including wives of such. In city districts there is a board of six trustees, elected by duly qualified electors. To each board is attached a secretary-treasurer to collect and disburse moneys for school purposes. Schools are supported in rural districts entirely by the government. In cities the salaries of teachers and all other expenses incurred by the trustees are borne and paid by the municipal corporations. The government pay a grant of ten dollars per head a year, based on the average actual daily attendance of the public school pupils, to each of the municipal corporations of the cities. Every child from seven to twelve must attend some school or be otherwise educated for six months in every year.

<hr/>

BIBLIOGRAPHICAL NOTE.

The machinery that regulates the public school system of a province can only be thoroughly understood by a close study of its law, and by practical experience of its working. This law is generally compiled and printed in convenient manuals published by the departments of education. These manuals also contain the regulations with respect to teachers, examinations, classification of schools, and course of studies in every class of school. The report of Mr. Miller, deputy minister of education for Ontario, on the educational system of his province, is especially worthy of mention in this connection, since it gives a summary which interests the general reader. The following compilations also have been found extremely useful by the writer: The "Code of Public Instruction," compiled and annotated by Mr. Paul de Cazes, F.R.S.C., D.L., secretary of the department in Quebec; a "Manual of the School Law of Quebec, under the regulations of the Protestant committee," by Rev. Elson I. Rexford, B.A., rector of the high school of Montreal; a "Conspectus of the Public Free School System of Nova Scotia," prepared for the Chicago exposition, by Dr. A. H. MacKay, F.R.S.C., superintendent of education. Mr Rexford has added to the value of his manual by giving an historical outline of school organization in the province of Quebec, from 1615 to the present time. These several works, when studied in connection with the very full reports annually published by the educational departments of the provinces, enable us to understand the actual position and practical working of the public schools in every section. The present writer has to express the obligations he is under to the superintendents of education in all the provinces for the facilities they have given him for the preparation of what is necessarily in so small a volume but a meagre summary of the educational system of the Dominion.

SEVENTH PART.

GOVERNMENT IN THE NORTHWEST
TERRITORIES.

[267]

CHAPTER I.

1. Territorial Area.— 2. Government. — 3. Administration of Justice.—4. Municipal Government.—5. School Government.

1.—Territorial Area.

The territories of Canada comprise a vast region stretching from the province of Manitoba to the Rocky mountains, and from the frontier of the United States to the waters of the north. It embraces more than two-thirds of the Dominion, 2,460,000 square miles. This region came into the possession of Canada by the purchase of the rights of the Hudson's Bay company, who had so long enjoyed a monopoly of the fur trade, and used their best efforts to keep it an unknown land. The government of the Dominion now holds complete jurisdiction over the territory. The provisional district of Keewatin was formed some years ago out of the eastern portion until the settlement of the boundary dispute between Ontario and the Dominion ; but since that question was settled it has only a nominal existence, while it still remains under the supervision of the lieutenant-governor of the province of Manitoba. In 1882 a large portion of the northwest region was divided into four districts for administrative purposes, Assiniboia, now the most populous district, contains about 89,000 square miles, Saskatchewan 101,000, Alberta 105,300,

[269]

Athabasca 122,000.   Beyond these districts lies an
immense and relatively unknown region of unorganized
territory, watered by the Peace, Slave and Mackenzie
rivers.

2.—The Government.

Until the winter of 1888, the territories were governed
by a lieutenant-governor and council, partly nominated
by the governor-general in council and partly elected by
the people.   In the session of 1888, the parliament of
Canada passed an act granting the territories a legislative assembly of twenty-two members elected by the
people, and by subsequent legislation the number has
been increased to twenty-six.   The lieutenant-governor
is appointed by the dominion government during
pleasure—practically for five years—and is assisted by
an executive committee or advisory council of four
members belonging to and appointed by the assembly,
simply for the purpose of advising the lieutenant-governor in relation to the expenditure of territorial funds.
Responsible government, as it exists in the provinces,
has not yet been extended to the territories.   The
assembly has a duration of four years and is called
together once every year at such time as the lieutenant-
governor appoints.   It elects its own speaker and is
governed by rules and usages similar to those that prevail in the assemblies of the provinces.   Each member
receives $500 a session, besides an allowance for travel-
ling expenses.   The parliament of Canada provides
nearly all the funds necessary for carrying on the government, and meeting expenses for local purposes.
Dominion and territorial elections are by ballot, the

electors must be actual male residents and householders of adult age, who are not aliens or unenfranchised Indians and who have resided within the district for twelve months before the election. The assembly has power to make ordinances or laws with respect to proceedings at territorial elections, direct taxation, establishment and tenure of territorial offices, prisons, municipal institutions, incorporation of companies for territorial objects, and generally all matters of a merely local or private nature given to the provincial legislatures by the British North America Act (see *above*, p. 163). The territories are represented in the senate by two senators, and in the house of commons by four members.

3.—Administration of Justice.

The civil and criminal laws of Canada are in force in the territories. The supreme court, consisting of five justices, are appointed by the Ottawa government and are removable upon an address from the senate and house of commons to the governor-general in council. It has within the territories all such powers as are incident to a superior court of civil and criminal jurisdiction in the provinces. Sheriffs are appointed by the Ottawa government, but the lieutenant-governor may appoint justices of the peace, and the governor-general in council police magistrates, who shall have all powers now vested in two justices of the peace under any law in Canada (see *above*, p. 180). Either French or English may be used in the proceedings of the courts. The mounted police, a large and efficient body of trained men, act as constables for the preservation of peace, the prevention of crime, the arrest of criminals, the conveyance of con-

victed persons to places of confinement, besides performing other duties necessary for the security and order of
the territories. Students who have been for three years
in the office of a duly enrolled advocate in the territories
are admitted to the practice of the law. Barristers and
advocates of the provinces are allowed to practise. The
lieutenant-governor can appoint notaries public (see
above, p. 195).

4.—Municipal System.

The organized territories possess a municipal system
based on that of Ontario. Each municipality of not less
than four hundred square miles is entitled to a reeve and
four councillors ; of more than four hundred, to a reeve
and six councillors. Towns may have a council, consisting of a mayor and six councillors, when the population
does not exceed three thousand; if above that population
councillors may be increased to eight. When towns have
a population of over five thousand they may be made
cities, with a mayor and ten aldermen. Mayors, reeves,
aldermen and councillors are elected annually by ballot.
As in the provinces, councillors and electors must be
British subjects, resident in a municipality, and assessed
as owners or occupants of real property. Electors
can also vote on personal property or income. Widows
and unmarried women, when ratepayers, can vote.
Judges, sheriffs, bailiffs, constables, clerks of the court,
dominion, territorial, and municipal officers, and persons
having contracts with or claims against the municipality, cannot act as councillors. Taxes are collected
on real or personal property, including incomes. The
exemptions cover the property of the dominion and

territorial government, Indian lands, municipal property, public educational institutions and lands immediately connected therewith to extent of half an acre, orphanages, houses of industry, jails and asylums, books of public libraries, incomes of farmers derived from their farms, incomes of merchants, mechanics and others derived from capital liable to taxation, personal property to value of $300, and household effects of every kind, except in unlicensed hotels and restaurants. Appeals may be made to a court of revision, composed of councillors, and thence to a judge of the supreme court. Bylaws are subject to same conditions as in the provinces (see *above*, p. 234). A clerk, treasurer, auditors, assessors, collectors, road overseers and other officers are appointed by the councils as in the provinces. The laws for the prevention of corrupt practices are very strict.

5.--School Government.

In the Northwest territories there is a council of public instruction, composed of the executive committee (see *above*, p. 270) and of four other members without votes, two Protestants and two Roman Catholics, appointed by the lieutenant-governor in council. The appointed members have no vote. A member of the executive committee, nominated by the lieutenant-governor in council, acts as chairman. A superintendent of education acts as secretary to the council. No religious instruction is permitted in any public school until half an hour before the close in the afternoon, when such exercises as have been arranged by the trustees are given, but only those children who have

18

the permission of their parents need remain. Duly qualified school inspectors are appointed by the lieutenant-governor in council. A minority of ratepayers in a district may establish a separate school therein. Schools are supported by local assessment and by grants of the government of the dominion, which have set apart sections of public land for that purpose (see *below*, p 277). All such grants are under the control of the legislative assembly, and are duly appropriated by it for school purposes. Local schools are managed by three resident trustees, elected by the ratepayers of the district. Each board has a secretary and a treasurer—the latter may be a member of the same. Education of children between seven and twelve is compulsory for a period of at least twelve weeks in each year. Kindergarten schools may be established in any section for the teaching of children between four and seven. Every teacher's certificate is granted by the council of public instruction, and must bear the signature of the superintendent.

CHAPTER II.

1. Public Lands.—2. Registration.—3. Indians.

1.—Public Lands.

The lands of Manitoba and the territories are owned by the dominion government, who have made very liberal provisions for the encouragement of settlement. Their administration and management is entrusted to

N.

31	32	33	34	35	36
30	29	28	27	26	25
19	20	21	22	23	24
18	17	16	15	14	13
7	8	9	10	11	12
6	5	4	3	2	1

W.　　　　　　　　　　　　　　　　*E.*

S.

[275]

the minister of interior (see *above*, p. 80), and to certain commissioners, officers and clerks, whose duties are de-fined by statute and the regulations of the department. Dominion lands are laid off in quadrilateral blocks or townships, each containing thirty-six sections of as nearly one mile square as the scientific survey permits, with such road allowances between sections as the governor-general in council prescribes. Sections are bounded and numbered as in the diagram on preceding page.

Each section is divided into quarter sections of one hundred and sixty acres, and consequently each town-ship, as a rule, comprises about 23,040 acres of land. Each such quarter section is again divided into quarter sections, or forty acres, numbered as in the following diagram :

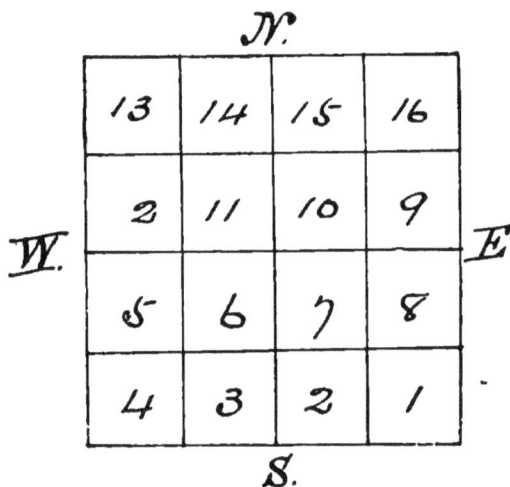

N.

13	*14*	*15*	*16*
2	*11*	*10*	*9*
5	*6*	*7*	*8*
4	*3*	*2*	*1*

W.   *E.*

S.

Sections eleven and twenty-nine (see first diagram) in every surveyed township throughout the extent of the dominion lands are set apart for the purposes of education in the territories. Provision is also made in the law for towns and cities. In order to give every possible encouragement to actual settlement in Manitoba and the territories the law provides that all surveyed even numbered sections, which have not been otherwise reserved for a special purpose, are to be held exclusively for "homesteads," or practically free homes. Any person who is the sole head of a family, or any male who is of the age of eighteen years, can on the payment of ten dollars obtain possession of a homestead of one quarter section, or one hundred and sixty acres of surveyed agricultural land, and secure a perfect title from the crown as its owner by actual residence and cultivation every six months from the date of entry until the end of three years. When he has complied with the terms of the law, which are intended to encourage actual settlers and prevent land falling into the hands of mere speculators, he receives a "patent" or title from the dominion government. A man who wishes to secure his complete title in a shorter time can do so by furnishing proof that he has lived on the land for at least twelve months from the date of his perfecting his entry, and that he has cultivated at least thirty acres. An actual settler may also purchase a quarter section adjoining his own when available, at the ordinary price, which is three dollars an acre; one-fourth of the purchase money to be in cash, and the balance in three equal yearly instalments at six per cent interest annually. Other advantages are given to settlers not necessary or possible to mention here.

2.—Registration.

The legal regulations for the sale and transfer of lands are very clear and simple. Five land registration districts have been made in the territories: Assiniboia, South Alberta, North Alberta, West Saskatchewan, and East Saskatchewan. The business of each land titles office is conducted by a registrar, appointed by the governor-general in council, and discharging all those duties performed by similar officers in the provinces with respect to the grant, sale, mortgage, lease and transfer of property. An inspector, appointed by the governor-general in council, inspects the books and records of the several land title offices from time to time.

3.—The Indians.

By the British North America Act the dominion government has sole control over the Indians and lands reserved for Indians in the provinces and territories of the Dominion. One of the departments of the government of Canada is that of Indian affairs, of which a superintendent general is the head. It has the management and charge of all matters relating to the Indians. The minister of the interior (see *above*, p. 80) generally fills the position of superintendent general, and has the assistance of a number of officers to manage the business of the department. In all the provinces and territories there are bands or remnants of the old tribes or "Nations" that once inhabited British North America, who live on lands specially reserved for their use and benefit. The law carefully guards their interests, and all property held for them can only be alienated or leased by their own consent, and then the proceeds are invested for their sole advantage. The law makes very satisfactory provision for the "enfranchisement" of the Indians; that is, the conferring upon them the rights and privileges of free citizens, whenever they can come up to the qualifications laid down to meet their case. Indians in the old provinces can vote at dominion and provincial elections on the conditions laid down in the statutes on the subject, but in the territories and Manitoba they have not yet reached that degree of civilization which would enable them to exercise the rights of white men. There are in British Columbia and the organized terri-tories some 46,000 Indians, in various stages of develop-ment. They are the wards of the Canadian government, which has always exercised a parental care over them. They are fed and clothed in large numbers. Before lands were laid out for settlement the Indian titles were extinguished by treaties of purchase, conducted between the representative of the Dominion and the councils of the several tribes. The Indians live on "reserves" set apart for them in valuable districts; indus-trial farms and other schools are provided by the govern-ment with the creditable hope of making them more useful members of the community. Agents live on the reserves, and inspectors visit the agencies from time to time to see that the interests of the Indians are protected in accordance with the general policy of the govern-ment. The sale of spirituous liquors is expressly for-bidden to the Indian population, and severe punishment is provided by the law for those who evade this wise regulation.

BIBLIOGRAPHICAL NOTE.

There are no books or essays to be quoted in connection with territorial government. The subject is new, and those who wish to study it thoroughly will have to go through the dominion statutes respecting Northwest government, Indians, public lands, mounted police, as well as through the ordinances of the Northwest assembly.   Much information is found in the Statistical Year Book of Canada.

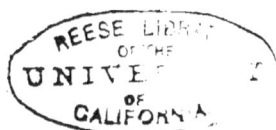

CONCLUSION.

THE DUTIES AND RESPONSIBILITIES OF CANADIAN CITIZENS.

I have now given an outline of the leading features of the government of Canada, and shall conclude with a few general observations addressed especially to my younger readers, on whom must largely rest the effective and pure administration of public affairs in the future of a country, still in the infancy of its development.

Whatever defects and weaknesses may exist in certain details of the Canadian federal structure—and this opens up subjects of controversy into which I cannot enter in a book like this—Canadians may fairly claim that it seems on the whole well adapted to meet the wants and necessities of the people of the Dominion. From the foundation to the crowning apex it has many attributes of strength. It is framed on principles which, as tested by British and American experience, are calculated to assist national development and give full liberty to local institutions. At the bottom of the edifice are those parish, township, county and municipal institutions which are eminently favourable to popular freedom and local improvement. Then comes the more important provincial organization, divided into those executive, legislative and judicial authorities which are essential to the working of all constitutions. Next comes the central government which assumes a national dignity and is intended as a guarantee of protection, unity and security

[281]

to the whole system. And above all is the imperial power — in other words, a sovereign who holds her exalted position, not by the caprice of a popular vote, but with all the guarantees of permanency with which the British constitution surrounds the throne.

In the system of parliamentary government, which has been developed in Canada in accordance with English principles, we have elements of undoubted strength as compared with those enjoyed by the people of the United States, where neither the president of the nation nor the governor of a state has a cabinet having seats in the legislative assemblies of the country and responsible for the work of administration and legislation. In Canada the governor-general, or the lieutenant-governor, his cabinet, and the popular branch of the legislature are governed, as in England, by a system of rules, conventions and understandings which enable them to work in harmony with one another. The crown, the cabinet, the legislature and the people have respectively certain rights and powers which, when properly and constitutionally brought into operation, give strength and elasticity to our system of government. In all cases there must be a ministry to advise the crown, assume responsibility for its acts, and obtain the support of the people and their representatives in parliament. As a last resort to bring into harmony the people, the legislature, and the crown, there is the exercise of the supreme prerogative of dissolution. A governor, acting always under the advice of responsible ministers, may at any time, generally speaking, grant an appeal to the people to test their opinion on vital public questions and bring the legislature into accord with the public mind. In short, the fundamental principle of popular sovereignty lies at the very basis of the Canadian system.

The following features of the Canadian system of government also give it strength and stability :—

A non-political and permanent civil service in the dominion and provincial governments—a system only partially adopted of very recent years by the national government of the United States, and now urged in almost all the old states of the union.

The appointment of all judges and public officials by the crown, on the advice of ministers responsible to parliament for every such executive act—in contradistinction to the elective system of the states of the federal republic, where even judges are, in most cases, elected by the people.

The independence of the judiciary of all party and political pressure, when once appointed, since they can be removed only by the crown, as a consequence of a successful impeachment by the dominion parliament, while in the several states their tenure is limited to a certain number of years—ten on the average.

The reference of questions, involving the constitutional rights of the Dominion and the provinces, to perfectly independent courts on whose unbiassed decision must always largely rest the security of a federal system.

But .however well devised a system of government may be, it is relatively worthless unless the men and women who compose the people of Canada are always fully alive to their duties and responsibilities. It has been well said that "eternal vigilance is the price of liberty," and if the people of Canada are indifferent to the character and ability of the men to whom, from time to time, they entrust the administration of public affairs —whether in the Dominion, a province, a city or other municipal division, or a school district—they must sooner or later themselves reap the results of their neglect. Good and safe government means active interest on the part of all classes of citizens, and not least on the part of those whose intelligence, education and standing give them a special right to be leaders in creating a sound public opinion in their respective communities.

A famous Greek writer told all of us our duty many centuries ago when he said that " man is born to be a citizen."

Let the young citizens of Canada have always before them a high ideal. Better to aim high than to sink low.

It is all important that the body politic should be kept pure and that public life should be considered a public trust. Canada is still young in political development, and the fact that her population has been as a rule a steady, fixed population, free from those dangerous elements which have come into the United States with such rapidity of late years, has kept her relatively free from many serious social and political dangers which have afflicted her neighbours, and to which I believe they themselves, having inherited English institutions, and being imbued with the spirit of English law, will always in the end rise superior. Great responsibility therefore rests in the first instance upon the people of Canada, who must select the best and purest among them to serve the country, and, secondly, upon the men whom the legislature chooses to discharge the trust of carrying on the government. No system of government or of laws can of itself make a people virtuous and happy unless their rulers recognize in the fullest sense their obligations to the state and exercise their powers with prudence and unselfishness, and endeavour to elevate public opinion. A constitution may be as perfect as human agencies can make it and yet be relatively worthless, while the large responsibilities and powers entrusted to the governing body—responsibilities and powers not set forth in acts of parliament— are forgotten in view of party triumph, personal ambition, or pecuniary gain. "The laws," says Burke, "reach but a very little way. Constitute government how you please, infinitely the greater part of it must depend upon the exercise of powers which are left at large to the prudence and uprightness of ministers of state. Even all the use and potency of the laws depend upon them. Without them your commonwealth is no better than a scheme upon paper, and not a living, active, effective organization."

In Canada, I quote the words of a Canadian poetess*—

" As yet the waxen mould is soft, the opening page is fair ;
   It's left for those who rule us now to leave their impress there—
   The stamp of true nobility, high honour, stainless truth ;
   The earnest quest of noble ends ; the generous heart of youth ;
   The love of country, soaring far above dull party strife ;
   The love of learning, art, and song—the crowning grace of life ;
   The love of science, soaring far through nature's hidden ways ;
   The love and fear of nature's God—a nation's highest praise."

---

* Miss Machar, of Kingston, well known as "Fidelis."

APPENDIX.

THE CONSTITUTION OF THE DOMINION OF CANADA

OR THE

BRITISH NORTH AMERICA ACT,

1867,

AND AMENDING ACTS.

[287]

APPENDIX.

THE BRITISH NORTH AMERICA ACT, 1867.

[Assented to by the Queen on the 27th March, 1867.

An Act for the Union of Canada, Nova Scotia and New Brunswick, and the Government thereof, and for purposes connected therewith.

WHEREAS the provinces of Canada, Nova Scotia and New Brunswick have expressed their desire to be federally united into one Dominion under the crown of the united kingdom of Great Britain and Ireland, with a constitution similar in principle to that of the united kingdom :

And whereas such a union would conduce to the welfare of the provinces and promote the interests of the British empire :

And whereas on the establishment of the union by authority of parliament it is expedient, not only that the constitution of the legislative authority in the Dominion be provided for, but also that the nature of the executive government therein be declared :

And whereas it is expedient that provision be made for the eventual admission into the union of other parts of British North America :

Be it therefore enacted and declared by the queen's most excellent majesty, by and with the advice and consent of the lords spiritual and temporal, and commons, in this present parliament assembled, and by the authority of the same, as follows :

I.—PRELIMINARY.

1. This act may be cited as the British North America Act, 1867.

2. The provisions of this act referring to her majesty the queen extend also to the heirs and successors of her majesty, kings and queens of the united kingdom of Great Britain and Ireland.

II.—UNION.

3. It shall be lawful for the queen, by and with the advice of her majesty's most honourable privy council, to declare by proclamation

19   [289]

that, on and after a day therein appointed, not being more than six months after the passing of this act, the provinces of Canada, Nova Scotia and New Brunswick shall form and be one Dominion under the name of Canada ; and on and after that day those three provinces shall form and be one Dominion under that name accordingly.

4. The subsequent provisions of this act shall, unless it is otherwise expressed or implied, commence and have effect on and after the union, that is to say, on and after the day appointed for the union taking effect in the queen's proclamation ; and in the same provisions, unless it is otherwise expressed or implied, the name Canada shall be taken to mean Canada as constituted under this act.

5. Canada shall be divided into four provinces, named Ontario, Quebec, Nova Scotia and New Brunswick.

6. The parts of the province of Canada (as it exists at the passing of this act) which formerly constituted respectively the provinces of Upper Canada and Lower Canada shall be deemed to be severed, and shall form two separate provinces. The part which formerly constituted the province of Upper Canada shall constitute the province of Ontario ; and the part which formerly constituted the province of Lower Canada shall constitute the province of Quebec.

7. The provinces of Nova Scotia and New Brunswick shall have the same limits as at the passing of this act.

8. In the general census of the population of Canada, which is hereby required to be taken in the year one thousand eight hundred and seventy-one, and in every tenth year thereafter, the respective populations of the four provinces shall be distinguished.

III.—EXECUTIVE POWER.

9. The executive government and authority of and over Canada is hereby declared to continue and be vested in the queen.

10. The provisions of this act referring to the governor-general extend and apply to the governor-general for the time being of Canada, or other the chief executive officer or administrator for the time being carrying on the government of Canada on behalf and in the name of the queen, by whatever title he is designated.

11. There shall be a council to aid and advise the government of Canada, to be styled the queen's privy council for Canada ; and the persons who are to be members of that council shall be from time to time chosen and summoned by the governor-general and sworn in as privy councillors, and members thereof may be from time to time removed by the governor-general.

12. All powers, authorities and functions, which under any act of

the parliament of Great Britain, or of the parliament of the united kingdom of Great Britain and Ireland, or of the legislature of Upper Canada, Lower Canada, Canada, Nova Scotia or New Brunswick, are at the union vested in or exercisable by the respective governors or lieutenant-governors of those provinces with the advice, or with the advice and consent, of the respective executive councils thereof, or in conjunction with those councils, or with any number of members thereof, or by those governors or lieutenant-governors individually, shall, as far as the same continue in existence and capable of being exercised after the union in relation to the government of Canada, be vested in and exercisable by the governor-general, with the advice, or with the advice and consent, of or in conjunction with the queen's privy council for Canada, or any members thereof, or by the governor-general individually, as the case requires, subject, nevertheless, (except with respect to such as exist under acts of the parliament of Great Britain or of the parliament of the united kingdom of Great Britain and Ireland) to be abolished or altered by the parliament of Canada.

13. The provisions of this act referring to the governor-general · in council shall be construed as referring to the governor-general acting by and with the advice of the queen's privy council for Canada.

14. It shall be lawful for the queen, if her majesty thinks fit, to authorize the governor-general from time to time to appoint any person or any persons jointly or severally to be his deputy or deputies within any part or parts of Canada, and in that capacity to exercise during the pleasure of the governor-general such of the powers, authorities and functions of the governor-general as the governor-general deems it necessary or expedient to assign to him or them, subject to any limitations or directions expressed or given by the queen; but the appointment of such a deputy or deputies shall not affect the exercise by the governor-general himself of any power, authority or function.

15. The command-in-chief of the land and naval militia, and of all naval and military forces, of and in Canada, is hereby declared to continue and be vested in the queen.

16. Until the queen otherwise directs, the seat of government of Canada shall be Ottawa.

IV.—LEGISLATIVE POWER.

17. There shall be one parliament for Canada, consisting of the queen, an upper house styled the senate, and the house of commons.

18. *The privileges, immunities and powers to be held, enjoyed and exercised by the senate and by the house of commons, and by

---

* Amended by a subsequent imperial Act (see *below*, p. 324).

the members thereof respectively, shall be such as are from time to time defined by act of the parliament of Canada, but so that the same shall never exceed those at the passing of this act held, enjoyed, and exercised by the commons house of parliament of the united kingdom of Great Britain and Ireland and by the members thereof.

19. The parliament of Canada shall be called together not later than six months after the union.

20. There shall be a session of the parliament of Canada once at least in every year, so that twelve months shall not intervene between the last sitting of the parliament in one session and its first sitting in the next session.

The Senate.

21. The senate shall, subject to the provisions of this act, consist of seventy-two members, who shall be styled senators.

22. In relation to the constitution of the senate, Canada shall be deemed to consist of three divisions—

1. Ontario ;
2. Quebec ;
3. The Maritime provinces, Nova Scotia and New Brunswick ; which three divisions shall (subject to the provisions of this act) be equally represented in the senate as follows : Ontario by twenty-four senators ; Quebec by twenty-four senators, and the Maritime provinces by twenty-four senators, twelve thereof representing Nova Scotia and twelve thereof representing New Brunswick.

In the case of Quebec, each of the twenty-four senators representing that province shall be appointed for one of the twenty-four electoral divisions of Lower Canada specified in schedule A to chapter one of the consolidated statutes of Canada.

23. The qualifications of a senator shall be as follows :—

(1) He shall be of the full age of thirty years.

(2) He shall be either a natural-born subject of the queen, or a subject of the queen naturalized by an act of the parliament of Great Britain, or of the parliament of the united kingdom of Great Britain and Ireland, or of the legislature of one of the provinces of Upper Canada, Lower Canada, Canada, Nova Scotia or New Brunswick before the union, or of the parliament of Canada after the union.

(3) He shall be legally or equitably seized as of freehold for his own use and benefit of lands or tenements held in free and common socage, or seized or possessed for his own use and benefit of lands or tenements held in franc-alleu or

in roture, within the province for which he is appointed, of the value of four thousand dollars, over and above all rents, dues, debts, charges, mortgages and encumbrances due or payable out of, or charged on or affecting the same ;

(4) His real and personal property shall be together worth four thousand dollars over and above his debts and liabilities ;

(5) He shall be resident in the province for which he is appointed ;

(6) In the case of Quebec, he shall have his real property qualification in the electoral division for which he is appointed, or shall be resident in that division.

24. The governor-general shall from time to time, in the queen's name, by instrument under the great seal of Canada, summon qualified persons to the senate ; and, subject to the provisions of this act, every person so summoned shall become and be a member of the senate and a senator.

25. Such persons shall be first summoned to the senate as the queen by warrant under her majesty's royal sign manual thinks fit to approve, and their names shall be inserted in the queen's proclamation of union.

26. If at any time, on the recommendation of the governor-general, the queen thinks fit to direct that three or six members be added to the senate, the governor-general may, by summons to three or six qualified persons (as the case may be), representing equally the three divisions of Canada, add to the senate accordingly.

27. In case of such addition being at any time made, the governor-general shall not summon any person to the senate, except on a further like direction by the queen on the like recommendation, until each of the three divisions of Canada is represented by twenty-four senators, and no more.

28. The number of senators shall not at any time exceed seventy-eight.

29. A senator shall, subject to the provisions of this act, hold his place in the senate for life.

30. A senator may, by writing under his hand, addressed to the governor-general, resign his place in the senate, and thereupon the same shall be vacant.

31. The place of a senator shall become vacant in any of the following cases :—

(1) If for two consecutive sessions of the parliament he fails to give his attendance in the senate :

(2) If he takes an oath or makes a declaration or acknowledgment of allegiance, obedience or adherence to a foreign power, or does an act whereby he becomes a subject or

citizen, or entitled to the rights or privileges of a subject or citizen of a foreign power :

(3) If he is adjudged bankrupt or insolvent, or applies for the benefit of any law relating to insolvent debtors, or becomes a public defaulter :

(4) If he is attainted of treason, or convicted of felony or of any infamous crime :

(5) If he ceases to be qualified in respect of property or of residence : provided that a senator shall not be deemed to have ceased to be qualified in respect of residence by reason only of his residing at the seat of the government of Canada while holding an office under that government requiring his presence there.

32. When a vacancy happens in the senate, by resignation, death or otherwise, the governor-general shall, by summons to a fit and qualified person, fill the vacancy.

33. If any question arises respecting the qualification of a senator or a vacancy in the senate, the same shall be heard and determined by the senate.

34. The governor-general may from time to time, by instrument under the great seal of Canada, appoint a senator to be speaker of the senate, and may remove him and appoint another in his stead.

35. Until the parliament of Canada otherwise provides, the presence of at least fifteen senators, including the speaker, shall be necessary to constitute a meeting of the senate for the exercise of its powers.

36. Questions arising in the senate shall be decided by a majority of voices, and the speaker shall in all cases have a vote, and when the voices are equal the decision shall be deemed to be in the negative.

The House of Commons.

37. The house of commons shall, subject to the provisions of this act, consist 'of one hundred and eighty-one members, of whom eighty-two shall be elected for Ontario, sixty-five for Quebec, nineteen for Nova Scotia, and fifteen for New Brunswick.

38. The governor-general shall from time to time, in the queen's name, by instrument under the great seal of Canada, summon and call together the house of commons.

39. A senator shall not be capable of being elected or of sitting or voting as a member of the house of commons.

40. Until the parliament of Canada otherwise provides, Ontario. Quebec, Nova Scotia and New Brunswick shall, for the purposes

of the election of members to serve in the house of commons, be divided into electoral districts as follows :—

1.—ONTARIO.

Ontario shall be divided into the counties, ridings of counties, cities, parts of cities, and towns enumerated in the first schedule to this act, each whereof shall be an electoral district, each such district as numbered in that schedule being entitled to return one member.

2.—QUEBEC.

Quebec shall be divided into sixty-five electoral districts, composed of the sixty-five electoral divisions into which Lower Canada is at the passing of this act divided under chapter two of the consolidated statutes of Canada, chapter seventy-five of the consolidated statutes for Lower Canada, and the act of the province of Canada of the twenty-third year of the queen, chapter one, or any other act amending the same in force at the union, so that each such electoral division shall be for the purposes of this act an electoral district entitled to return one member.

3.—NOVA SCOTIA.

Each of the eighteen counties of Nova Scotia shall be an electoral district. The county of Halifax shall be entitled to return two members, and each of the other counties one member.

4.—NEW BRUNSWICK.

Each of the fourteen counties into which New Brunswick is divided, including the city and county of St. John, shall be an electoral district. The city of St. John shall also be a separate electoral district. Each of those fifteen electoral districts shall be entitled to return one member.

41. Until the parliament of Canada otherwise provides, all laws in force in the several provinces at the union relative to the following matters or any of them, namely :—the qualifications and disqualifications of persons to be elected or to sit or vote as members of the house of assembly or legislative assembly in the several provinces, the voters at elections of such members, the oaths to be taken by voters, the returning officers, their powers and duties, the proceedings at elections, the periods during which elections may be continued, the trial of controverted elections, and proceedings incident thereto, the vacating of seats of members, and the execution of new writs in case of seats vacated otherwise than by dissolution — shall respectively apply to elections of

members to serve in the house of commons for the same several provinces.

Provided that, until the parliament of Canada otherwise provides, at any election for a member of the house of commons for the district of Algoma, in addition to persons qualified by the law of the province of Canada to vote, every male British subject, aged twenty-one years or upwards, being a householder, shall have a vote.

42. For the first election of members to serve in the house of commons the governor-general shall cause writs to be issued by such person, in such form and addressed to such returning officers as he thinks fit.

The person issuing writs under this section shall have the like powers as are possessed at the union by the officers charged with the issuing of writs for the election of members to serve in the respective house of assembly or legislative assembly of the province of Canada, Nova Scotia or New Brunswick ; and the returning officers to whom writs are directed under this section shall have the like powers as are possessed at the union by the officers charged with the returning of writs for the election of members to serve in the same respective house of assembly or legislative assembly.

43. In case a vacancy in the representation in the house of commons of any electoral district happens before the meeting of the parliament or after the meeting of the parliament before provision is made by the parliament in this behalf, the provisions of the last foregoing section of this act shall extend and apply to the issuing and returning of a writ in respect of such vacant district.

44. The house of commons, on its first assembling after a general election, shall proceed with all practicable speed to elect one of its members to be speaker.

45. In case of a vacancy happening in the office of speaker, by death, resignation or otherwise, the house of commons shall, with all practicable speed, proceed to elect another of its members to be speaker.

46. The speaker shall preside at all meetings of the house of commons.

47. Until the parliament of Canada otherwise provides, in case of the absence for any reason, of the speaker from the chair of the house of commons for a period of forty-eight consecutive hours, the house may elect another of its members to act as speaker, and the member so elected shall, during the continuance of such absence of the speaker, have and execute all the powers, privileges and duties of speaker.

48. The presence of at least twenty members of the house of commons shall be necessary to constitute a meeting of the house for the exercise of its powers ; and for that purpose the speaker shall be reckoned as a member.

49. Questions arising in the house of commons shall be decided by a majority of voices other than that of the speaker, and when the voices are equal, but not otherwise, the speaker shall have a vote.

50. Every house of commons shall continue for five years from the day of the return of the writs for choosing the house (subject to be sooner dissolved by the governor-general), and no longer.

51. On the completion of the census in the year one thousand eight hundred and seventy-one, and of each subsequent decennial census, the representation of the four provinces shall be readjusted by such authority, in such manner, and from such time as the parliament of Canada from time to time provides, subject and according to the following rules :—

(1) Quebec shall have the fixed number of sixty-five members :

(2) There shall be assigned to each of the other provinces such a number of members as will bear the same proportion to the number of its population (ascertained at such census) as the number of sixty-five bears to the number of the population of Quebec (so ascertained) :

(3) In the computation of the number of members for a province a fractional part not exceeding one-half of the whole number requisite for entitling the province to a member shall be disregarded ; but a fractional part exceeding one-half of that number shall be equivalent to the whole number :

(4) On any such readjustment the number of members for a province shall not be reduced unless the proportion which the number of the population of the province bore to the number of the aggregate population of Canada at the then last preceding readjustment of the number of members for the province is ascertained at the then latest census to be diminished by one-twentieth part or upwards :

(5) Such readjustment shall not take effect until the termination of the then existing parliament.

52. The number of members of the house of commons may be from time to time increased by the parliament of Canada, provided the proportionate representation of the provinces prescribed by this act is not thereby disturbed.

Money Votes; Royal Assent.

53. Bills for appropriating any part of the public revenue, or for imposing any tax or impost, shall originate in the house of commons.

54. It shall not be lawful for the house of commons to adopt or pass any vote, resolution, address, or bill for the appropriation of any part of the public revenue, or of any tax or impost, to any purpose that has not been first recommended to that house by message of the governor-general in the session in which such vote, resolution, address, or bil! is proposed.

55. Where a bill passed by the houses of the parliament is presented to the governor-general for the queen's assent, he shall declare, according to his discretion, but subject to the provisions of this act and to her majesty's instructions, either that he assents thereto in the queen's name, or that he withholds the queen's assent, or that he reserves the bill for the signification of the queen's pleasure.

56. Where the governor-general assents to a bill in the queen's name, he shall by the first convenient opportunity send an authentic copy of the act to one of her majesty's principal secretaries of state, and if the queen in council within two years after receipt thereof by the secretary of state thinks fit to disallow the act, such disallowance (with a certificate of the secretary of state of the day on which the act was received by him) being signified by the governor-general, by speech or message to each of the houses of the parliament or by proclamation, shall annul the act from and after the day of such signification.

57. A bill reserved for the signification of the queen's pleasure shall not have any force unless and until within two years from the day on which it was presented to the governor-general for the queen's assent, the governor-general signifies, by speech or message to each of the houses of the parliament or by proclamation, that it has received the assent of the queen in council.

An entry of every such speech, message or proclamation shall be made in the journal of each house, and a duplicate thereof duly attested shall be delivered to the proper officer to be kept among the records of Canada.

V.—PROVINCIAL CONSTITUTIONS.

Executive Power.

58. For each province there shall be an officer, styled the lieutenant-governor, appointed by the governor-general in council by instrument under the great seal of Canada.

59. A lieutenant-governor shall hold office during the pleasure of the governor-general ; but any lieutenant-governor appointed after

the commencement of the first session of the parliament of Canada shall not be removable within five years from his appointment, except for cause assigned which shall be communicated to him in writing within one month after the order for his removal is made, and shall be communicated by message to the senate and to the house of commons within one week thereafter if the parliament is then sitting, and if not then within one week after the commencement of the next session of the parliament.

60. The salaries of the lieutenant-governors shall be fixed and provided by the parliament of Canada.

61. Every lieutenant-governor shall, before assuming the duties of his office, make and subscribe before the governor-general or some person authorized by him, oaths of allegiance and office similar to those taken by the governor-general.

62. The provisions of this act referring to the lieutenant-governor extend and apply to the lieutenant-governor for the time being of each province or other the chief executive officer or administrator for the time being carrying on the government of the province, by whatever title he is designated.

63. The executive council of Ontario and of Quebec shall be composed of such persons as the lieutenant-governor from time to time thinks fit, and in the first instance of the following officers, namely : the attorney-general, the secretary and registrar of the province, the treasurer of the province, the commissioner of crown lands, and the commissioner of agriculture and public works, with, in Quebec, the speaker of the legislative council and the solicitor-general.

64. The constitution of the executive authority in each of the provinces of Nova Scotia and New Brunswick shall, subject to the provisions of this act, continue as it exists at the union until altered under the authority of this act.

65. All powers, authorities and functions, which under any act of the parliament of Great Britain, or of the parliament of the united kingdom of Great Britain and Ireland, or of the legislature of Upper Canada, Lower Canada, or Canada, were or are before or at the union vested in or exercisable by the respective governors or lieutenant-governors of those provinces, with the advice, or with the advice and consent, of the respective executive councils thereof, or in conjunction with those councils or with any number of members thereof, or by those governors or lieutenant-governors individually, shall, as far as the same are capable of being exercised after the union in relation to the government of Ontario and Quebec respectively, be vested in and shall or may be exercised by the lieutenant-governor of Ontario and Quebec respectively, with the advice or with the advice and consent of

or in conjunction with the respective executive councils or any members thereof, or by the lieutenant-governor individually, as the case requires, subject nevertheless (except with respect to such as exist under acts of the parliament of Great Britain or of the parliament of the united kingdom of Great Britain and Ireland), to be abolished or altered by the respective legislatures of Ontario and Quebec.

66. The provisions of this act referring to the lieutenant-governor in council shall be construed as referring to the lieutenant-governor of the province acting by and with the advice of the executive council thereof.

67. The governor-general in council may from time to time appoint an administrator to execute the office and functions of lieutenant-governor during his absence, illness, or other inability.

68. ·Unless and until the executive government of any province otherwise directs with respect to that province, the seats of government of the provinces shall be as follows, namely : of Ontario, the city of Toronto ; of Quebec, the city of Quebec ; of Nova Scotia, the city of Halifax; and of New Brunswick, the city of Fredericton.

Legislative Power.

I.—ONTARIO.

69. There shall be a legislature for Ontario, consisting of the lieutenant-governor and of one house, styled the legislative assembly of Ontario.

70. The legislative assembly of Ontario shall be composed of eighty-two members, to be elected to represent the eighty-two electoral districts set forth in the first schedule to this act.

2.—QUEBEC.

71. There shall be a legislature for Quebec, consisting of the lieutenant-governor and two houses, styled the legislative council of Quebec and the legislative assembly of Quebec.

72. The legislative council of Quebec shall be composed of twenty-four members, to be appointed by the lieutenant-governor in the queen's name by instrument under the great seal of Quebec, one being appointed to represent each of the twenty-four electoral divisions of Lower Canada in this act referred to, and each holding office for the term of his life, unless the legislature of Quebec otherwise provides under the provisions of this act.   ·

73. The qualifications of the legislative councillors of Quebec shall be the same as those of the senators for Quebec.

1357913

5791357913

74. The place of a legislative councillor of Quebec shall become vacant in the cases, *mutatis mutandis*, in which the place of senator becomes vacant.

75. When a vacancy happens in the legislative council of Quebec by resignation, death, or otherwise, the lieutenant-governor, in the queen's name, by instrument under the great seal of Quebec, shall appoint a fit and qualified person to fill the vacancy.

76. If any question arises respecting the qualifications of a legislative councillor of Quebec, or a vacancy in the legislative council of Quebec, the same shall be heard and determined by the legislative council.

77. The lieutenant-governor may, from time to time, by instrument under the great seal of Quebec, appoint a member of the legislative council of Quebec to be speaker thereof, and may remove him and appoint another in his stead.

78. Until the legislature of Quebec otherwise provides, the presence of at least ten members of the legislative council, including the speaker, shall be necessary to constitute a meeting for the exercise of its powers.

79. Questions arising in the legislative council of Quebec shall be decided by a majority of voices, and the speaker shall in all cases have a vote, and when the voices are equal the decision shall be deemed to be in the negative.

80. The legislative assembly of Quebec shall be composed of sixty-five members, to be elected to represent the sixty-five electoral divisions or districts of Lower Canada in this act referred to, subject to alteration thereof by the legislature of Quebec : provided that it shall not be lawful to present to the lieutenant-governor of Quebec for assent any bill for altering the limits of any of the electoral divisions or districts mentioned in the second schedule to this act, unless the second and third readings of such bill have been passed in the legislative assembly with the concurrence of the majority of the members representing all those electoral divisions or districts, and the assent shall not be given to such bill unless an address has been presented by the legislative assembly to the lieutenant-governor stating that it has been so passed.

3.—ONTARIO AND QUEBEC.

81. The legislatures of Ontario and Quebec, respectively, shall be called together not later than six months after the union.

82. The lieutenant-governors of Ontario and of Quebec shall, from time to time, in the queen's name, by instrument under the great seal of the province, summon and call together the legislative assembly of the province.

83. Until the legislature of Ontario or of Quebec otherwise provides, a person accepting or holding in Ontario, or in Quebec, any office, commission or employment, permanent or temporary, at the nomination of the lieutenant-governor, to which an annual salary, or any fee, allowance, emolument or profit of any kind or amount whatever from the province is attached, shall not be eligible as a member of the legislative assembly of the respective province, nor shall he sit or vote as such; but nothing in this section shall make ineligible any person being a member of the executive council of the respective province, or holding any of the following offices, that is to say: the offices of attorney-general, secretary and registrar of the province, treasurer of the province, commissioner of crown lands, and commissioner of agriculture and public works, and in Quebec, solicitor-general, or shall disqualify him to sit or vote in the house for which he is elected, provided he is elected while holding such office.

84. Until the legislatures of Ontario and Quebec respectively otherwise provide, all laws which at the union are in force in those provinces respectively, relative to the following matters or any of them, namely: the qualifications and disqualifications of persons to be elected or to sit or vote as members of the assembly of Canada, the qualifications or disqualifications of voters, the oaths to be taken by voters, the returning officers, their powers and duties, the proceedings at elections, the periods during which such elections may be continued, and the trial of controverted elections and the proceedings incident thereto, the vacating of the seats of members, and the issuing and execution of new writs in case of seats vacated otherwise than by dissolution, shall respectively apply to elections of members to serve in the respective legislative assemblies of Ontario and Quebec.

Provided that until the legislature of Ontario otherwise provides, at any election for a member of the legislative assembly of Ontario for the district of Algoma, in addition to persons qualified by the law of the province of Canada to vote, every male British subject aged twenty-one years or upwards, being a householder, shall have a vote.

85. Every legislative assembly of Ontario and every legislative assembly of Quebec shall continue for four years from the day of the return of the writs for choosing the same (subject, nevertheless, to either the legislative assembly of Ontario or the legislative assembly of Quebec being sooner dissolved by the lieutenant-governor of the province), and no longer.

86. There shall be a session of the legislature of Ontario and of that of Quebec once at least in every year, so that twelve months shall not intervene between the last sitting of the legislature in

each province in one session and its first sitting in the next session.

87. The following provisions of this act respecting the house of commons of Canada, shall extend and apply to the legislative assemblies of Ontario and Quebec, that is to say, the provisions relating to the election of a speaker originally and on vacancies, the duties of the speaker, the absence of the speaker, the quorum, and the mode of voting, as if those provisions were here re-enacted and made applicable in terms to each such legislative assembly.

4.—NOVA SCOTIA AND NEW BRUNSWICK.

88. The constitution of the legislature of each of the provinces of Nova Scotia and New Brunswick shall, subject to the provisions of this act, continue as it exists at the union until altered under the authority of this act ; and the house of assembly of New Brunswick existing at the passing of this act shall, unless sooner dissolved, continue for the period for which it was elected.

5.—ONTARIO, QUEBEC AND NOVA SCOTIA.

89. Each of the lieutenant-governors of Ontario, Quebec, and Nova Scotia, shall cause writs to be issued for the first election of members of the legislative assembly thereof in such form and by such person as he thinks fit, and at such time and addressed to such returning officer as the governor-general directs, and so that the first election of member of assembly for any electoral district or any subdivision thereof shall be held at the same time and at the same places as the election for a member to serve in the house of commons of Canada for that electoral district.

6.—THE FOUR PROVINCES.

90. The following provisions of this act respecting the parliament of Canada, namely : the provisions relating to appropriation and tax bills, the recommendation of money votes, the assent to bills, the disallowance of acts and the signification of pleasure on bills reserved—shall extend and apply to the legislatures of the several provinces as if those provisions were here re-enacted and made applicable in terms to the respective provinces and the legislatures thereof, with the substitution of the lieutenant-governor of the province for the governor-general, of the governor-general for the queen, and for a secretary of state, of one year for two years, and of the province for Canada.

Powers of the Parliament.

91. It shall be lawful for the queen, by and with the advice and consent of the senate and house of commons, to make laws for the peace, order and good government of Canada, in relation to all matters not coming within the classes of subjects by this act assigned exclusively to the legislatures of the provinces; and for greater certainty, but not so as to restrict the generality of the foregoing terms of this section, it is hereby declared that (notwithstanding anything in this act) the exclusive legislative authority of the parliament of Canada extends to all matters coming within the classes of subjects next hereinafter enumerated, that is to say :—

(1) The public debt and property.
(2) The regulation of trade and commerce.
(3) The raising of money by any mode or system of taxation.
(4) The borrowing of money on the public credit.
(5) Postal service.
(6) The census and statistics.
(7) Militia, military and naval service and defence.
(8) The fixing of and providing for the salaries and allowances of civil and other officers of the government of Canada.
(9) Beacons, buoys, lighthouses and Sable island.
(10) Navigation and shipping.
(11) Quarantine and the establishment and maintenance of marine hospitals.
(12) Sea coast and inland fisheries.
(13) Ferries between a province and any British or foreign country, or between two provinces.
(14) Currency and coinage.
(15) Banking, incorporation of banks and the issue of paper money.
(16) Savings banks.
(17) Weights and measures.
(18) Bills of exchange and promissory notes.
(19) Interest.
(20) Legal tender.
(21) Bankruptcy and insolvency.
(22) Patents of invention and discovery.
(23) Copyrights.

(24) Indians and lands reserved for the Indians.

(25) Naturalization and aliens.

(26) Marriage and divorce.

(27) The criminal law, except the constitution of the courts of criminal jurisdiction, but including the procedure in criminal matters.

(28) The establishment, maintenance and management of penitentiaries.

(29) Such classes of subjects as are expressly excepted in the enumeration of the classes of subjects by this act assigned exclusively to the legislatures of the provinces.

And any matter coming within any of the classes of subjects enumerated in this section shall not be deemed to come within the class of matters of a local or private nature comprised in the enumeration of the classes of subjects by this act assigned exclusively to the legislatures of the provinces.

Exclusive Powers of Provincial Legislatures.

92. In each province the legislature may exclusively make laws in relation to matters coming within the classes of subjects next hereinafter enumerated, that is to say :—

(1) The amendment from time to time, notwithstanding anything in this act, of the constitution of the province, except as regards the office of lieutenant-governor.

(2) Direct taxation within the province in order to the raising of a revenue for provincial purposes.

(3) The borrowing of money on the sole credit of the province.

(4) The establishment and tenure of provincial offices, and the appointment and payment of provincial officers.

(5) The management and sale of the public lands belonging to the province, and of the timber and wood thereon.

(6) The establishment, maintenance, and management of public and reformatory prisons in and for the province.

(7) The establishment, maintenance, and management of hospitals, asylums, charities, and eleemosynary institutions in and for the province, other than marine hospitals.

(8) Municipal institutions in the province.

(9) Shop, saloon, tavern, auctioneer, and other licenses, in order to the raising of a revenue for provincial, local, or municipal purposes.

20

(10) Local works and undertakings, other than such as are of the following classes :—

(a) Lines of steam or other ships, railways, canals, telegraphs, and other works and undertakings connecting the province with any other or others of the provinces, or extending beyond the limits of the province :

(b) Lines of steamships between the province and any British or foreign country :

(c) Such works as, although wholly situate within the province, are before or after their execution declared by the parliament of Canada to be for the general advantage of Canada or for the advantage of two or more of the provinces.

(11) The incorporation of companies with provincial objects.

(12) Solemnization of marriage in the province.

(13) Property and civil rights in the province.

(14) The administration of justice in the province, including the constitution, maintenance and organization of provincial courts, both of civil and of criminal jurisdiction, and including procedure in civil matters in those courts.

(15) The imposition of punishment by fine, penalty, or imprisonment for enforcing any law of the province made in relation to any matter coming within any of the classes of subjects enumerated in this section.

(16) Generally all matters of a merely local or private nature in the province.

Education.

93. In and for each province the legislature may exclusively make laws in relation to education, subject and according to the following provisions :—

(1) Nothing in any such law shall prejudicially affect any right or privilege with respect to denominational schools which any class of persons have by law in the province at the union.

(2) All the powers, privileges, and duties at the union by law conferred and imposed in Upper Canada on the separate schools and school trustees of the queen's Roman Catholic subjects, shall be and the same are hereby extended to the dissentient schools of the queen's Protestant and Roman Catholic subjects in Quebec.

(3) Where in any province a system of separate or dissentient schools exists by law at the union, or is thereafter estab-

lished by the legislature of the province, an appeal shall lie to the governor-general in council from any act or decision of any provincial authority affecting any right or privilege of the Protestant or Roman Catholic minority of the queen's subjects in relation to education.

(4) In case any such provincial law as from time to time seems to the governor-general in council requisite for the due execution of the provisions of this section is not made, or in case any decision of the governor-general in council on any appeal under this section is not duly executed by the proper provincial authority in that behalf, then and in every such case, and as far only as the circumstances of each case require, the parliament of Canada may make remedial laws for the due execution of the provisions of this section, and of any decision of the governor-general in council under this section.

Uniformity of Laws in Ontario, Nova Scotia, and New Brunswick.

94. Notwithstanding anything in this act, the parliament of Canada may make provision for the uniformity of all or any of the laws relative to property and civil rights in· Ontario, Nova Scotia and New Brunswick, and of the procedure of all or any of the courts in those three provinces, and from and after the passing of any act in that behalf, the power of the parliament of Canada to make laws in relation to any matter comprised in any such act shall, notwithstanding anything in this act, be unrestricted ; but any act of the parliament of Canada making provision for such uniformity shall not have effect in any province unless and until it is adopted and enacted as law by the legislature thereof.

Agriculture and Immigration.

95. In each province the legislature may make laws in relation to agriculture in the province, and to immigration into the province ; and it is hereby declared that the parliament of Canada may from time to time make laws in relation to agriculture in all or any of the provinces, and to immigration into all or any of the provinces ; ánd any law of the legislature of a province, relative to agriculture or to immigration, shall have effect in and for the province, as long and as far only as it is not repugnant to any act of the parliament of Canada.

VII.—JUDICATURE.

96. The governor-general shall appoint the judges of the superior, district and county courts in each province, except those of the courts of probate in Nova Scotia and New Brunswick.

97. Until the laws relative to property and civil rights in Ontario, Nova Scotia and New Brunswick, and the procedure of the courts in those provinces, are made uniform, the judges of the courts of those provinces appointed by the governor-general shall be selected from the respective bars of those provinces.

98. The judges of the courts of Quebec shall be selected from the bar of that province.

99. The judges of the superior courts shall hold office during good behaviour, but shall be removable by the governor-general on address of the senate and house of commons.

100. The salaries, allowances and pensions of the judges of the superior, district and county courts (except the courts of probate in Nova Scotia and New Brunswick), and of the admiralty courts in cases where the judges thereof are for the time being paid by salary, shall be fixed and provided by the parliament of Canada.

101. The parliament of Canada may, notwithstanding anything in this act, from time to time provide for the constitution, maintenance and organization of a general court of appeal for Canada, and for the establishment of any additional courts for the better administration of the laws of Canada.

VIII.—REVENUES, DEBTS, ASSETS, TAXATION.

102. All duties and revenues over which the respective legislatures of Canada, Nova Scotia and New Brunswick before and at the union had and have power of appropriation, except such portions thereof as are by this act reserved to the respective legislatures of the provinces, or are raised by them in accordance with the special powers conferred on them by this act, shall form one consolidated revenue fund, to be appropriated for the public service of Canada in the manner and subject to the charges in this act provided.

103. The consolidated revenue fund of Canada shall be permanently charged with the costs, charges and expenses incident to the collection, management and receipt thereof, and the same shall form the first charge thereon, subject to be reviewed and audited in such manner as shall be ordered by the governor-general in council until the parliament otherwise provides.

104. The annual interest of the public debts of the several provinces of Canada, Nova Scotia and New Brunswick at the union shall form the second charge on the consolidated revenue fund of Canada.

105. Unless altered by the parliament of Canada, the salary of the governor-general shall be ten thousand pounds sterling money of the united kingdom of Great Britain and Ireland, payable out of

the consolidated revenue fund of Canada, and the same shall form the third charge thereon.

106. Subject to the several payments by this act charged on the consolidated revenue fund of Canada, the same shall be appropriated by the parliament of Canada for the public service.

107. All stocks, cash, bankers' balances, and securities for money belonging to each province at the time of the union, except as in this act mentioned, shall be the property of Canada, and shall be taken in reduction of the amount of the respective debts of the provinces at the union.

108. The public works and property of each province enumerated in the third schedule to this act shall be the property of Canada.

109. All lands, mines, minerals, and royalties belonging to the several provinces of Canada, Nova Scotia and New Brunswick at the union, and all sums then due or payable for such lands, mines, minerals, or royalties, shall belong to the several provinces of Ontario, Quebec, Nova Scotia and New Brunswick in which the same are situate or arise, subject to any trusts existing in respect thereof, and to any interest other than that of the province in the same.

110. All assets connected with such portions of the public debt of each province as are assumed by that province shall belong to that province.

111. Canada shall be liable for the debts and liabilities of each province existing at the union.

112. Ontario and Quebec conjointly shall be liable to Canada for the amount (if any) by which the debt of the province of Canada exceeds at the union sixty-two million five hundred thousand dollars, and shall be charged with interest at the rate of five per centum per annum thereon.

113. The assets enumerated in the fourth schedule to this act, belonging at the union to the province of Canada, shall be the property of Ontario and Quebec conjointly.

114. Nova Scotia shall be liable to Canada for the amount (if any) by which its public debt exceeds at the union eight million dollars, and shall be charged with the interest at the rate of five per centum per annum thereon.

115. New Brunswick shall be liable to Canada for the amount (if any) by which its public debt exceeds at the union seven million dollars, and shall be charged with interest at the rate of five per centum per annum thereon.

116. In case the public debts of Nova Scotia and New Brunswick do not at the union amount to eight million and seven million dollars respectively, they shall respectively receive, by half-

yearly payments in advance from the government of Canada, interest at five per centum per annum on the difference between the actual amounts of their respective debts and such stipulated amounts.

117. The several provinces shall retain all their respective public property not otherwise disposed of in this act, subject to the right of Canada to assume any lands or public property required for fortifications or for the defence of the country.

118. The following sums shall be paid yearly by Canada to the several provinces for the support of their governments and legislatures :—

Ontario	$80,000
Quebec	70,000
Nova Scotia	60,000
New Brunswick...........................	50,000
	$260,000

and an annual grant in aid of each province shall be made, equal to eighty cents per head of the population, as ascertained by the census of one thousand eight hundred and sixty-one, and in the case of Nova Scotia and New Brunswick, by each subsequent decennial census until the population of each of those two provinces amounts to four hundred thousand souls, at which rate such grant shall thereafter remain. Such grants shall be in full settlement of all future demands on Canada, and shall be paid half-yearly in advance to each province ; but the government of Canada shall deduct from such grants, as against any province, all sums chargeable as interest on the public debt of that province in excess of the several amounts stipulated in this act.

119. New Brunswick shall receive by half-yearly payments in advance from Canada, for a period of ten years from the union, an additional allowance of sixty-three thousand dollars per annum ; but as long as the public debt of that province remains under seven million dollars, a deduction equal to the interest at five per centum per annum on such deficiency shall be made from that allowance of sixty-three thousand dollars.

120. All payments to be made under this act, or in discharge of liabilities created under any act of the provinces of Canada, Nova Scotia and New Brunswick, respectively, and assumed by Canada shall, until the parliament of Canada otherwise directs, be made in such form and manner as may from time to time be ordered by the governor-general in council.

121. All articles of the growth, produce or manufacture of any one of the provinces shall, from and after the union, be admitted free into each of the other provinces.

122. The customs and excise laws of each province shall, subject to the provisions of this act, continue in force until altered by the parliament of Canada.

123. Where customs duties are at the union leviable on any goods, wares or merchandises in any two provinces, those goods, wares and merchandises may, from and after the union, be imported from one of those provinces into the other of them on proof of payment of the customs duty leviable thereon in the province of exportation, and on payment of such further amount (if any) of customs duty as is leviable thereon in the province of importation.

124. Nothing in this act shall affect the right of New Brunswick to levy the lumber dues provided in chapter fifteen of title three of the revised statutes of New Brunswick, or in any act amending that act before or after the union, and not increasing the amount of such dues ; but the lumber of any of the provinces other than New Brunswick shall not be subject to such dues.

125. No lands or property belonging to Canada or any province shall be liable to taxation.

126. Such portions of the duties and revenues over which the respective legislatures of Canada, Nova Scotia and New Brunswick had before the union power of appropriation as are by this act reserved to the respective governments or legislatures of the provinces, and all duties and revenues raised by them in accordance with the special powers conferred upon them by this act, shall in each province form one consolidated revenue fund to be appropriated for the public service of the province.

IX.—MISCELLANEOUS PROVISIONS.

General.

127. If any person being, at the passing of this act, a member of the legislative council of Canada, Nova Scotia or New Brunswick, to whom a place in the senate is offered, does not within thirty days thereafter, by writing under his hand, addressed to the governor-general of the province of Canada or to the lieutenant-governor of Nova Scotia or New Brunswick (as the case may be), accept the same, he shall be deemed to have declined the same ; and any person who, being at the passing of this act a member of the legislative council of Nova Scotia or New Brunswick, accepts a place in the senate, shall thereby vacate his seat in such legislative council.

128. Every member of the senate or house of commons of Canada shall, before taking his seat therein, take and subscribe before the governor-general or some person authorized by him, and every member of a legislative council or legislative assembly of any province shall, before taking his seat therein, take and subscribe before the lieutenant-governor of the province, or some person authorized by him, the oath of allegiance contained in the fifth schedule to this act ; and every member of the senate of Canada and every member of the legislative council of Quebec shall also, before taking his seat therein, take and subscribe before the governor-general, or some person authorized by him, the declaration of qualification contained in the same schedule.

129. Except as otherwise provided by this act, all laws in force in Canada, Nova Scotia or New Brunswick at the union, and all courts of civil and criminal jurisdiction, and all legal commissions, powers and authorities, and all officers, judicial, administrative and ministerial, existing therein at the union, shall continue, in Ontario, Quebec, Nova Scotia and New Brunswick, respectively, as if the union had not been made ; subject, nevertheless (except with respect to such as are enacted by or exist under acts of the parliament of Great Britain, or of the parliament of the united kingdom of Great Britain and Ireland), to be repealed, abolished or altered by the parliament of Canada, or by the legislature of the respective province, according to the authority of the parliament or of that legislature under this act.

130. Until the parliament of Canada otherwise provides, all officers of the several provinces having duties to discharge in relation to matters other than those coming within the classes of subjects by this act assigned exclusively to the legislatures of the provinces, shall be officers of Canada, and shall continue to discharge the duties of their respective offices under the same liabilities, responsibilities and penalties, as if the union had not been made.

131. Until the parliament of Canada otherwise provides, the governor-general in council may from time to time appoint such officers as the governor-general in council deems necessary or proper for the effectual execution of this act.

132. The parliament and government of Canada shall have all powers necessary or proper for performing the obligations of Canada or of any province thereof, as part of the British empire, towards foreign countries, arising under treaties between the empire and such foreign countries.

133. Either the English or the French language may be used by any person in the debates of the houses of the parliament of Canada and of the houses of the legislature of Quebec ; and both those languages shall be used in the respective records and

journals of those houses; and either of those languages may be used by any person or in any pleading or process in or issuing from any court of Canada established under this act, and in or from all or any of the courts of Quebec.

The acts of the parliament of Canada and of the legislature of Quebec shall be printed and published in both those languages.

Ontario and Quebec.

134. Until the legislature of Ontario or of Quebec otherwise provides, the lieutenant-governors of Ontario and Quebec may each appoint, under the great seal of the province, the following officers, to hold office during pleasure, that is to say : the attorney-general, the secretary and registrar of the province, the treasurer of the province, the commissioner of crown lands, and the commissioner of agriculture and public works, and, in the case of Quebec, the solicitor-general ; and may by order of the lieutenant-governor in council from time to time prescribe the duties of those officers, and of the several departments over which they shall preside or to which they shall belong, and of the officers and clerks thereof, and may also appoint other and additional officers to hold office during pleasure, and may from time to time prescribe the duties of those officers, and of the several departments over which they shall preside or to which they shall belong, and of the officers and clerks thereof.

135. Until the legislature of Ontario or Quebec otherwise provides, all rights, powers, duties, functions, responsibilities or authorities at the passing of this act vested in or imposed on the attorney-general, solicitor-general, secretary and registrar of the province of Canada, minister of finance, commissioner of crown lands, commissioner of public works and minister of agriculture and receiver general, by any law, statute or ordinance of Upper Canada, Lower Canada or Canada, and not repugnant to this act, shall be vested in or imposed on any officer to be appointed by the lieutenant-governor for the discharge of the same or any of them ; and the commissioner of agriculture and public works shall perform the duties and functions of the office of minister of agriculture at the passing of this act imposed by the law of the province of Canada as well as those of the commissioner of public works.

136. Until altered by the lieutenant-governor in council, the great seals of Ontario and Quebec respectively shall be the same, or of the same design, as those used in the provinces of Upper Canada and Lower Canada respectively before their union as the province of Canada.

137. The words "and from thence to the end of the then next ensuing session of the legislature," or words to the same effect used

in any temporary act of the province of Canada not expired before the union, shall be construed to extend and apply to the next session of the parliament of Canada, if the subject matter of the act is within the powers of the same as defined by this act, or to the next sessions of the legislatures of Ontario and Quebec, respectively, if the subject matter of the act is within the powers of the same as defined by this act.

138. From and after the union the use of the words "Upper Canada" instead of "Ontario," or "Lower Canada" instead of Quebec," in any deed, writ, process, pleading, document, matter or thing, shall not invalidate the same.

139. Any proclamation under the great seal of the province of Canada, issued before the union, to take effect at a time which is subsequent to the union, whether relating to that province, or to Upper Canada, or to Lower Canada, and the several matters and things therein proclaimed, shall be and continue of like force and effect as if the union had not been made.

140. Any proclamation which is authorized by any act of the legislature of the province of Canada to be issued under the great seal of the province of Canada, whether relating to that province or to Upper Canada or to Lower Canada, and which is not issued before the union, may be issued by the lieutenant-governor of Ontario or of Quebec, as its subject matter requires, under the great seal thereof, and from and after the issue of such proclamation the same and the several matters and things therein proclaimed shall be and continue of the like force and effect in Ontario or Quebec as if the union had not been made.

141. The penitentiary of the province of Canada shall, until the parliament of Canada otherwise provides, be and continue the penitentiary of Ontario and of Quebec.

142. The division and adjustment of the debts, credits, liabilities, properties and assets of Upper Canada and Lower Canada shall be referred to the arbitrament of three arbitrators, one chosen by the government of Ontario, one by the government of Quebec and one by the government of Canada ; and the selection of the arbitrators shall not be made until the parliament of Canada and the legislatures of Ontario and Quebec have met; and the arbitrator chosen by the government of Canada shall not be a resident either in Ontario or in Quebec.

143. The governor-general in council may from time to time order that such and so many of the records, books and documents of the province of Canada as he thinks fit shall be appropriated and delivered either to Ontario or to Quebec, and the same shall thenceforth be the property of that province ; and any copy thereof

or extract therefrom, duly certified by the officer having charge of the original thereof, shall be admitted as evidence.

144. The lieutenant-governor of Quebec may from time to time, by proclamation under the great seal of the province, to take effect from a day to be appointed therein, constitute townships in those parts of the province of Quebec in which townships are not then already constituted, and fix the metes and bounds thereof.

X.—INTERCOLONIAL RAILWAY.

145. Inasmuch as the provinces of Canada, Nova Scotia and New Brunswick have joined in a declaration that the construction of the Intercolonial railway is essential to the consolidation of the union of British North America, and to the assent thereto of Nova Scotia and New Brunswick, and have consequently agreed that provision should be made for its immediate construction by the government of Canada : therefore, in order to give effect to that agreement, it shall be the duty of the government and parliament of Canada to provide for the commencement, within six months after the union, of a railway connecting the river St. Lawrence with the city of Halifax in Nova Scotia, and for the construction thereof without intermission, and the completion thereof with all practicable speed.

XI.—ADMISSION OF OTHER COLONIES.

146. It shall be lawful for the queen, by and with the advice of her majesty's most honourable privy council, on addresses from the houses of the parliament of Canada, and from the houses of the respective legislatures of the colonies or provinces of Newfoundland, Prince Edward Island and British Columbia, to admit those colonies or provinces, or any of them, into the union, and on address from the houses of the parliament of Canada to admit Rupert's Land and the Northwestern territory, or either of them, into the union, on such terms and conditions in each case as are in the addresses expressed and as the queen thinks fit to approve, subject to the provisions of this act ; and the provisions of any order in council in that behalf shall have effect as if they had been enacted by the parliament of the united kingdom of Great Britain and Ireland.

147. In case of the admission of Newfoundland and Prince Edward Island, or either of them, each shall be entitled to a representation in the senate of Canada of four members, and (notwithstanding anything in this act), in case of the admission of Newfoundland, the normal number of senators shall be seventy-six and their maximum number shall be eighty-two ; but Prince Edward Island, when admitted, shall be deemed to be comprised in the

third of the three divisions into which Canada is, in relation to the constitution of the senate, divided by this act, and accordingly, after the admission of Prince Edward Island, whether Newfoundland is admitted or not, the representation of Nova Scotia and New Brunswick in the senate shall, as vacancies occur, be reduced from twelve to ten members respectively, and the representation of each of those provinces shall not be increased at any time beyond ten, except under the provisions of this act, for the appointment of three or six additional senators under the direction of the queen.

SCHEDULES.

THE FIRST SCHEDULE.

Electoral Districts of Ontario.

A.

EXISTING ELECTORAL DIVISIONS.

COUNTIES.

(1) Prescott.
(2) Glengarry.
(3) Stormont.
(4) Dundas.
(5) Russell.

(6) Carleton.
(7) Prince Edward.
(8) Halton.
(9) Essex.

RIDINGS OF COUNTIES.

(10) North Riding of Lanark
(11) South Riding of Lanark.
(12) North Riding of Leeds and North Riding of Grenville.
(13) South Riding of Leeds.
(14) South Riding of Grenville.
(15) East Riding of Northumberland.
(16) West Riding of Northumberland (excepting therefrom the township of South Monaghan).
(17) East Riding of Durham.
(18) West Riding of Durham.
(19) North Riding of Ontario.

(20) South Riding of Ontario.

(21) East Riding of York.

(22) West Riding of York.

(23) North Riding of York.

(24) North Riding of Wentworth.

(25) South Riding of Wentworth.

(26) East Riding of Elgin.

(27) West Riding of Elgin.

(28) North Riding of Waterloo.

(29) South Riding of Waterloo.

(30) North Riding of Brant.

(31) South Riding of Brant.

(32) North Riding of Oxford.

(33) South Riding of Oxford.

(34) East Riding of Middlesex.

CITIES, PARTS OF CITIES AND TOWNS.

(35) West Toronto.

(36) East Toronto.

(37) Hamilton.

(38) Ottawa.

(39) Kingston.

(40) London.

(41) Town of Brockville, with the township of Elizabethtown thereto attached.

(42) Town of Niagara, with the township of Niagara thereto attached.

(43) Town of Cornwall, with the township of Cornwall thereto attached.

B.

NEW ELECTORAL DIVISIONS.

(44) The provisional judicial district of Algoma.

The county of Bruce, divided into two ridings, to be called respectively the north and south ridings :—

(45) The north riding of Bruce to consist of the townships of Bury, Lindsay, Eastnor, Albemarle, Amable, Arran, Bruce, Elderslie and Saugeen, and the village of Southampton.

(46) The south riding of Bruce to consist of the townships of Kincardine (including the village of Kincardine), Greenock, Brant, Huron, Kinloss, Culross and Carrick.

The county of Huron, divided into two ridings, to be called respectively the north and south ridings :—

(47) The north riding to consist of the townships of Ashfield, Wawanosh, Turnberry, Howick, Morris, Grey, Colborne, Hullett (including the village of Clinton), and McKillop.

(48) The south riding to consist of the town of Goderich, and the townships of Goderich, Tuckersmith, Stanley, Hay, Usborne and Stephen.

The county of Middlesex, divided into three ridings, to be called respectively the north, west and east ridings :—

(49) The north riding to consist of the townships of McGillivray and Biddulph (taken from the county of Huron), and Williams East, Williams West, Adelaide and Lobo.

(50) The west riding to consist of the townships of Delaware, Carradoc, Metcalfe, Mosa and Ekfrid, and the village of Strathroy.

[The east riding to consist of the townships now embraced therein, and be bounded as it is at present].

(51) The county of Lambton to consist of the townships of Bosanquet, Warwick, Plympton, Sarnia, Moore, Enniskillen and Brooke, and the town of Sarnia.

(52) The county of Kent to consist of the townships of Chatham, Dover, East Tilbury, Romney, Raleigh and Harwich, and the town of Chatham.

(53) The county of Bothwell to consist of the townships of Sombra, Dawn and Euphemia (taken from the county of Lambton), and the townships of Zone, Camden with the gore thereof, Orford and Howard (taken from the county of Kent).

The county of Grey, divided into two ridings, to be called respectively the south and north ridings :—

(54) The south riding to consist of the townships of Bentinck, Glenelg, Artemesia, Osprey, Normanby, Egremont, Proton and Melancthon.

(55) The north riding to consist of the townships of Collingwood, Euphrasia, Holland, St. Vincent, Sydenham, Sullivan, Derby and Keppel, Sarawak and Brooke, and the town of Owen Sound.

The county of Perth, divided into two ridings, to be called respectively the south and north ridings :—

(56) The north riding to consist of the townships of Wallace, Elma, Logan, Ellice, Mornington and North Easthope, and the town of Stratford.

(57) The south riding to consist of the townships of Blanchard, Downie, South Easthope, Fullerton, Hibbert, and the villages of Mitchell and Ste. Mary's.

The county of Wellington, divided into three ridings, to be called respectively north, south and centre ridings :—

(58) The north riding to consist of the townships of Amaranth, Arthur, Luther, Minto, Maryborough, Peel, and the village of Mount Forest.

(59) The centre riding to consist of the townships of Garafraxa, Erin, Eramosa, Nichol and Pilkington, and the villages of Fergus and Elora.

(60) The south riding to consist of the town of Guelph and the townships of Guelph and Puslinch.

The county of Norfolk, divided into two ridings, to be called respectively the south and north ridings :—

(61) The south riding to consist of the townships of Charlotteville, Houghton, Walsingham and Woodhouse, and with the gore thereof.

(62) The north riding to consist of the townships of Middleton, Townsend and Windham, and the town of Simcoe.

(63) The county of Haldimand to consist of the townships of Oneida, Seneca, Cayuga North, Cayuga South, Rainham, Walpole and Dunn.

(64) The county of Monck to consist of the townships of Canborough and Moulton, and Sherbrooke, and the village of Dunnville (taken from the county of Haldimand), the townships of Caister and Gainsborough (taken from the county of Lincoln), and the townships of Pelham and Wainfleet (taken from the county of Welland).

(65) The county of Lincoln to consist of the townships of Clinton, Grantham, Grimsby and Louth, and the town of St. Catharines.

(66) The county of Welland to consist of the townships of Bertie, Crowland, Humberstone, Stamford, Thorold and Willoughby, and the villages of Chippewa, Clifton, Fort Erie, Thorold and Welland.

(67) The county of Peel to consist of the townships of Chinguacousy, Toronto and the Gore of Toronto, and the villages of Brampton and Streetsville.

(68) The county of Cardwell to consist of the townships of Albion and Caledon (taken from the county of Peel), and the townships of Adjala and Mono (taken from the county of Simcoe).

The county of Simcoe, divided into two ridings, to be called respectively the south and north ridings :—

(69) The south riding to consist of the townships of West Gwillimbury, Tecumseth, Innisfil, Essa, Tossorontio, Mulmur, and the village of Bradford.

(70) The north riding to consist of the townships of Nottawasaga, Sunnidale, Vespra, Flos, Oro, Medonte, Orillia and Matchedash, Tiny and Tay, Balaklava and Robinson, and the towns of Barrie and Collingwood.

The county of Victoria, divided into two ridings, to be called respectively the south and north ridings :—

(71) The south riding to consist of the townships of Ops, Mariposa, Emily, Verulam, and the town of Lindsay.

(72) The north riding to consist of the townships of Anson, Bexley, Carden, Dalton, Digby, Eldon, Fenelon, Hindon, Laxton, Lutterworth, Macaulay and Draper, Sommerville and Morrison, Muskoka, Monck and Watt (taken from the county of Simcoe), and any other surveyed townships lying to the north of the said north riding.

The county of Peterborough, divided into two ridings, to be called respectively the west and east ridings :—

(73) The west riding to consist of the townships of South Monaghan (taken from the county of Northumberland), North Monaghan, Smith and Ennismore, and the town of Peterborough.

(74) The east riding to consist of the townships of Asphodel, Belmont and Methuen, Douro, Dummer, Galway, Harvey, Minden, Stanhope and Dysart, Otonabee and Snowden, and the village of Ashburnham, and any other surveyed townships lying to the north of the said east riding.

The county of Hastings, divided into three ridings, to be called respectively the west, east and north ridings :—

(75) The west riding to consist of the town of Belleville, the township of Sydney, and the village of Trenton.

(76) The east riding to consist of the townships of Thurlow, Tyendinaga and Hungerford.

(77) The north riding to consist of the townships of Rawdon, Huntingdon, Madoc, Elzevir, Tudor, Marmora and Lake, and the village of Stirling, and any other surveyed townships lying to the north of the said north riding.

(78) The county of Lennox to consist of the townships of Richmond, Adolphustown, North Fredericksburgh, South Fredericksburgh, Ernest Town and Amherst Island, and the village of Napanee.

(79) The county of Addington to consist of the townships of Camden, Portland, Sheffield, Hinchinbrooke, Kaladar, Kennebec, Olden, Oso, Anglesea, Barrie, Clarendon, Palmerston, Effingham, Abinger, Miller, Canonto, Denbigh, Loughborough and Bedford.

(80) The county of Frontenac to consist of the townships of Kingston, Wolfe Island, Pittsburgh and Howe Island, and Storrington.

The county of Renfrew, divided into two ridings, to be called respectively the south and north ridings :—

(81) The south riding to consist of the townships of McNab, Bagot, Blithfield, Brougham, Horton, Admaston, Grattan, Matawatchan, Griffith, Lyndoch, Raglan, Radcliffe, Brudenell, Sebastopol, and the villages of Arnprior and Renfrew.

(82) The north riding to consist of the townships of Ross, Bromley, Westmeath, Stafford, Pembroke, Wilberforce, Alice, Petawawa, Buchanan, South Algona, North Algona, Fraser, McKay, Wylie, Rolph, Head, Maria, Clara, Haggerty, Sherwood, Burns and Richards, and any other surveyed townships lying northwesterly of the said north riding.

Every town and incorporated village existing at the union, not specially mentioned in the schedule, is to be taken as part of the county or riding within which it is locally situate

---

THE SECOND SCHEDULE.

Electoral Districts of Quebec Specially Fixed.

COUNTIES OF—

Pontiac.

Ottawa.

Argenteuil.

Huntingdon.

Missisquoi.

Brome.

Shefford.

Stanstead.

Compton.

Wolfe and Richmond.

Megantic.

Town of Sherbrooke.

THE THIRD SCHEDULE.

Provincial Public Works and Property to be the Property of Canada.

(1) Canals with lands and water power connected therewith.

(2) Public harbours.

(3) Lighthouses and piers, and Sable Island.

(4) Steamboats, dredges, and public vessels.

(5) Rivers and lake improvements.

(6) Railways and railway stocks, mortgages, and other debts due by railway companies.

(7) Military roads.

(8) Custom houses, post offices, and all other public buildings, except such as the government of Canada appropriate for the use of the provincial legislatures and governments.

(9) Property transferred by the imperial government, and known as ordnance property.

(10) Armouries, drill sheds, military clothing and munitions of war, and lands set apart for general public purposes.

21

THE FOURTH SCHEDULE.

Assets to be the Property of Ontario and Quebec conjointly.

Upper Canada building fund.
Lunatic asylums.
Normal school.
Court houses in
   Aylmer.
   Montreal. } Lower Canada.
   Kamouraska.
Law society, Upper Canada.
Montreal turnpike trust.
University permanent fund.
Royal institution.
Consolidated municipal loan fund, Upper Canada.
Consolidated municipal loan fund, Lower Canada.
Agricultural society, Upper Canada.
Lower Canada legislative grant.
Quebec fire loan.
Temiscouata advance account.
Quebec turnpike trust.
Education, east.
Building and jury fund, Lower Canada.
Municipalities fund.
Lower Canada superior education income fund.

THE FIFTH SCHEDULE.

OATH OF ALLEGIANCE.

I, *A. B.*, do swear, that I will be faithful and bear true allegiance to her majesty Queen Victoria.

NOTE.—*The name of the king or queen of the united kingdom of Great Britain and Ireland for the time being is to be substituted from time to time, with proper terms of reference thereto.*

DECLARATION OF QUALIFICATION.

I, *A. B.*, do declare and testify, that I am by law duly qualified to be appointed a member of the senate of Canada [*or as the case may be*], and that I am legally or equitably seised as of freehold for my own use and benefit of lands or tenements held in free and common socage [*or* seised or possessed for my own use and benefit of lands or tenements held in franc-alleu or in roture (*as the case may be*)], in the province of Nova Scotia [*or as the case may be*] of the value of four thousand dollars over or above all rents, dues, debts, mortgages, charges and encumbrances, due and payable out of or charged on or affecting the same, and that I have not collusively or colourably obtained a title to or become possessed of the said lands and tenements or any part thereof for the purpose of enabling me to become a member of the senate of Canada [*or as the case may be*], and that my real and personal property are together worth four thousand dollars over and above my debts and liabilities.

THE BRITISH NORTH AMERICA ACT, 1871.

[Assented to by the Queen on the 29th June, 1871.

An Act respecting the establishment of Provinces in the Dominion of Canada.

WHEREAS doubts have been entertained respecting the powers of the parliament of Canada to establish provinces in territories admitted, or which may hereafter be admitted into the Dominion of Canada, and to provide for the representation of such provinces in the said parliament, and it is expedient to remove such doubts, and to vest such powers in the said parliament :

Be it enacted by the queen's most excellent majesty, by and with the advice and consent of the lords spiritual and temporal, and commons, in this present parliament assembled, and by the authority of the same, as follows :—

1. This act may be cited for all purposes as "The British North America Act, 1871."

2. The parliament of Canada may from time to time establish new provinces in any territories forming for the time being part of the Dominion of Canada, but not included in any province thereof, and may at the time of such establishment, make provision for the constitution and administration of any such province, and for the passing of laws for the peace, order, and good government of such province, and for its representation in the said parliament.

3. The parliament of Canada may from time to time, with the consent of the legislature of any province of the said Dominion, increase, diminish or otherwise alter the limits of such province, upon such terms and conditions as may be agreed to by the said legislature, and may, with the like consent, make provision respecting the effect and operation of any such increase or diminution or alteration of territory in relation to any province affected thereby.

4. The parliament of Canada may from time to·time make provision for the administration, peace, order and good government of any territory not for the time being included in any province.

5. The following acts passed by the said parliament of Canada, and intituled respectively : " An act for the temporary government of Rupert's Land and the Northwestern Territory when united with Canada," and "An act to amend and continue the act thirty-two and thirty-three Victoria, chapter three, and to establish and provide for the government of the province of Manitoba," shall be and be deemed to have been valid and effectual for all purposes whatsoever from the date at which they respectively received the assent, in the queen's name, of the governor-general of the said Dominion of Canada.

6. Except as provided by the third section of this act, it shall not be competent for the parliament of Canada to alter the provisions of the last mentioned act of the said parliament, in so far as it relates to the province of Manitoba, or of any other act hereafter establishing new provinces in the said Dominion, subject always to the right of the legislature of the province of Manitoba to alter from time to time the provisions of any law respecting the qualification of electors and members of the legislative assembly, and to make laws respecting elections in the said province.

THE PARLIAMENT OF CANADA ACT, 1875.

[Assented to by the Queen on the 19th July, 1875.

An Act to remove certain doubts with respect to the powers of the Parliament of Canada under section eighteen of the British North America Act, 1867.

WHEREAS by section eighteen of the British North America Act, 1867, it is provided as follows :

" The privileges, immunities and powers to be held, enjoyed and exercised by the senate and by the house of commons, and by the members thereof respectively, shall be such as are from time to time defined by act of parliament of Canada, but so that the same shall never exceed those at the passing of this act, held, enjoyed and exercised by the commons house of parliament of the united kingdom of Great Britain and Ireland and by the members thereof."

And whereas doubts have arisen with regard to the power of defining by an act of the parliament of Canada, in pursuance of the said section, the said privileges, powers, or immunities; and it is expedient to remove such doubts:

Be it therefore enacted by the queen's most excellent majesty, by and with the advice and consent of the lords spiritual and temporal, and commons, in this present parliament assembled, and by the authority of the same, as follows:—

1. Section eighteen of the British North America Act, 1867, is hereby repealed without prejudice to anything done under that section, and the following section shall be substituted for the section so repealed:

The privileges, immunities and powers to be held, enjoyed and exercised by the senate and by the house of commons, and by the members thereof, respectively, shall be such as are from time to time defined by act of the parliament of Canada, but so that any act of the parliament of Canada defining such privileges, immunities and powers shall not confer any privileges, immunities or powers exceeding those at the passing of such act, held, enjoyed and exercised by the commons house of parliament of the united kingdom of Great Britain and Ireland and by the members thereof.

2. The act of the parliament of Canada passed in the thirty-first year of the reign of her present majesty, chapter twenty-four, intituled "An act to provide for oaths to witnesses being adminis- tered in certain cases for the purposes of either house of parliament," shall be deemed to be valid, and to have been valid as from the date at which the royal assent was given thereto by the governor- general of the Dominion of Canada.

3. This act may be cited as "The Parliament of Canada Act, 1875."

THE BRITISH NORTH AMERICA ACT, 1886.

[Assented to by the Queen on the 25th June, 1886.

An Act respecting the representation in the Parliament of Canada of Territories which for the time being form part of the Do- minion of Canada, but are not included in any Province.

WHEREAS it is expedient to empower the parliament of Canada to provide for the representation in the senate and house of commons of Canada, or either of them, of any territory which for the time being forms part of the Dominion of Canada, but is not included in any province:

326

Be it therefore enacted by the queen's most excellent majesty, by and with the advice and consent of the lords spiritual and temporal, and commons, in this present parliament assembled, and by the authority of the same, as follows :—

1. The parliament of Canada may, from time to time, make provisions for the representation in the senate and house of commons of Canada, or in either of them, of any territories which for the time being form part of the J ominion of Canada, but are not included in any province thereof.

2. Any act passed by the parliament of Canada before the passing of this act for the purpose mentioned in this act shall, if not disallowed by the queen, be, and shall be deemed to have been, valid and effectual from the date at which it received the assent, in her majesty's name, of the governor-general of Canada.

It is hereby declared that any act passed by the parliament of Canada, whether before or after the passing of this act, for the purpose mentioned in this act, or in the British North America Act, 1871, has effect, notwithstanding anything in the British North America Act, 1867, and the number of senators or the number of members of the house of commons specified in the last-mentioned act is increased by the number of senators or of members, as the case may be, provided by any such act of the parliament of Canada, for the representation of any provinces or territories of Canada.

3. This act may be cited as the British North America Act, 1886.

This act and the British North America Act, 1867, and the British North America Act, 1871, shall be construed together, and may be cited together as the British North America Acts, 1867 to 1886.

ANALYTICAL INDEX.

ANALYTICAL INDEX.

[The references in all cases, except the British North America Act of 1867, are to pages.]

A.

ACADIE; meaning of, 27; formerly comprised Nova Scotia, New Brunswick, and part of Maine, *ib.*

Act of Settlement; fixed the succession to the throne of England, 46.

Adjournment of debate; rules relating to, 111.

Adjournment of house; rules relating to, 111.

Adjutant-general of militia; his position, 140.

Administration; definition of, 6.

Admiralty court of Canada; how constituted, 131.

Advocate; profession of, 194.

Alberta; one of the territorial districts of the Northwest, 39; its area, 269.

Alderman; origin of name of, 239; elected in certain municipal divisions, 223-225.

Amendments; how proposed in parliament, 110-113.

Appeals; in criminal cases, 207.

Arms of the dominion, 88-89.

Arms of the provinces, 149.

Assessment rolls; courts for revision of, 180.

Assessors of municipalities, 237.

Assiniboia; one of the territorial districts of the Northwest, 39; its area, 269.

Assize; court of, 197.

Athabasca; one of the territorial districts of the Northwest, 39; its area, 269.

Attorney; profession of, 195.

Attorney-general; in the provinces, 148, 151-152.

Auditors of councils, 230.

Autographs; of Champlain, 13; of governor-general Murray, 15; of Lord Durham, 23; of governors-general from 1867-1895, 75; of signers of Quebec federal resolutions of 1864, 37-38; of Queen Victoria, 60.

B.

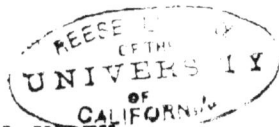

ANALYTICAL INDEX. 333

Criminals ; extradition of, 208.

Criminal courts of Canada, 197-201.

Criminal law ; in Canada, 172-176.

Criminal offences ; trial of, 203 ; appeals in cases of trial of, 191-207 ; not allowed to judicial committee of privy council, 66, 191 ; speedy trial of, 208.

Crown lands ; of the dominion, 214 ; of the provinces, 213-214 ; in the Northwest, 275-278 ; origin of the term, 215.

Crown ; its meaning, 41, *note.*

Currency ; Canadian, 136.

D.

DEBATE in parliament; rules regulating, 110-111.

Debentures ; meaning of, 238.

Debt of the Dominion of Canada ; its amount, gross and net, 134-135.

Defendant in a legal suit ; meaning of, 201.

Definitions of words and phrases used in this book ; government, 2 ; law of the land, 4 ; executive, judicial and legislative powers, 5 ; administration, 6 ; parliament, 7.

Deputy-reeve ; municipal officer in Ontario, 222-223.

Direct taxation in Canada, 211.

Disallowance of legislative acts ; by imperial government, 67 ; by dominion government, 168.

Divisional courts of appeal in Ontario, 183.

Divorce ; courts of, in Canada, 188 ; powers of senate with respect to, 94, 189.

Division courts for the collection of debts ; in Ontario, 178.

Division on motions ; in parliament, 112-113.

Dominion of Canada ; derivation of name of, 8 ; composed of provinces and territories, *ib.;* population of, 8-9 ; its periods of political development, 12 ; French rule from 1608-1760, 13-15 ; English rule from 1760-1791, 15-17 ; immigration of the United Empire loyalists, 18 ; representative institutions in Upper and Lower Canada from 1792-1840, 18-26 ; constitutional history of maritime provinces from 1714-1867, 27-31 ; summary of political rights of, 32 ; federal union of, 35 ; admission of British Columbia, 38 ; acquisition of the Northwest and formation of Manitoba, 39 ; how it is governed, 41 ; imperial control over, 64-68 ; general government of, 73-138 ; executive power in, 73-86 ; legislative power of, 92-127 ; judicial power in, 128-132 ; revenue and expenditure of, 133-136 ; currency of, 136-137 ; militia and defence of, 137-141 ; great seal of, 86 ; arms of, 88 ; flags of, 89 ; consolidated fund of, 135 ; laws of, 214 ; Northwest territorial government by, 269-272.

G.

H.

I.

Indians in Canada ; their rights, 278 ; where they can vote, 100, 160, 279; how protected, 279.

Indictment, meaning of, 203.

Intendant in French Canada, 14.

J.

JUDICIAL APPOINTMENTS, 164.

Judicial committee of the privy council ; its origin, 63 ; its functions, 65.

Judicial power ; definition of, 6.

Judicial tenure of office in Canada, 132 ; compared with the system in the United States, 283.

Jury ; common or petty, its English origin, 198 ; its Canadian history, 199 ; how constituted in Canada, 200 ; number required for a verdict, 201.

K.

KEEWATIN ; one of the territorial districts of the Northwest, 39.

Kindergarten schools ; their origin, 245.

King's bench ; court of, its origin and meaning, 197-198.

Kingston ; military college at, 140.

L.

LANDS OF CANADA ; see *crown lands ; dominion lands.*

Land question ; in French Canada, 25 ; in Prince Edward Island, 30.

Law of the land ; definition of, 4.

Law societies in Canada, 194.

Legal profession ; study of, 194.

Legislative power ; definition of, 6 ; in England, 55 ; in the dominion, 123 ; in the provinces, 163 ; in the Northwest territories, 271.

Legislatures; provincial, how constituted, 155-159; number of members in, 159 ; voting qualifications of electors for members of, 160-161 ; legislative powers of, 163-168.

Lieutenant-governors of provinces ; how appointed, 147 ; their duties and responsibilities, 147-148 ; advised by an executive council, 148-152 ; flags of, 153.

Lower Canada ; its constitutional history, 18-26 ; comes into the Dominion as Quebec, 35 ; autographs of delegates from, to Quebec conference of 1864, 36.

Loyalists, United Empire ; founded Upper Canada, 19 ; settled in Nova Scotia and New Brunswick, 19, 28.

M.

MAGISTRATES ; police, their duties, 179-181.

Magna Charta ; what it affirmed, 58.

Major-general commanding the militia of Canada, 141.

Manhood suffrage ; in the provinces, 160-161.

Manitoba ; province of, once a part of Rupert's Land, 39 ; its constitutional history, *ib.;* its executive council, 151 ; its legislature, 156-159 ; its franchise, 160 ; its arms, 154 ; its municipal divisions, 225 ; its courts, 179, 182, 184, 185, 187, 188, 190 ; its schools, 261.

Mayor ; origin of name of, 239 ; head of councils of cities and towns, 222.

Members of parliament ; number of, in the dominion senate, 94 ; in the house of commons, 95 ; in provincial legislatures, 159 ; indemnity to, 97, 156 ; travelling expenses, *ib.*

Meetings of municipal councils, 232.

Mileage rate ; to members of the house of commons, 97 ; to members of provincial legislatures, 156.

Military districts of Canada, 140.

Militia and defence of Canada, 138-141.

Militia service of Canada, 140.

Mines and minerals belong to the provinces, 148, 214.

Minister of agriculture of Canada ; his duties, 80.

Minister of education in Ontario ; his duties, 149.

Minister of finance in Canada ; his duties, 79.

Minister of the interior of Canada ; his duties, 80.

Minister of justice of Canada; his duties, 79.

Minister of militia and defence of Canada ; his duties, 80, 138.

Minister of public works of Canada ; his duties, 80.

Minister of railways and canals of Canada ; his duties, 80.

Minister of trade and commerce of Canada ; his duties, 79.

Ministerial responsibility ; its origin and development, 49-54 ; in Canada, 25, 81, 149.

Ministers not in the cabinet ; controllers of customs and inland revenue, solicitor-general, 81.

Ministries of the provinces ; how constituted, 151-152.

Ministry of the dominion ; members composing, 78-181.

Monarchical government ; meaning of, 3.

Money matters ; in parliament, 116.

Montfort, Simon de ; founder of house of commons, 57.

Motions in parliament ; their form and use, 110 ; debate on, *ib.;* divisions on, 112.

22

N.

O.

P.

Q.

QUEBEC act of 1774; first constitution given to Canada by imperial parliament, 16.

Quebec conference of 1864 ; first lays basis of federal union of Canada, 35 ; delegates from provinces to, 36-37 ; autographs of, *ib.*

Quebec ; province of, its early history, 13-26; enters confederation, 35 ; its executive council, 151; its legislature, 155-159; its franchise, 160 ; its arms, 154; its legal system, 173-174 ; its courts, 178, 179, 182, 183, 187, 188, 190 ; its municipal divisions, 224 ; its school government, 250.

Queen ; the, head of the executive government of Great Britain, 45 ; her hereditary right to the crown, 46 ; her titles, *ib. ;* her royal standard, *ib. ;* all acts of government done in her name, 48 ; her prerogatives, *ib. ;* "the queen can do no wrong," *ib. ;* origin of her advisory council, 49-54 ; her responsible councillors, 50-53 ; the crown in parliament, 55 ; her laborious duties, 60-61 ; her autograph, 60 ; her courts of justice, 62 ; head of the executive government in Canada, 74 ; represented by a governor-general, *ib.*

Queen's bench ; its origin as a court, 198 ; in Ontario, 183 ; in Quebec, *ib.*

Queen's counsel ; learned in the law, 195.

Questions or motions in parliament ; how proposed, 110.

Quorum ; of senate, 294 ; of house of commons, 297 ; of municipal councils, 232.

R.

RAILWAY belt of lands ; granted by British Columbia to dominion government, 214.

Recorders of Canada, 180, 181, 182 and *note.*

Red ensign of Canada ; sketch of, 90.

Reeve ; origin of name, 239.

Referendum ; Swiss, its meaning and use, 236.

Registrars of lands, 216.

Religious exercises in schools ; in British Columbia, 264 ; in Manitoba, 261 ; in Prince Edward Island, 260 ; in Ontario, 248 ; in Quebec, 251 ; in Northwest territories, 273.

Remanded ; meaning of, 181.

Representative government ; meaning of, 3.

Representative institutions in Upper and Lower Canada ; their history, 18-26 ; in the maritime provinces, 27-31.

Responsible government ; its meaning, 3 ; when and how established, 12, 23, 25, 29 ; its conventions and usages, 83.

S.

T.

Thomson, Poulett ; afterwards Lord Sydenham, governor-general of Canada, 25.

Town ; origin of name, 239 ; now a municipal division, 222. See *municipal institutions in Canada.*

Treasurer ; in provincial cabinets, 151-152 ; in municipalities, 230.

Treaties ; when relating to, how made, 67.

Treaty of Paris of 1763 ; cedes Canada to England, 15.

Trial by jury in Canada ; its origin, 199 ; in civil cases, 200, 201, 202 ; in criminal cases, *ib.*, 205.

Trial of civil cases ; in Canada, 201.

Trial of criminal cases ; in Canada, 203.

Trustees, school ; duties of, 247.

U.

UNION JACK ; sketch of, 89.

United Empire Loyalists ; their coming into Canada, 18.

University ; provincial, in Manitoba, 263 ; New Brunswick, 259 ; in Ontario, 250.

Upper Canada ; province of, its constitutional history, 12-26 ; enters confederation as province of Ontario, 35 ; see *Ontario.*

Utrecht ; treaty of, 27-32.

V.

VANCOUVER ISLAND ; its early history, 38 ; united with British Columbia, *ib. ;* see *British Columbia.*

Verdict ; in civil actions, 202 ; in criminal cases, 207.

Victoria, Queen ; her autograph, 46 ; her laborious duties as sovereign, 46-47 ; see *sovereign.*

Village ; a municipal division, 222.

Voters' lists ; courts for revision of, 187, 188.

Voters' qualifications ; at dominion elections, 99-101 ; at provincial elections, 160-161 ; at municipal elections, 228.

W.

WARDEN ; head of county council, 222-228 ; his duties and responsibilities, 229.

Warrant ; meaning of, 191.

Westminster palace or parliament house of Great Britain and Ireland ; illustration of, 56.

Witenagemot ; national assembly of England before Norman conquest, 57 ; meaning of the name, 47.

Women ; vote at municipal elections in Ontario, 228 ; in Manitoba, *ib. ;* in British Columbia, *ib. ;* in Northwest territories, 272.

www.ingramcontent.com/pod-product-compliance
Lightning Source LLC
Chambersburg PA
CBHW030916270326
41929CB00008B/714